Generating Wealth Quickly

Generating Wealth Quickly

Matthew Petchinsky

1 1 1

Generating Wealth Quickly:
How to Generate $100,000 in 24 Hours
By: Matthew Petchinsky

Introduction: The $100,000 in 24 Hours Mindset

When you hear the phrase "make $100,000 in 24 hours," it can seem like an audacious claim—something out of reach for most people. Yet, for those who have mastered the right mindset and strategies, this is not only possible, but achievable in a systematic and repeatable way. Before diving into the specifics of generating this kind of income, it's critical to understand the most important factor behind such massive, rapid success: **your mindset**.

The ability to make $100,000 in a single day isn't just about having the right tools or a perfect product. It starts with the foundation of a **high-income mindset**—a belief system that enables you to attract wealth, identify opportunities, and take bold, calculated actions. This introduction will explore how cultivating the right mindset breaks down old, limiting beliefs and sets the stage for financial breakthroughs.

Defining the High-Income Mindset and Belief System

The high-income mindset is the fundamental psychological framework that separates people who achieve extraordinary financial success from those who struggle to earn and scale. In essence, this mindset revolves around seeing the potential for **limitless earning**—not just through hard work, but through smart work, value creation, and leveraging opportunities that align with your skills and passions.

A person with a high-income mindset understands that:

- **Money is abundant:** There's no scarcity of wealth; instead, there's a need to position yourself in the right places and with the right offers. Money is constantly circulating, and the key is learning how to tap into these flows.

- **Wealth comes from value, not time:** Traditional thinking tells us that money is tied to hours worked. However, with a high-income mindset, you realize that income is directly linked to the value you bring to others, the problems you solve, and the transformations you enable. This is how you detach from time-based earnings and shift into value-based income.
- **Action is key, but smart action is critical:** It's not about working harder or longer than anyone else. It's about strategic actions. Those with a high-income mindset focus on leverage—how can they make the biggest impact with the least amount of effort, by working smarter, outsourcing, automating, or scaling effectively?
- **Opportunities are everywhere:** Where others see risks, setbacks, or challenges, individuals with a high-income mindset see opportunities. They constantly ask themselves, "How can I turn this situation into a win?" and seek out ways to grow even during adversity.

This mindset drives boldness, a willingness to take risks, and the confidence to position yourself in high-reward situations. When you adopt this perspective, the idea of making $100,000 in a single day doesn't feel unrealistic—it feels like a strategic, attainable goal.

Breaking the Myth: Large Sums of Money Take a Long Time to Earn

One of the most common misconceptions about wealth is that it takes years—or even decades—of hard work and effort to accumulate. Most people grow up with the belief that making large sums of money requires grinding through long hours, moving up a corporate ladder, or building businesses slowly over time. While gradual wealth accumulation is one path, it is by no means the only one.

In the digital age, **speed to wealth** is more achievable than ever. Here are some myths that need to be dismantled if you're going to step into the mindset of earning $100,000 in just 24 hours:

• Myth 1: You Need to Work for Years to Earn Big

Traditional thinking suggests that money is something that is earned in slow increments. We are often taught that salaries grow annually and that success is a slow climb. The truth is, especially in today's economy, you can accelerate your earning potential. The internet and digital platforms have removed many barriers to entry. You can launch a product or service, tap into a global market, and scale rapidly in ways that were unthinkable just 20 years ago.

In many cases, people who make massive amounts of money quickly are simply those who positioned themselves to take advantage of an opportunity, not those who have been grinding for years. The moment you realize that big financial wins don't require long timelines, your world opens up to new possibilities.

• Myth 2: Large Sums Require Complex Systems and Expensive Resources

Another limiting belief is that making big money requires enormous infrastructures—factories, physical products, large teams, or complex systems. In reality, many individuals and businesses today generate large sums with minimal overhead. They leverage digital products, online platforms, and scalable marketing strategies to multiply their impact and income with minimal resources.

Digital products, for example, can be created once and sold repeatedly without the limitations of physical inventory. Services can be offered in group settings, multiplying the value you deliver while keeping your time investment low. Today's technology enables automations, ads, and outsourcing to do much of the work for you. With the right tools, it's possible to make $100,000 in one day without having a single employee or a complicated business setup.

- **Myth 3: You Need to Be a Millionaire to Make $100,000 Quickly**

Many people believe you need to start rich or have access to massive amounts of capital to achieve these kinds of rapid results. While having resources certainly helps, the most important asset in your journey to making $100,000 in 24 hours is your **ability to create value**. You don't need a million-dollar startup fund, but you do need a valuable offer, a clear market, and the ability to communicate why people need what you have.

Whether you're selling a high-ticket service, a digital product, or a limited-time offer, people will pay for solutions that meet their urgent needs. By identifying these high-impact problems and offering tailored solutions, you can command high prices and scale rapidly, even starting from humble beginnings.

- **Myth 4: Big Success Is Reserved for the Lucky or Well-Connected**

It's easy to think that making large sums of money fast is only for celebrities, influencers, or those with a wide network. The reality is that **value speaks louder than connections**. In the digital world, you can reach thousands—if not millions—of people with the right marketing strategy. Platforms like Facebook Ads, Google Ads, and social media allow you to connect with people across the globe, without needing an existing following.

Your ability to market, position your offer, and demonstrate its value can often matter more than who you know. Many individuals who have generated six or seven figures quickly started with little more than a solid idea, an effective offer, and a willingness to scale aggressively.

Building the $100,000 in 24 Hours Mentality

To successfully earn $100,000 in a single day, you need to be laser-focused, driven by clarity, and operate with a deep sense of possibility.

The journey starts with your belief system: if you believe you can do it, you're more likely to take the necessary actions to make it happen. If you think it's impossible, you're likely to overlook opportunities and dismiss strategies that could lead to your success.

Here are key mindset principles to internalize as you embark on this journey:

1. **Believe in abundance, not scarcity**: There is no limit to how much money you can earn. There is only the question of how you will tap into the existing wealth flows.
2. **See time as a resource, not a limitation**: You don't need months or years to achieve financial success. The right offer, launched at the right time, can generate massive returns in a fraction of the time most people expect.
3. **Take bold, decisive action**: The mindset that leads to $100,000 in 24 hours is not passive. It requires you to act with conviction, take calculated risks, and capitalize on opportunities quickly.
4. **Focus on leverage**: The most successful people don't work harder—they work smarter. They create systems that multiply their efforts, whether through automation, outsourcing, or scalable products.

By reshaping your beliefs about money, time, and value, you'll be equipped with the mental framework needed to not only make $100,000 in a single day but also to replicate that success in future ventures. This is your foundation—once it's solid, the strategies and techniques to achieve this goal will fall into place.

Part 1: Laying the Foundation

Chapter 1: Understanding the Market Opportunity

In order to generate $100,000 in 24 hours, you must first position yourself within markets that support large-scale, rapid transactions. Not every industry or market is designed for this kind of accelerated revenue generation, and the key to success lies in choosing the right niche or product category that allows for scalability, high demand, and quick monetary exchange. This chapter will provide a thorough analysis of markets that support rapid financial gains and the factors that make them conducive to generating significant income in a short amount of time.

The Anatomy of a Lucrative Market

Before diving into specific markets, it's important to understand what makes a market ideal for rapid transactions and large financial gains. Here are some key characteristics:

1. **Scalability:**
   - A scalable market is one where you can serve an increasing number of customers or clients without a proportional increase in costs. This allows you to multiply your earnings quickly without the need to hire more employees, acquire more resources, or spend more time. Digital products are a prime example of a scalable market because once the product is created, it can be sold to an unlimited number of customers without significant additional costs.

2. **High Demand:**
   - A lucrative market is one where there is a strong demand for the product or service. The more urgent or essential the need, the faster the transaction. High-demand markets also tend to have a larger customer base, which means that even

if you're targeting a small percentage of that market, you can achieve significant sales.

3. **High Perceived Value:**
   - A market that allows for rapid, large-scale transactions typically offers products or services with high perceived value. These are products that solve a major pain point, offer a significant transformation, or provide a unique solution that customers are willing to pay a premium for. High-ticket items (such as consulting, coaching, or advanced digital solutions) fall into this category because they deliver more than just a product—they provide a solution to a pressing problem.

4. **Quick Transaction Process:**
   - Markets that support large-scale rapid transactions often have streamlined sales processes, allowing customers to quickly make purchasing decisions and complete transactions. This can be achieved through automated sales funnels, digital product delivery, and easy-to-use payment systems. The quicker the transaction, the more likely you are to reach your $100,000 goal in 24 hours.

Identifying High-Potential Markets

Now that we understand the core principles behind a lucrative market, let's explore specific markets that are particularly conducive to generating $100,000 in a single day. Each of these markets has its own unique set of advantages, and by choosing the one that best aligns with your skills, resources, and audience, you can significantly increase your chances of success.

1. Digital Products

Why It Works: Digital products are among the most scalable and profitable options for generating rapid income. Once a digital product is created—whether it's an ebook, online course, software, or template—it can be sold an infinite number of times with minimal additional costs. Digital products also have the advantage of being easy to distribute, allowing for instant delivery and satisfaction for the customer, which further encourages rapid purchases.

Key Advantages:

- **No Inventory Costs:** Unlike physical products, digital products don't require inventory management or shipping, allowing you to keep overhead costs extremely low.
- **High Profit Margins:** Since there are little to no production or distribution costs after the initial creation, the majority of your sales revenue becomes profit.
- **Instant Delivery:** Digital products can be delivered instantly upon purchase, meaning there is no delay for the customer, which increases the likelihood of impulse buying.
- **Global Audience:** Digital products can be sold to anyone with an internet connection, which vastly increases your market reach.

Examples of Digital Products That Sell Fast:

- Online courses and training programs.
- Ebooks and guides on niche topics.
- Software or app subscriptions.
- Digital templates (e.g., business, design, or marketing templates).
- Membership sites or digital communities.

Market Opportunity: The e-learning and online education market is projected to be worth over $325 billion by 2025, making it a ripe opportunity for rapid income generation, particularly in high-demand areas such as business, finance, health, personal development, and tech.

2. High-Ticket Consulting and Coaching

Why It Works: In the world of high-ticket services, individuals are willing to pay thousands—or even tens of thousands—of dollars for specialized expertise, guidance, or mentorship. Consulting and coaching are particularly lucrative because they address specific problems and offer tailored solutions. Clients seeking rapid results are often willing to pay a premium for expert advice, especially if it can help them achieve significant business, financial, or personal breakthroughs.

Key Advantages:

- **High Perceived Value:** Personalized consulting and coaching are seen as high-value services because they are customized to the client's unique needs and often lead to measurable results.
- **High Price Point:** Because the service is highly personalized and impactful, you can charge significant fees—sometimes as much as $5,000, $10,000, or even $20,000 per client.
- **Small Client Base, Large Revenue:** Unlike markets where you need thousands of customers to reach your goal, high-ticket consulting allows you to reach $100,000 with only a few clients.

Examples of High-Ticket Services:

- Business consulting for entrepreneurs, startups, or established companies looking to scale.
- Life coaching for individuals seeking personal transformation.
- Financial coaching or investment consulting for high-net-worth individuals.
- Marketing consulting for businesses aiming to improve their sales or brand presence.
- Health and wellness coaching for clients seeking physical and mental well-being.

Market Opportunity: The coaching and consulting industry is booming, with an estimated value of over $20 billion in the U.S. alone. Entrepreneurs, business owners, and individuals looking for personal development are willing to pay for expert guidance, particularly when it promises high returns.

3. Affiliate Marketing

Why It Works: Affiliate marketing is a powerful way to generate significant income without creating a product yourself. As an affiliate marketer, you promote other people's products or services and earn a commission for each sale generated through your unique affiliate link. With high-commission products (often digital or high-ticket items), you can earn substantial commissions on each sale, allowing you to scale rapidly.

Key Advantages:

- **No Product Creation:** You don't need to spend time or money developing your own product, which means you can focus solely on marketing and sales.
- **High Commissions:** Many affiliate programs offer commissions of 30-70%, particularly in digital product spaces such as online courses, software, or memberships.
- **Scalability:** You can promote products to a large audience using paid advertising, email marketing, or content marketing, allowing you to scale quickly.
- **Leveraging Others' Success:** As an affiliate, you're promoting products that have already been proven successful, which reduces the risk associated with selling new or untested products.

Examples of Affiliate Products That Sell Fast:

- Online courses and certifications.
- SaaS (Software as a Service) products with recurring commissions.
- High-ticket products like investment programs, luxury items, or business tools.
- Membership sites or subscription services.

Market Opportunity: Affiliate marketing is expected to grow to a $12 billion industry globally. High-ticket affiliate programs, in particular, offer the potential to generate significant income with just a few sales, allowing you to hit your $100,000 goal quickly.

4. High-Ticket Webinars

Why It Works: Webinars have become a staple in the digital marketing world, particularly for high-ticket sales. A well-structured webinar allows you to demonstrate your expertise, provide immense value, and pitch your high-ticket product or service to a live audience. By focusing on a specific problem and offering a transformational solution, webinars are a powerful tool for closing high-ticket deals quickly.

Key Advantages:

- **Interactive and Engaging:** Webinars offer real-time interaction, which builds trust with your audience and allows for immediate feedback and engagement.
- **Perfect for High-Ticket Offers:** Webinars provide the perfect platform for explaining the value of high-ticket offers, making it easier to justify premium pricing.
- **Leverage Existing Audience:** Webinars allow you to sell to both warm leads (people who already know you) and cold leads (people introduced through ads or partnerships) in a way that feels personal and high-value.

Examples of Webinar Topics That Sell Fast:

- Business or marketing strategies for scaling revenue.
- Personal development coaching (e.g., confidence, relationships, leadership).
- Investment strategies or financial growth programs.
- Health and fitness transformations.

Market Opportunity: Webinars continue to grow in popularity due to their ability to convert attendees into paying customers. The online education and business coaching markets are ideal for this model, allowing you to sell high-ticket products or services to a global audience.

Conclusion

Understanding the market opportunity is critical when aiming to generate $100,000 in a single day. By focusing on scalable, high-demand markets with high perceived value, you position yourself for success. Whether you're selling digital products, offering high-ticket services, leveraging affiliate marketing, or using webinars to close sales, the key is to identify a market where rapid, large-scale transactions are possible and align your product or service to meet that demand.

By targeting the right market and understanding the mechanics behind it, you're laying the foundation for a highly successful $100,000 launch within 24 hours. The next chapters will explore specific strategies for crafting offers, driving traffic, and executing a high-impact launch, all of which will help you realize your financial goal.

Chapter 2: Choosing the Right Niche

One of the most crucial decisions you will make when trying to generate $100,000 in 24 hours is choosing the right niche. A niche is a specific segment of the market that you focus on, defined by a unique set of problems, desires, and characteristics. Picking the right niche can make the difference between rapid success and slow, painful progress. In this chapter, we'll dive deep into how to identify a **lucrative** and **scalable** niche that sets you up for fast financial growth, and how to ensure that your chosen niche aligns with the goals of generating substantial income in a short amount of time.

Why Choosing the Right Niche is Critical

The online business landscape is vast and competitive, which makes specialization critical. By narrowing your focus to a specific niche, you can tailor your offer to meet the specific needs of a well-defined group of people. This allows you to:

- **Stand out from the crowd:** Specialization allows you to cut through the noise of general competitors and attract customers who are looking for precise solutions.
- **Build authority faster:** In a niche, you can become known as an expert more quickly than if you try to appeal to a broad market.
- **Charge premium prices:** Targeting a niche allows you to offer highly specialized products and services that command higher prices because they directly address unique pain points.
- **Scale faster:** By honing in on a specific audience with scalable needs, you can create products and services that are easy to reproduce or deliver repeatedly without a proportional increase in time or effort.

A well-chosen niche is not only lucrative but also scalable, meaning it allows you to grow your business quickly without exhausting resources or adding unnecessary complexity. The ideal niche will provide a continuous demand for your products or services, allowing you to leverage that demand into rapid growth.

Step 1: Identifying Lucrative Niches

When choosing a niche, profitability should be a top priority. A niche is considered lucrative when it has a large enough customer base willing to pay for high-value solutions. Here's how you can identify a lucrative niche:

1. Solve a Specific Problem

The foundation of every lucrative niche lies in the problems it solves. People spend money when they believe a product or service can solve a significant pain point in their lives or deliver meaningful results. A lucrative niche often addresses urgent problems, such as health, financial stability, business growth, or personal relationships.

To identify lucrative problems:

- **Look for recurring pain points**: Seek out issues that people experience regularly or ones that are getting worse over time. The more pressing or chronic the problem, the more people will be willing to pay for a solution.
- **Focus on high-emotion problems**: Pain points that evoke strong emotions (fear, frustration, desire, or hope) tend to create higher perceived value, leading to greater willingness to invest in a solution.
- **Find where people are already spending money**: Research markets where people are already spending large amounts of money to solve specific problems. For instance, the weight loss industry is a multi-billion-dollar niche because people are constantly seeking solutions to achieve their health goals.

2. Passion Meets Profit

When choosing a niche, balance passion with profitability. While it's important to choose a niche you are genuinely interested in, it must also have a proven potential to generate significant revenue. Passion alone won't make money; your niche must have demand and purchasing power.

To assess whether your passion aligns with profit:

- **Ask: Are people paying for solutions in this area?** Even if you're passionate about a topic, there's no point pursuing it if no one is willing to spend money on it. Look for existing markets with a healthy number of products and services, indicating that customers are actively purchasing.
- **Evaluate the pricing potential**: Some niches may have demand but come with a low price ceiling. For example, while crafting is a passion for many, the individual products in that space often sell at a low price point. Compare that to financial coaching or business consulting, where people are willing to pay thousands of dollars for results. Pick a niche where customers expect to pay premium prices for valuable outcomes.

3. Identify High-Spending Audiences

Not every audience spends money the same way. Some groups are more willing and able to invest in products and services than others. The most lucrative niches are often those that cater to audiences with significant disposable income and a strong willingness to pay for premium solutions.

High-spending audiences often include:

- **Business owners and entrepreneurs**: This group consistently seeks ways to improve their operations, generate more revenue, and optimize efficiency. Products like online courses, software solutions, or consulting services aimed at businesses often command high prices.
- **Health and wellness enthusiasts**: People are willing to spend considerable amounts on products and services that improve their physical or mental well-being, especially if they promise fast

or significant results (e.g., fitness coaching, supplements, or mental health programs).

- **Investors and finance-focused individuals**: The financial industry attracts individuals looking to grow their wealth, who are often willing to invest large sums in training, coaching, or financial tools that promise high returns.

To find high-spending audiences:

- **Look for existing products/services and analyze pricing**: Research top-selling products in your potential niche and note their price points. If the audience is willing to pay significant amounts for similar offers, there's potential for high earnings.
- **Study customer behavior in forums, groups, and social media**: Places like Reddit, Facebook Groups, or niche-specific forums are gold mines for understanding how much people in your target audience are willing to invest in solving their problems.

4. Examine Competition Levels

While high competition can sometimes indicate a saturated market, it can also be a sign that the niche is highly lucrative. However, you must evaluate how easy or difficult it will be to stand out in a competitive niche and how to carve out your own space by offering something unique.

To assess competition:

- **Look for existing market leaders**: If you see businesses or individuals dominating the niche, analyze what makes them successful. What problems are they solving, and how do they position themselves?
- **Identify gaps in the market**: Even in competitive niches, there are often gaps where customer needs are unmet. These gaps can

be as simple as delivering better customer service, providing faster results, or offering a more tailored solution than competitors.

- **Examine niche saturation**: If a niche is too saturated and everyone is offering similar products, it may be hard to differentiate yourself. However, if you can offer a fresh angle—such as a unique process, tool, or delivery method—there is still room for success.

Step 2: Ensuring Scalability

Scalability is the second critical factor in choosing a niche that supports fast financial growth. A scalable niche allows you to grow without the limitations of time, effort, or physical resources. For example, digital products or services that can be sold to a global audience without incremental cost increases are highly scalable.

1. Favor Digital Over Physical Products

While physical products have their place in the market, they come with inherent limitations, including inventory management, shipping, and manufacturing costs. Digital products, on the other hand, are highly scalable because they can be delivered instantly, with zero shipping or production delays.

Scalable digital product examples include:

- **Online courses or training programs**: Once created, courses can be sold to an unlimited number of students without needing additional resources.
- **Membership sites**: Subscription-based models allow customers to access exclusive content, training, or tools, providing a recurring income stream without the need for constant content creation.
- **Software as a Service (SaaS)**: SaaS products are highly scalable because they can be sold to an unlimited number of users while only needing occasional updates or customer support.

2. Look for Automated or Semi-Automated Services

If you choose a service-based niche, it's important to find ways to automate or semi-automate the process so that it can be delivered to multiple clients simultaneously. High-ticket services can be scalable when packaged in a way that reduces your direct involvement in every transaction.

Examples of scalable service models include:

- **Group coaching or consulting**: Instead of offering one-on-one sessions, you can create group programs where multiple clients receive the same value in a shared setting. This allows you to scale your impact and income without significantly increasing your time commitment.
- **Hybrid programs**: Combine digital content with live coaching or support. For example, an online course with a monthly group Q&A session can create a high-value service with limited personal involvement.

3. Leverage Affiliate and Partner Networks

Scalability can be significantly enhanced by tapping into existing networks of affiliates or partners. Affiliate marketing allows other individuals or businesses to promote your product for a commission, enabling you to reach new audiences without spending extra time or resources on marketing.

To leverage affiliate networks:

- **Offer high commissions**: Affiliates are more likely to promote products that offer them a significant commission (30-70%), which can lead to rapid sales and increased exposure for your niche.
- **Work with partners in related industries**: Partner with complementary businesses or influencers who have an established audience in your niche. For example, if your niche is health and

wellness, you could partner with a fitness brand or a nutrition coach to cross-promote products.

Step 3: Testing and Validating Your Niche

Before you fully commit to a niche, it's important to test and validate that it is both profitable and scalable. You don't want to invest a lot of time and resources into a niche that won't deliver the results you're seeking.

1. Conduct Market Research

Market research helps you assess the viability of your niche and ensures that there is sufficient demand for your product or service. Use tools like:

- **Google Trends**: See how search volume is trending for key terms in your niche to determine whether demand is increasing or decreasing.
- **Keyword Research Tools (e.g., SEMrush, Ahrefs)**: Use keyword research tools to assess how competitive and profitable your niche is. Look for keywords with high search volume and low to moderate competition.
- **Industry Reports**: Access industry reports from reliable sources like Statista, IBISWorld, or Nielsen to understand how much money is being spent in your niche and what the future growth potential looks like.

2. Validate with a Minimum Viable Product (MVP)

Before fully launching, test your niche by offering a Minimum Viable Product (MVP)—a simplified version of your product or service that can gauge market interest. This allows you to validate demand without spending excessive time or resources.

- **Pre-Sell Your Product**: If possible, pre-sell your product or service to see if people are willing to pay for it before you even create the full version. This ensures that there is genuine demand and that your niche is profitable.

- **Collect Feedback**: Once you have initial customers, collect feedback to understand how well your product or service solves their problem and whether they would recommend it to others.

Conclusion

Choosing the right niche is a critical step in generating $100,000 in 24 hours. By selecting a niche that is both lucrative and scalable, you position yourself for rapid financial growth. The key is to find a niche that addresses urgent, high-value problems for a willing-to-pay audience, and that allows for easy scaling through digital products, automation, or affiliate networks. By conducting thorough market research and testing your idea before fully committing, you can ensure that your niche will support your financial goals and set you up for long-term success.

Chapter 3: The Power of Urgency

When aiming to generate $100,000 in 24 hours, one of the most powerful psychological triggers you can leverage is **urgency**. Urgency motivates potential buyers to act quickly, reducing procrastination and decision-making delays. The faster people make a purchase, the more likely you are to reach your financial target within a limited timeframe.

In this chapter, we will explore how to create urgency in your offers, the psychological basis behind its effectiveness, and specific techniques for implementing scarcity and urgency in your marketing. By mastering these tactics, you can drive rapid sales and push your customers to take immediate action.

The Psychology Behind Urgency

Urgency is effective because it taps into human psychology. People are more likely to take action when they feel that an opportunity may be missed or a consequence is imminent. This behavior is driven by several psychological principles:

1. Fear of Missing Out (FOMO)

FOMO is a powerful motivator. When potential buyers believe they may miss out on a valuable offer, they are more likely to make an immediate decision. People naturally want to avoid the regret of missing a good deal, so when they see that time is limited or that others are taking advantage of an offer, they feel compelled to act quickly.

2. Loss Aversion

People are more motivated by the fear of losing something than the potential for gaining something. When you frame your offer as something that could be lost if they don't act quickly—whether it's a discount, bonus, or product availability—people are more likely to take action because they don't want to lose the perceived benefit.

3. Perceived Scarcity

Scarcity increases the perceived value of your offer. When something is limited in availability, it becomes more desirable. This principle is frequently used in marketing to make products or services feel more exclusive, which drives people to act fast to secure their place before it's too late.

4. Instant Gratification

Many people are driven by the desire for instant results or rewards. If your offer promises a fast solution to a pressing problem, or if the customer can see immediate benefits, they are more likely to purchase quickly to experience that gratification sooner.

By understanding these psychological triggers, you can craft marketing messages and sales strategies that create urgency, encouraging buyers to act immediately rather than procrastinating or waiting for a "better time."

Techniques to Create Urgency and Scarcity

Now that you understand the psychological principles behind urgency, let's explore specific techniques you can use to create urgency and scarcity in your sales process. These methods can be implemented in your marketing materials, sales pages, emails, and even during live events like webinars to encourage fast purchases.

1. Limited-Time Offers

One of the most straightforward ways to create urgency is to offer something for a limited time. When people know that they only have a small window of time to take advantage of your offer, they are far more likely to act quickly.

How to Implement:

- **Countdown Timers:** Use a countdown timer on your sales page, in your emails, or during webinars to visually reinforce the urgency. The ticking clock serves as a constant reminder that time is running out. For example, "This offer expires in 24 hours!" followed by a live timer creates a sense of immediacy.
- **Flash Sales:** Run a flash sale where your product or service is discounted for a very short period—typically 24 to 72 hours. The short duration increases the pressure on potential buyers to act fast before the price goes back up.

- **Time-Sensitive Bonuses:** Include an additional bonus or benefit for people who act within a specific timeframe. For example, "Purchase within the next 24 hours and get a free 1-hour consultation," or "Buy today and receive exclusive access to our members-only community." These bonuses add extra value to the offer, incentivizing immediate action.

2. Limited Availability

Another highly effective strategy is to limit the availability of your product or service. Scarcity makes your offer feel exclusive and more valuable because people don't want to miss out on something that is rare or limited.

How to Implement:

- **Limited Quantity**: For physical products, clearly state that you only have a certain number of items available for purchase. For example, "Only 50 units left!" or "Limited to the first 100 buyers." Even for digital products, you can limit the number of sales by saying something like "Only 100 spots available for this program," or "This offer is only available to the first 50 people."
- **Exclusive Offer**: Make it clear that this is a one-time-only opportunity, and the product or service will not be offered again. Use language like, "Once it's gone, it's gone forever," or "This is a limited-edition offer, never to be repeated." This makes the product feel more valuable because it won't be available again in the future.
- **Early-Bird Access**: Offer limited access to early-bird buyers before the main offer goes live to the general public. This makes early-bird customers feel special and gives them an incentive to act quickly before the full launch.

3. Price Increases

Gradually increasing the price of your product or service over time is an excellent way to drive sales quickly. People are much more likely to buy now if they know the price will go up later.

How to Implement:

- **Tiered Pricing:** Introduce a tiered pricing strategy where the price increases at specific intervals. For example, "The price goes up by $50 every 24 hours," or "Get in at $299 before the price increases to $499 tomorrow." This encourages people to buy now to secure the best price.
- **Expiring Discounts:** Offer a special discounted price for a limited time, after which the product will return to its full price. For example, "Save 30% if you purchase by midnight," or "This price will never be this low again."
- **Early-Bird Pricing:** Offer a lower price for early adopters who act quickly. For instance, "Get the early-bird discount of 20% before the price increases on launch day." Early-bird pricing works particularly well for course launches or software, where early customers get rewarded for buying before the full launch.

4. Bonus Incentives for Fast Action

Offering bonus incentives for fast action is a great way to enhance the perceived value of your offer and make people feel like they're getting more for their money. By tying these bonuses to a limited time, you encourage quick decision-making.

How to Implement:

- **Fast-Action Bonuses:** Reward buyers who act within the first few hours of your launch or sales period. For example, "Purchase within the first 3 hours and get an exclusive bonus ebook," or "First 10 buyers receive a free 1:1 coaching session." These bonuses should be valuable and relevant to the product or service being offered, making them highly attractive.

- **Scarcity-Based Bonuses:** Limit the number of bonuses available. For instance, "Only the first 20 customers will receive access to this bonus training." This tactic plays on both urgency and scarcity, making buyers want to be among the first to act.

- **Stacking Bonuses:** Offer additional bonuses for customers who take action sooner. For example, "Buy within the first 12 hours and get three bonuses; buy within the next 24 hours and get two bonuses." This way, early buyers get more value, and the diminishing bonus stack reinforces the urgency.

5. One-Time-Only Offers (OTO)

One-Time-Only (OTO) offers are exclusive deals presented to potential customers right after they express interest or make a purchase. These offers capitalize on the momentum of a potential buyer's decision to drive additional sales, but they are only available for a very short time.

How to Implement:

- **Post-Purchase Upsell:** After someone buys a product or service, immediately present them with a one-time offer for an upgrade or complementary product. For example, "Get this exclusive add-on for just $99, but only if you buy it now!" These offers create urgency by presenting a valuable addition that won't be available again.

- **Exit-Intent Offers:** If someone tries to leave your sales page without purchasing, trigger a one-time offer with a discount or bonus. For example, "Wait! Before you go, get 10% off if you complete your purchase in the next 10 minutes." This taps into their indecision and presents a last-chance opportunity to act quickly.

6. Urgent Social Proof

Social proof is one of the most effective tools for driving conversions, and when combined with urgency, it becomes even more powerful. Social proof provides reassurance to potential buyers that others are purchasing the product and experiencing positive results, increasing their desire to act quickly.

How to Implement:

- **Real-Time Sales Notifications:** Use tools that display real-time notifications of recent purchases on your website, such as "John just purchased this product 5 minutes ago!" Seeing others buying creates a sense of urgency as customers don't want to be left behind.

- **Limited Spots or Seats Left:** If you are offering a webinar, course, or consulting service, display how many spots are left in real-time. For example, "Only 3 spots remaining!" This emphasizes that availability is dwindling and that they need to act fast to secure their place.

- **Testimonials with Time Sensitivity:** Feature testimonials from satisfied customers who emphasize how quickly they took advantage of the offer and the benefits they've gained from acting fast. For example, "I'm so glad I purchased during the early-bird period and got the bonus coaching call!"

7. Use Urgent Copywriting

Your copywriting plays a vital role in creating urgency. By using specific language that conveys a sense of urgency, you can encourage potential buyers to take action sooner rather than later.

How to Implement:

- **Time-Sensitive Phrases:** Use phrases such as "Act Now," "Limited Time Only," "Hurry," "Don't Miss Out," "Last Chance," "Only Available Today," and "Ending Soon" throughout your sales copy. These phrases instill a sense of urgency and push readers to make quicker decisions.

- **Focus on the Consequences of Inaction:** Highlight what buyers will miss out on if they don't act now. For example, "If you wait, you risk losing access to this exclusive offer forever," or "Miss this chance, and you'll have to pay full price next time."
- **Create Urgency in the Headline:** Your headline should grab attention and emphasize urgency right from the start. Use powerful headlines like, "Only 24 Hours Left to Claim This Life-Changing Offer," or "This Deal Expires at Midnight Tonight."

Combining Techniques for Maximum Impact

To maximize urgency, it's often effective to combine several techniques. For example, you might run a flash sale with a countdown timer, offer a limited quantity of bonuses, and introduce a tiered pricing model. The more ways you can reinforce the urgency, the more likely you are to drive fast sales.

Conclusion

Urgency is one of the most powerful tools you can use to drive immediate sales and hit your $100,000 goal in 24 hours. By using techniques like limited-time offers, scarcity, fast-action bonuses, price increases, and social proof, you create a psychological need for potential buyers to act quickly. The key is to make your offer feel time-sensitive and valuable, leveraging the fear of missing out and the desire for instant gratification. As you integrate these techniques into your sales strategy, you'll not only increase conversion rates but also build momentum toward your goal of generating massive income in a short time frame.

Chapter 4: Setting Your Goal and Strategy

The key to generating $100,000 in 24 hours is not just about creating a great product or marketing campaign; it's about setting a clear, actionable goal and developing a strategic plan to achieve it. In this chapter, we will break down how to reverse engineer your $100,000 target into manageable steps. By understanding the numbers behind your goal, identifying the right tactics, and executing a well-thought-out plan, you can significantly increase your chances of reaching your financial target.

This chapter provides a step-by-step blueprint for setting your goal, identifying the right offers and customers, and executing a high-impact 24-hour strategy that maximizes sales.

Step 1: Reverse Engineering the $100,000 Goal

The first step in achieving a financial target is to break it down into smaller, more manageable components. By reverse engineering the $100,000 goal, you can get a clearer picture of exactly what needs to happen to hit that number.

1. Identify Your Revenue Sources

You need to determine what products, services, or offers will generate your revenue. Typically, these can include:

- **Digital products** (e.g., ebooks, online courses, templates, software)
- **High-ticket services** (e.g., coaching, consulting, done-for-you services)
- **Affiliate marketing** (selling someone else's product for a commission)
- **Membership sites or subscriptions** (recurring revenue)

The goal is to figure out what combination of these revenue sources will add up to $100,000. For instance, you may decide to sell a high-ticket coaching program alongside a digital course, or run a webinar that promotes a premium product.

2. Break Down the Numbers

Next, break down the math of how you'll reach $100,000 in 24 hours. You can sell a few high-ticket offers, hundreds of mid-range products, or thousands of low-cost items. Let's explore different pricing structures and sales quantities to see how this works:

- **High-Ticket Strategy**: Sell fewer, higher-priced products.
    - Sell 5 units of a $20,000 offer.
    - Sell 10 units of a $10,000 offer.
    - Sell 20 units of a $5,000 offer.
- **Mid-Range Strategy**: Sell moderately priced products.
    - Sell 50 units of a $2,000 product.
    - Sell 100 units of a $1,000 product.
    - Sell 200 units of a $500 product.
- **Low-Ticket Strategy**: Sell a high volume of lower-priced products.
    - Sell 1,000 units of a $100 product.
    - Sell 2,000 units of a $50 product.
    - Sell 10,000 units of a $10 product.

You can also combine these strategies. For example:

- Sell 10 high-ticket products at $5,000 each ($50,000) and 500 low-ticket products at $100 each ($50,000).

By understanding how many units you need to sell at each price point, you can start planning the type of offers and promotions required to achieve this goal.

3. Set Conversion Rate Goals

Your next step is to estimate the number of potential customers you'll need to reach in order to sell the desired number of products. This involves understanding your conversion rates—how many people who see your offer will actually make a purchase.

Average online conversion rates vary, but here are some typical benchmarks:

- **Sales pages**: 2-5%
- **Webinars**: 5-10%
- **Email marketing**: 1-3%
- **Facebook ads**: 1-2%

Let's assume you have a $1,000 product and want to sell 100 units to make $100,000. If your sales page converts at 2%, you'll need to drive 5,000 targeted visitors to the page. If your webinar converts at 10%, you'll need 1,000 webinar attendees.

This step is crucial for understanding how much traffic and how many leads you need to generate in order to hit your goal.

Step 2: Crafting Your Offer

The next step is to design an irresistible offer that will compel people to buy during your 24-hour window. Your offer should be tailored to the needs and desires of your audience, and it should present a clear, high-value solution to a problem they are eager to solve.

1. Identify a High-Demand Problem

To create a compelling offer, you need to solve a problem that your target audience finds urgent and important. This can be a business, financial, personal, or health-related problem, but the key is that people are willing to pay to solve it quickly.

Examples of high-demand problems include:

- Business owners wanting to scale their revenue.
- Individuals looking to improve their health or fitness rapidly.
- Professionals seeking ways to increase their productivity or efficiency.

Make sure the problem you choose is one that people are actively seeking a solution for, and that they're willing to pay to solve it.

2. Create a High-Value Solution

Once you've identified a problem, your next step is to offer a solution that provides significant value. The higher the perceived value of your solution, the more people will be willing to pay for it, and the faster they'll be to act. Your offer needs to clearly communicate the benefits your customers will receive and the transformation they can expect.

Some components of a high-value offer include:

- **Clear, measurable outcomes**: What specific results will your customers achieve? For example, "Double your business revenue in 30 days" or "Lose 10 pounds in 4 weeks."
- **Bonuses and extras**: Add bonuses that enhance the core offer, such as additional training, one-on-one coaching sessions, or exclusive access to resources.
- **Time-sensitive value**: If possible, create a sense of urgency by offering time-sensitive bonuses or discounts for fast action, as discussed in the previous chapter.

3. Use Strategic Pricing

Your pricing strategy is key to generating the most revenue possible. For high-ticket offers, you need to price your product or service based on the value you deliver rather than the cost of production. People are willing to pay more if the perceived value and the results are high.

Some pricing strategies include:

- **Value-based pricing**: Price your offer according to the value and outcome it delivers to the customer, not the cost of materials or time spent. For example, if your coaching program helps businesses generate $50,000 in new revenue, charging $5,000 is reasonable.
- **Tiered pricing**: Offer multiple pricing tiers to cater to different budget levels. For instance, you could have a basic version of your product for $1,000, a mid-tier option with bonuses for $2,500, and a premium version with one-on-one access for $5,000.
- **Anchor pricing**: Introduce a high-priced option first to make the subsequent, lower-priced options seem more affordable in comparison. This technique often leads people to choose the mid-tier option because it appears to offer the most value for the price.

Step 3: Building the Audience

To generate $100,000 in 24 hours, you'll need a large, engaged audience who are ready to buy as soon as your offer goes live. Building and priming this audience ahead of your launch is critical to hitting your sales target quickly.

1. Leverage Your Existing Audience

If you already have an audience—such as an email list, social media following, or existing customers—this is your best source of initial buyers. These people are familiar with you, trust your expertise, and are more likely to make a purchase.

Strategies for engaging your existing audience:

- **Pre-launch content**: Share teasers and valuable content related to your offer in the weeks leading up to your launch. This can be through blog posts, emails, social media, or videos that demonstrate your expertise and build anticipation.
- **Exclusive access**: Offer early access or special bonuses to your existing audience to reward their loyalty and encourage fast action.

For example, "My email subscribers get 24-hour early access to the program."

2. Drive New Traffic with Paid Advertising

If you don't have a large audience, or if you want to scale up quickly, paid advertising is one of the fastest ways to drive new traffic to your offer.

Paid advertising platforms include:

- **Facebook and Instagram Ads**: Target specific demographics and interests that align with your offer.
- **Google Ads**: Reach people who are actively searching for solutions to the problem you solve.
- **YouTube Ads**: Use video ads to engage potential customers with a compelling message that introduces your offer.

Paid advertising can generate significant traffic in a short amount of time, but it's important to optimize your campaigns to ensure you're attracting high-quality leads who are likely to convert.

3. Use Partnerships and Affiliates

Partnering with other influencers, businesses, or affiliates can help you reach a much larger audience in a short period of time. By offering affiliates a commission on each sale they generate, you can tap into their audiences without doing all the marketing yourself.

How to implement an affiliate strategy:

- **Offer generous commissions**: Affiliate marketers are more likely to promote your product if they know they'll receive a significant commission—typically 30-50% of the sale price.
- **Create an affiliate toolkit**: Make it easy for your affiliates to promote your offer by providing them with swipe copy, promotional materials, and graphics they can use in their marketing efforts.

- **Leverage influencer partnerships**: Partner with influencers in your niche who have engaged audiences. Offer them exclusive access to your product and a commission on sales made through their referral links.

Step 4: Crafting a High-Converting Sales Funnel

A well-designed sales funnel guides potential customers through the buying process and maximizes your chances of converting them into paying customers. To generate $100,000 in 24 hours, your funnel needs to be optimized for both speed and conversion.

1. Use a Multi-Channel Approach

Don't rely on just one marketing channel to generate sales. Use multiple channels—such as social media, email, webinars, and paid ads—to reach different segments of your audience. The more touchpoints your audience has with your offer, the more likely they are to buy.

2. Set Up Automated Follow-Up Sequences

Use automated email sequences to follow up with potential customers who don't buy immediately. This can include:

- **Cart abandonment emails**: If someone adds your product to their cart but doesn't complete the purchase, send them an email reminding them to finalize the transaction.
- **Urgency-based reminders**: Send follow-up emails in the final hours of your 24-hour window to remind people that the offer is about to expire. Use countdown timers and language that reinforces urgency.

3. Optimize Your Checkout Process

A smooth, user-friendly checkout process can significantly improve your conversion rates. Ensure that your payment system is easy to use, mobile-friendly, and secure. Reduce friction by offering multiple payment options (credit cards, PayPal, etc.) and minimizing the number of steps required to complete the purchase.

Step 5: Launching and Monitoring Your Campaign

Once your strategy is in place, it's time to launch. The launch phase is where all your preparation comes together, and it's crucial to monitor your progress in real-time to ensure everything is running smoothly.

1. Create Pre-Launch Buzz

In the days leading up to your 24-hour launch, build excitement by sharing sneak peeks of your offer, countdowns, and reminders on social media and via email. Make your audience feel like something big is coming, and they need to be ready to act as soon as the offer goes live.

2. Execute Your 24-Hour Sales Push

During the 24-hour window, use all the marketing channels at your disposal to drive traffic and sales:

- **Run social media ads** that target your warm audience and retarget website visitors.
- **Send email blasts** to your list, highlighting the urgency of the offer and including clear calls-to-action.
- **Go live on social media or host a webinar** to engage your audience in real time and answer any questions they may have.

3. Monitor and Optimize in Real-Time

Keep a close eye on your metrics throughout the 24 hours. Track the following:

- **Traffic sources**: Which channels are driving the most traffic and conversions?
- **Conversion rates**: Are your sales pages converting at the expected rates? If not, consider tweaking your copy or calls-to-action.
- **Abandoned carts**: Follow up with people who abandon their carts by sending targeted reminders.

By monitoring your campaign in real-time, you can make adjustments and optimize your strategy to maximize sales before the 24 hours are up.

Conclusion

Setting a goal to generate $100,000 in 24 hours requires a clear, actionable strategy. By reverse engineering your target, crafting a high-value offer, building an engaged audience, and optimizing your sales funnel, you can significantly increase your chances of hitting your goal. Remember, the key is to stay focused, execute each step meticulously, and monitor your progress in real-time. With the right plan in place, hitting $100,000 in 24 hours is not only possible but achievable.

Chapter 5: Leveraging Existing Assets

When aiming to generate $100,000 in 24 hours, one of your most powerful tools is your ability to leverage existing assets. These assets—whether they be your network, skills, or existing resources—can be the driving force behind rapid success. Many entrepreneurs make the mistake of looking outside themselves for solutions when, in fact, their greatest potential lies in what they already possess.

This chapter will guide you through assessing and utilizing the assets you have at your disposal to maximize your earning potential. By leveraging your network, honing your skills, and strategically using available resources, you can significantly increase the likelihood of reaching your financial goal in a short period.

Step 1: Assessing Your Existing Assets

Before diving into creating new offers or developing marketing strategies, it's important to conduct a thorough inventory of what you already have. Understanding your existing assets can save you time, reduce costs, and give you a clearer path toward reaching your $100,000 goal.

1. Audit Your Network

Your network is one of the most valuable assets you can leverage. Whether it's personal relationships, business contacts, or online followers, tapping into your network can give you a major advantage.

How to Assess Your Network:

- **Identify your warm audience:** These are people who already know, like, and trust you. This could include current clients, past customers, email subscribers, social media followers, and professional acquaintances. Warm audiences are more likely to buy from you because they are already familiar with your brand or expertise.

- **Segment your network by influence and relevance:** Consider who in your network has the potential to amplify your reach. This could be influencers, business partners, or colleagues who have access to large or engaged audiences that would be interested in your offer. Also, assess who in your network might be directly interested in your product or service.
- **Evaluate your existing relationships:** Are there any high-value relationships you can leverage for collaborations, joint ventures, or endorsements? A well-placed recommendation from an influential person in your industry can drive significant traffic and sales in a short time.

Examples of Leveraging Your Network:

- **Partnerships and collaborations:** Collaborate with influencers or industry leaders in your niche to co-promote your offer. Offer them a commission or revenue share for their support.
- **Affiliate marketing:** Activate affiliates in your network to promote your product or service. You can offer a commission (30-50%) for each sale they drive.
- **Direct outreach:** Reach out to key contacts in your network personally and invite them to participate in your launch. Personalized emails or messages to trusted contacts can lead to early sales or referrals.

2. Audit Your Skills and Expertise

Your skills and expertise are intangible assets that can be directly monetized. Assess your capabilities and determine how you can package them into high-value offers that meet the needs of your target audience.

How to Assess Your Skills:

- **Identify your core strengths:** What are you uniquely good at? This could be anything from business strategy and coaching to technical skills like web design or software development. Pinpoint the skills that can solve high-value problems for your audience.

- **Review past successes:** Look back at previous work, projects, or achievements. What did you do well? What feedback did you receive from clients or customers? Past successes can give you insight into what people are willing to pay for and where you can offer the most value.
- **Match your skills to market demand:** Ensure that your skills align with a pressing market need. For example, if you have expertise in digital marketing, and businesses are seeking ways to boost their online presence, you can leverage that skill to create a high-ticket service offering.

Examples of Leveraging Your Skills:

- **Offer high-ticket services:** Package your expertise into high-ticket coaching, consulting, or done-for-you services. High-ticket offers can help you reach your $100,000 goal quickly by serving fewer clients at a higher price point.
- **Create a digital product based on your skills:** Turn your knowledge into an online course, ebook, or training program. Digital products are scalable and allow you to serve many customers simultaneously without additional effort.
- **Host workshops or webinars:** Use your skills to provide real-time value to your audience through live workshops or webinars. Charge a premium for access, or use the webinar as a way to sell high-ticket services or products.

3. Audit Your Existing Resources

Existing resources can include content, products, tools, and platforms that you already have at your disposal. By repurposing or enhancing these resources, you can save time and avoid reinventing the wheel.

How to Assess Your Resources:

- **Evaluate existing content:** Do you have past blog posts, videos, social media content, or training materials that can be repurposed for your new offer? For example, a collection of blog posts can be turned into an ebook, or a series of videos can become a paid online course.

- **Review past offers:** If you've successfully sold products or services in the past, consider whether you can improve or relaunch them for this new campaign. Can you add bonuses, offer a new version, or bundle past products to create a high-value package?

- **Examine your platforms:** Take stock of the platforms you already own or have access to. This includes your website, email marketing platform, social media accounts, and any other digital channels where you can promote your offer. These are valuable tools for reaching your audience without needing to invest in new systems.

Examples of Leveraging Existing Resources:

- **Repurpose content into a new offer:** Take existing content—such as blog posts, podcasts, or videos—and compile them into a new product. This could be an ebook, a course, or a membership site with access to all your past content.

- **Repackage previous products:** If you've launched products or services before, consider bundling them with new bonuses or updates to create a fresh, high-value offer. For instance, if you have an online course, you could add a group coaching component to make it more attractive.

- **Use existing platforms for marketing:** Rather than investing in new tools, maximize your existing resources. Use your website, social media pages, and email list to promote your offer. Set up automated email sequences and retargeting ads to engage people who've shown interest but haven't yet purchased.

Step 2: Strategically Leveraging Your Network

Your network is one of the most effective assets you can use to boost sales. Leveraging your relationships in a strategic way can amplify your reach, build credibility, and accelerate your path to generating $100,000 in 24 hours.

1. Activate Your Inner Circle

Start by reaching out to your closest connections—those who are already familiar with your work and trust your expertise. Your inner circle includes existing clients, past customers, colleagues, and close professional contacts. These people are more likely to support your launch and help spread the word.

How to Activate Your Inner Circle:

- **Exclusive early access:** Offer your inner circle early access to your product or service before the official launch. This makes them feel valued and gives them an opportunity to purchase before the general public. For example, "As one of my valued clients, I'm offering you first access to this offer before it goes live."
- **Request testimonials or endorsements:** Ask past clients or colleagues for testimonials that you can use in your marketing materials. You can also request that they endorse or share your offer with their network.
- **Offer special bonuses:** Reward your inner circle for supporting your launch. This could be in the form of exclusive bonuses, discounts, or VIP access to additional content.

2. Leverage Affiliate Marketing

Affiliate marketing is a powerful way to extend your reach by incentivizing others to promote your product or service. Affiliates are typically paid a commission for each sale they generate, which motivates them to share your offer with their audience.

How to Set Up an Affiliate Program:

- **Create a compelling offer for affiliates:** Your affiliate offer should be attractive and clearly communicate the benefits of promoting your product. Offer competitive commissions (typically 30-50%) and emphasize the high value of your product or service.
- **Provide marketing materials:** Make it easy for affiliates to promote your product by providing them with ready-made marketing materials, including email swipe files, social media posts, and banners.
- **Track and pay commissions:** Use affiliate tracking software to track sales generated by your affiliates and automate commission payments. Popular affiliate platforms include ClickBank, ShareASale, and CJ Affiliate.

3. Collaborate with Influencers

Influencer collaborations can rapidly increase your exposure by allowing you to tap into new audiences. Influencers have built trust with their followers, which means their endorsement of your product can lead to immediate sales.

How to Collaborate with Influencers:

- **Find influencers in your niche:** Look for influencers who have an engaged audience in your target market. This can include social media influencers, bloggers, YouTubers, or podcasters. Micro-influencers (with 10,000 to 100,000 followers) can often deliver high engagement rates.
- **Offer a mutually beneficial deal:** Propose a collaboration that benefits both you and the influencer. This could be through affiliate commissions, a flat fee, or cross-promotion. For example, offer

to promote their content in exchange for them promoting your product.

- **Give influencers early access:** Provide influencers with early access to your product or service, allowing them to review and recommend it to their audience during your 24-hour launch window.

Step 3: Maximizing Your Skills

Your unique skills and expertise are valuable assets that can set you apart from competitors and allow you to offer high-ticket services or products. To maximize these skills, focus on delivering exceptional value to your customers.

1. Position Yourself as an Expert

When people perceive you as an expert in your field, they are more likely to trust your recommendations and invest in your offers. Use your skills to position yourself as an authority in your niche.

How to Establish Expert Authority:

- **Content marketing:** Share valuable, actionable content that demonstrates your expertise. This could include blog posts, social media content, webinars, or podcasts. Provide solutions to key problems that your audience faces, which builds trust and credibility.
- **Case studies and success stories:** Showcase your expertise through case studies or testimonials from past clients or customers. Highlight the results you've helped them achieve, and use this social proof to attract new customers.
- **Guest appearances:** Increase your visibility by guest posting on high-traffic blogs, being interviewed on podcasts, or speaking at virtual events. These opportunities allow you to reach new audiences and establish yourself as a thought leader in your industry.

2. Create High-Value, High-Ticket Offers

To quickly generate significant revenue, focus on creating high-ticket offers that are closely aligned with your skills. High-ticket offers are premium products or services that deliver exceptional value and command premium prices.

How to Create High-Ticket Offers:

- **Identify a specific, high-value problem:** Pinpoint a pressing problem that your target audience is willing to pay a premium to solve. For example, business owners might be willing to pay $10,000 for a service that will increase their revenue by six figures.
- **Offer personalized solutions:** High-ticket offers often involve personalized or customized solutions. For instance, you could offer one-on-one coaching, consulting, or done-for-you services that provide a tailored experience.
- **Include bonuses and support:** Increase the perceived value of your high-ticket offer by including additional bonuses, such as exclusive content, follow-up support, or access to a private community.

Step 4: Leveraging Existing Resources

Using existing resources—whether it's content, platforms, or tools—can streamline your marketing efforts and reduce the amount of time and money you need to invest.

1. Repurpose Existing Content

If you've been producing content over the years, such as blog posts, videos, or podcasts, you can repurpose this material into new offers or marketing materials.

How to Repurpose Content:

- **Bundle content into a digital product:** Take a series of blog posts, training videos, or webinars and bundle them into a comprehensive digital product, such as an online course or ebook.
- **Turn webinars into an evergreen product:** If you've hosted live webinars, you can package the recordings into an on-demand training program that customers can purchase and access anytime.
- **Use content as lead magnets:** Offer existing content, such as checklists, templates, or guides, as lead magnets to grow your email list and nurture potential buyers before your 24-hour launch.

2. Utilize Existing Platforms

Maximize the platforms you already own—such as your website, email list, or social media accounts—to promote your offer and engage your audience.

How to Leverage Platforms:

- **Email marketing:** Your email list is a direct line of communication to people who are already interested in what you offer. Use your email list to send pre-launch teasers, countdown emails, and special offers.
- **Retargeting ads:** Use retargeting ads on platforms like Facebook and Google to reach people who have visited your website but haven't purchased. Retargeting keeps your offer top-of-mind and can lead to higher conversions.
- **Automated systems:** Set up automation tools to streamline your marketing. For example, use an email sequence to nurture leads and guide them through the buying process, or set up an automated sales funnel to capture leads and close sales.

Conclusion

Leveraging your existing assets is a powerful strategy for generating $100,000 in 24 hours. By assessing and utilizing your network, skills, and resources, you can amplify your reach, increase credibility, and create high-value offers that meet the needs of your target audience. Whether it's activating your network, collaborating with affiliates, positioning yourself as an expert, or repurposing existing content, these strategies will help you boost your success and achieve your financial goal in a short timeframe.

Chapter 6: Building Your Offer: High-Value, High-Ticket

To achieve your goal of generating $100,000 in 24 hours, you need to create an irresistible, high-value, high-ticket offer that people are eager to buy. High-ticket offers command premium prices because they deliver substantial value, solve significant problems, and promise meaningful transformations. By positioning your offer as a solution to your audience's most pressing challenges, you can justify higher price points and drive rapid sales within a short period.

In this chapter, we'll explore how to craft a high-ticket offer that delivers immense value, connects with your target audience's needs, and positions you as the best solution available. We'll break down the components of a value-packed offer, how to build perceived value, and strategies for pricing and structuring your offer for maximum success.

Step 1: Understanding the Psychology of High-Ticket Buyers

Before crafting your offer, it's important to understand what motivates high-ticket buyers. These are individuals or businesses who are willing to invest significant amounts of money in a solution that promises a clear return on investment (ROI) or transformative outcomes. High-ticket buyers are not just looking for products or services—they're looking for **results**.

1. They Want a Solution to a High-Value Problem

High-ticket buyers are often facing urgent or significant challenges. Whether it's scaling a business, improving their health, or increasing their financial stability, they're willing to pay more for a solution that will save them time, eliminate pain points, and deliver results quickly.

2. They Want an Expert, Not a Generalist

High-ticket buyers seek out experts who specialize in solving their specific problem. They don't want a generalist who offers vague promises; they want someone with a proven track record who understands their unique situation. Positioning yourself as a niche expert is key to attracting high-ticket buyers.

3. They Expect Personalized or Tailored Solutions

When paying premium prices, buyers expect personalized attention or customization. They want a solution that's tailored to their specific needs and circumstances, whether it's through one-on-one coaching, customized strategies, or direct access to you as the expert.

4. They Expect High Perceived Value

High-ticket buyers expect an offer that not only solves their problem but also feels exclusive, premium, and luxurious. They're more likely to buy when they feel that they're getting an experience that others cannot easily access, reinforcing the perceived value of your offer.

Step 2: Identifying the Core Problem and Offering a High-Value Solution

The foundation of any high-ticket offer is solving a core problem that is deeply felt by your target audience. The bigger the problem, the more people are willing to pay for a solution that resolves it effectively.

1. Identify a High-Value Problem

To create a compelling high-ticket offer, you need to identify the most significant problem your target audience is facing. This should be a problem that your audience views as urgent, impactful, and worth solving as soon as possible.

Examples of high-value problems:

- **Business owners struggling to scale**: They're overwhelmed with operational tasks and want to grow their revenue without burning out.
- **Health and wellness seekers facing chronic issues**: They may be dealing with weight loss, fitness, or mental health challenges and are ready to invest in a solution that delivers fast, measurable results.
- **Entrepreneurs seeking financial freedom**: They're looking for a roadmap to achieving financial independence and want clear, actionable strategies to get there.

To identify a high-value problem:

- **Survey or interview your audience**: Ask your current customers or followers what their biggest challenges are, what's keeping them from success, and what they're willing to invest in to solve those problems.
- **Monitor forums and social media**: Platforms like Reddit, Quora, and Facebook Groups are full of people asking questions and discussing their struggles. Look for patterns in the types of problems people are experiencing.
- **Look at competitors**: Identify what high-ticket solutions your competitors are offering. If others are solving similar problems at a premium price, it's a sign that the market values that solution.

2. Craft a Solution That Delivers Tangible Results

Once you've identified a high-value problem, the next step is to create a solution that addresses it in a way that delivers clear, measurable results. High-ticket offers must be outcome-driven. Buyers are not paying for time or effort—they're paying for results.

Your solution should:

- **Promise a clear transformation**: Describe the specific outcome buyers will achieve after working with you or using your product. For example, instead of offering "business coaching," promise to help them "double their revenue in 6 months."
- **Include measurable goals**: Provide quantifiable metrics for success. For example, "lose 10 pounds in 4 weeks," "cut operational costs by 30%," or "gain 1,000 new leads in 90 days."
- **Demonstrate urgency and speed**: High-ticket buyers often want results quickly. If you can deliver a solution faster than your competitors, it adds to the perceived value. Highlight how your approach saves time and delivers faster results.

Step 3: Building Perceived Value with Premium Components

The perceived value of your offer is what justifies a high price tag. While the core solution is crucial, adding premium components can elevate your offer's value in the eyes of potential buyers. The more exclusive, comprehensive, and tailored your offer feels, the more people will be willing to invest in it.

1. Personalized Access to You or Your Team

One of the most powerful ways to increase the value of your offer is to include direct access to you as the expert. Whether through one-on-one coaching, personalized consulting sessions, or direct email support, offering personalized attention significantly boosts the value of your offer.

How to offer personalized access:

- **One-on-one coaching**: Provide private coaching sessions tailored to each client's unique needs. For example, a high-ticket business coaching program might include weekly one-on-one calls where you help the client implement custom strategies.
- **Personalized consulting or done-for-you services**: For clients who want faster results, you can offer a done-for-you service where you or your team directly handle certain tasks for them.
- **Unlimited email or Voxer access**: Offer VIP access to your clients, where they can contact you anytime with questions or challenges. This level of access makes clients feel supported throughout their journey and adds significant value to your offer.

2. Exclusive Content and Resources

Adding exclusive content or resources that your clients can't find elsewhere can further increase the perceived value of your offer. These could be resources you've developed based on your expertise or content you've created specifically for your high-ticket clients.

Premium components to consider:

- **Private training sessions**: Offer live or recorded training sessions that are only available to clients in your high-ticket program. These sessions could cover advanced topics that go beyond what's publicly available.
- **Exclusive templates or frameworks**: Provide ready-made templates, checklists, or frameworks that clients can use to implement your strategies faster and more effectively.
- **Members-only resources**: Create a private library of resources—such as ebooks, videos, or guides—that clients can access for additional learning and support. Make sure these resources are comprehensive and packed with value.

3. Bonuses and Add-Ons

Bonuses can significantly enhance the perceived value of your offer by making buyers feel like they're getting more than they paid for. When choosing bonuses, focus on adding items that complement the core offer and make it easier for the client to achieve their desired outcome.

Types of bonuses to consider:

- **Bonus coaching sessions**: Include a limited number of bonus one-on-one coaching sessions to help clients accelerate their results.
- **Done-for-you templates**: Provide templates or documents that clients can use to implement your teachings immediately (e.g., sales scripts, marketing funnels, or workout plans).
- **Exclusive community access**: Give clients access to a private community of like-minded individuals. This could be a Facebook Group, Slack channel, or forum where they can ask questions, get feedback, and network with others in your program.

4. Premium Delivery and Customer Experience

How you deliver your high-ticket offer can also contribute to its perceived value. High-ticket buyers expect a premium customer experience that makes them feel special and supported.

Enhance the delivery of your offer by:

- **Creating a premium onboarding process**: Start with an in-depth onboarding process that sets clear expectations and gives clients a personalized roadmap for success. This could include a detailed intake form, an onboarding call, or access to an exclusive members' area.
- **Offering lifetime access**: If your offer includes digital products, such as an online course or training program, give clients lifetime access to the content. This ensures they can revisit the material whenever they need to, adding long-term value to the purchase.
- **Providing white-glove service**: High-ticket clients should feel like they're getting VIP treatment. This could include priority customer support, personalized follow-up after coaching sessions, or regular progress check-ins.

Step 4: Pricing Your High-Ticket Offer

Pricing is one of the most important factors in building a high-ticket offer. You want to price your offer based on the value it delivers rather than the time or effort it takes to create. Pricing your offer too low can undermine its perceived value, while pricing it too high without sufficient value can deter potential buyers.

1. Value-Based Pricing

Value-based pricing means setting the price of your offer based on the outcomes and transformation it provides, rather than the cost of creating it. High-ticket offers should focus on the return on investment (ROI) the buyer will get from your solution.

To set value-based pricing:

- **Determine the financial value of the outcome**: For example, if you're offering a business coaching program that helps clients increase their revenue by $50,000, it's reasonable to charge $5,000-$10,000 for your program.

- **Price according to transformation**: Think about the emotional and life-changing results your clients will experience. For example, if you're offering health coaching that helps people lose weight and regain confidence, those emotional benefits are worth a premium price.

- **Compare your pricing to competitors**: While you don't want to price your offer solely based on what others are charging, it's helpful to understand the range of prices in your industry. Your offer should be priced competitively but reflect the additional value you're providing.

2. Tiered Pricing Options

Offering tiered pricing can make your high-ticket offer accessible to different segments of your audience while still maintaining premium pricing for those who want more personalized attention.

Examples of tiered pricing:

- **Basic, mid-tier, and premium packages**: Create multiple pricing tiers that offer varying levels of access and support. For example, your basic package could include access to an online course, while the mid-tier package includes group coaching, and the premium package includes one-on-one coaching.

- **Early-bird or fast-action discounts**: Encourage fast sales by offering a limited-time discount for people who purchase your high-ticket offer within a specific time frame. This creates urgency and rewards buyers for taking immediate action.

- **Payment plans**: To make your high-ticket offer more accessible, provide a payment plan option. For example, instead of charging $5,000 upfront, you could offer five monthly payments of

$1,100. This makes it easier for buyers to afford the premium price without diminishing the perceived value.

Step 5: Communicating the Value of Your High-Ticket Offer

Creating a high-ticket offer is one thing; communicating its value effectively is another. Buyers need to understand why your offer is worth the investment and what makes it stand out from other options. Clear, persuasive messaging is key to driving sales.

1. Focus on Outcomes, Not Features

While it's important to explain what's included in your offer (e.g., coaching sessions, templates, bonuses), your messaging should focus primarily on the outcomes and results that buyers will experience.

Your messaging should answer the question:

- **What transformation will buyers experience after purchasing your offer?** For example:
- Instead of "6 coaching calls," say "Get personalized guidance to create a scalable business strategy that doubles your revenue in 6 months."
- Instead of "Access to a private community," say "Join an exclusive group of high-performing entrepreneurs and get support and feedback from like-minded individuals."

2. Use Testimonials and Social Proof

Testimonials from past clients or success stories can significantly boost the credibility of your offer. High-ticket buyers want to know that you have a proven track record of delivering results.

How to leverage testimonials:

- **Feature success stories prominently**: Display testimonials from clients who have achieved significant results through your offer. Include specific details about their transformation (e.g., "I tripled my revenue in 3 months thanks to this coaching program!").

- **Include video testimonials**: Video testimonials are particularly effective because they feel more personal and trustworthy. Encourage past clients to share their experiences on video, highlighting the specific benefits of working with you.

3. Address Objections and Build Trust

High-ticket buyers are naturally more cautious about making large purchases. Address common objections head-on to build trust and reduce the perceived risk of investing in your offer.

Address common objections such as:

- **"I'm not sure if this will work for me"**: Include case studies and examples of how your offer has helped people in similar situations achieve results.
- **"The price is too high"**: Justify the price by highlighting the long-term benefits and ROI that buyers will receive. Emphasize the value of the transformation compared to the cost.
- **"I'm worried about taking the leap"**: Offer a guarantee or risk-reversal strategy to reduce the fear of making a large investment. For example, you could offer a money-back guarantee if buyers don't see measurable results within a certain timeframe.

Conclusion

Building a high-value, high-ticket offer is one of the most effective strategies for reaching your $100,000 goal in 24 hours. By crafting a solution that addresses a high-value problem, offering premium components, and pricing your offer based on the transformation it delivers, you can create an irresistible package that buyers are eager to invest in. Remember, high-ticket buyers are looking for outcomes and results, so your offer should be outcome-driven, personalized, and supported by strong social proof. By clearly communicating the value of your offer and addressing objections, you'll position yourself as the best choice for your audience's most pressing needs, making it easier to close sales and hit your financial target.

Part 2: Rapid Product Creation

Chapter 7: Identifying Pain Points and Solutions

At the heart of every successful high-ticket offer is a deep understanding of your audience's most pressing **pain points**—the urgent problems that cause them frustration, stress, or anxiety. When people face significant challenges in their lives or businesses, they are often willing to invest large sums of money in a solution that can relieve their pain quickly and effectively. Identifying and addressing these urgent pain points is crucial to building an irresistible offer that people are eager to buy.

In this chapter, we'll explore how to identify the most painful and urgent problems your target audience faces, and how to position your offer as the solution they are willing to pay big money to solve. We'll dive into the psychology behind pain points, research methods for uncovering these problems, and strategies for crafting solutions that speak directly to your audience's needs.

Step 1: Understanding the Psychology of Pain Points

A **pain point** is a specific problem that your target audience is experiencing. The more urgent or emotionally charged the problem, the more likely people are to seek out a solution—and the more willing they are to pay a premium for that solution. When you address these pain points directly in your marketing and offers, you tap into a deep emotional need for relief, which drives purchasing decisions.

1. Emotional Drivers of Pain Points

Pain points are not just surface-level problems; they are often tied to deep emotional drivers such as fear, frustration, uncertainty, and desire for change. People's willingness to spend money on a solution is directly related to how much emotional discomfort the problem causes them.

For example:

- **Fear**: A business owner might fear going out of business if they don't increase their revenue. This fear can drive them to pay for high-ticket coaching or consulting to help them grow their business.

- **Frustration**: An individual struggling with weight loss may feel frustrated after trying numerous diets without success. They are more likely to invest in a high-end fitness or health program that promises real results.
- **Uncertainty**: An entrepreneur may feel uncertain about how to scale their business. This uncertainty can lead them to invest in a mentorship program that provides clear, actionable strategies for growth.

By understanding the emotional drivers behind your audience's pain points, you can position your offer as the solution that alleviates their discomfort, reduces stress, and delivers the transformation they seek.

2. Urgency of the Problem

The **urgency** of a pain point plays a significant role in how quickly someone will act to resolve it. The more immediate and pressing the problem, the more likely a potential buyer will be to seek a solution quickly and pay a higher price for that solution. Urgent pain points often have consequences if left unresolved, which can motivate faster purchasing decisions.

Examples of urgent pain points include:

- A business on the verge of bankruptcy if sales don't improve within the next quarter.
- A health condition that worsens without immediate intervention.
- An upcoming deadline for launching a product or project, leading to stress and time pressure.

Urgent problems often come with higher stakes, making people more willing to invest in a high-ticket solution that promises fast, effective results.

Step 2: Researching Your Audience's Pain Points

To identify the most pressing pain points for your target audience, you need to conduct thorough research. This research allows you to understand the challenges your audience is facing, how these challenges impact their lives, and what solutions they are already seeking.

1. Engage with Your Audience Directly

One of the best ways to uncover pain points is by engaging directly with your audience. By speaking with your existing customers, followers, or target market, you can gain valuable insights into their most pressing challenges.

Methods for Engaging Your Audience:

- **Surveys and Polls**: Send surveys to your email list or social media followers asking them about their biggest challenges. Include open-ended questions like, "What is the biggest problem you're currently facing in your business?" or "What keeps you up at night?"
- **Interviews**: Conduct one-on-one interviews with existing clients or potential customers. Ask them to describe their pain points in detail, including how these problems impact their lives and what solutions they've tried before.
- **Social Media Engagement**: Use social media platforms to ask your audience about their challenges. You can post polls, ask questions in comments, or start conversations in Facebook Groups, Twitter, or Instagram Stories.

The goal is to gather qualitative data that gives you a deep understanding of the emotional and practical challenges your audience faces. The more specific you can get, the better you'll be able to craft solutions that resonate.

2. Analyze Online Communities and Forums

Online communities, forums, and social media platforms are rich sources of information about your audience's pain points. These platforms allow people to openly discuss their problems, ask for advice, and share their frustrations. By analyzing these conversations, you can gain insights into what people are struggling with and how urgent those struggles are.

Where to Find Pain Points:

- **Reddit**: Reddit is full of niche communities where people discuss their challenges in various industries, from entrepreneurship to health to personal finance. Search for relevant subreddits in your niche and look for recurring themes in posts and comments.
- **Quora**: Quora is a question-and-answer platform where users ask for advice on specific problems. Search for questions related to your niche to see what issues people are seeking solutions for.
- **Facebook Groups**: Facebook Groups are great for uncovering pain points because they allow for real-time discussions. Join groups where your target audience hangs out and pay attention to the questions and problems they post about.
- **LinkedIn Groups**: If you're in a B2B niche, LinkedIn Groups are a valuable resource for understanding business-related challenges. Look for discussions around common business problems like scaling, marketing, or operational inefficiencies.

As you analyze these platforms, take note of common complaints, questions, and frustrations. This will help you identify the most urgent and widespread problems that people are actively looking to solve.

3. Study Competitors and Industry Trends

Competitor research can also help you identify pain points in your market. By analyzing what your competitors are offering and how they position their solutions, you can uncover gaps in the market or areas where customers may still feel unsatisfied.

How to Study Competitors:

- **Analyze competitor offers**: Look at the products or services your competitors are selling and how they frame the problems they solve. Pay attention to customer reviews and testimonials to see if there are any recurring complaints or unmet needs.
- **Review marketing materials**: Study your competitors' marketing campaigns, sales pages, and email sequences to see how they describe the pain points they address. Are there any areas where you can differentiate your offer by solving an overlooked problem?
- **Look for market trends**: Stay up-to-date on industry trends by following relevant blogs, news sites, or industry reports. This can help you identify emerging pain points or shifts in the market that create new opportunities for high-ticket offers.

Competitor research not only helps you understand what's currently being offered but also highlights opportunities to offer something unique or improved.

Step 3: Prioritizing the Most Urgent Pain Points

Once you've gathered a list of potential pain points, the next step is to prioritize the ones that are the most urgent, impactful, and financially valuable. Not all problems are created equal—some pain points are more pressing, while others may be minor annoyances that people are less willing to pay for.

1. Focus on High-Impact Pain Points

High-impact pain points are problems that have a significant effect on your audience's lives or businesses. These are the types of problems that, if left unresolved, will continue to cause stress, financial loss, or other negative consequences.

Questions to ask when prioritizing pain points:

- **What are the financial consequences of not solving this problem?**
    - ◦ For example, a business owner who is losing money due to poor marketing will be more motivated to invest in a solution because the problem has direct financial consequences.
- **What emotional impact does this problem have?**
    - ◦ Emotional pain points, such as stress, overwhelm, or frustration, are often just as powerful as financial ones. If your audience is feeling burned out or demoralized, they'll be more willing to invest in a solution that offers relief.
- **How widespread is this problem?**
    - ◦ Look for problems that affect a large portion of your audience. The more people who are experiencing the pain point, the larger your potential customer base.

2. Target Problems with High Perceived Value

People are willing to pay more for solutions to problems that they perceive as valuable. High-perceived-value problems are those that, once solved, create a significant improvement in the buyer's life or business.

Examples of high-perceived-value problems:

- **Business scaling**: Entrepreneurs who need help scaling their business see this as a high-value problem because it directly affects their revenue and growth potential. They are often willing to pay premium prices for coaching, consulting, or software solutions that help them scale faster.
- **Health transformations**: People struggling with chronic health issues, weight loss, or fitness goals perceive these problems as life-changing. They are more likely to invest in high-ticket health programs or personal training to achieve their desired outcomes.
- **Financial freedom**: Those seeking financial independence or better money management perceive these problems as critical to

their future. They will invest in financial coaching, courses, or tools that promise to improve their financial situation.

3. Prioritize Problems with Immediate Need

Some problems have a greater sense of urgency because they have immediate or time-sensitive consequences. People are more willing to spend money when they feel they need to act quickly to avoid negative outcomes.

Examples of urgent problems:

- **Business owners facing a revenue decline**: If a business is losing customers or revenue, the owner will feel the need to fix the problem immediately to avoid financial ruin.
- **Professionals facing deadlines**: A professional who needs to meet an important deadline (e.g., launching a new product, completing a major project) may be willing to invest in services or tools that help them achieve their goals on time.
- **Health concerns that worsen over time**: Someone experiencing a health issue that could get worse without intervention is more likely to act quickly. This could include someone with chronic pain or a fitness goal they need to meet by a specific date.

By focusing on pain points with an immediate need for resolution, you can position your offer as a time-sensitive solution, creating urgency and increasing the likelihood of fast sales.

Step 4: Crafting Solutions to Pain Points

Once you've identified the most pressing and valuable pain points, the next step is to craft a solution that addresses these problems in a way that is both comprehensive and easy to implement. Your solution should be outcome-driven, meaning it leads to a clear and measurable result for the buyer.

1. Design an Outcome-Driven Solution

Your offer should be built around a specific outcome that directly solves your audience's pain point. High-ticket buyers are paying for results, so your offer must promise a clear transformation.

To design an outcome-driven solution:

- **Define the end result**: What will the buyer achieve after using your product or service? Be specific about the transformation they can expect. For example, "Double your revenue in 6 months," or "Lose 15 pounds in 30 days."
- **Outline the steps to get there**: Break down the process you will guide the buyer through to achieve the desired result. This could include modules in an online course, milestones in a coaching program, or deliverables in a done-for-you service.
- **Focus on ease of implementation**: Your solution should feel easy to implement, even if it involves complex strategies. High-ticket buyers want to know that they can achieve the desired outcome without feeling overwhelmed or lost.

2. Incorporate Personalized or Tailored Solutions

High-ticket buyers often expect a level of customization or personalization in the solution they purchase. By offering tailored solutions, you increase the perceived value and differentiate your offer from generic, one-size-fits-all options.

Ways to offer personalization:

- **One-on-one coaching or consulting**: Provide personalized guidance and support based on the client's unique situation. This could include one-on-one coaching calls, custom strategies, or personalized feedback on their progress.

- **Customizable templates or resources**: If you're offering a digital product, include customizable templates, checklists, or tools that allow buyers to adapt the solution to their needs.
- **VIP access or support**: Offer exclusive access to a VIP support team, or provide priority email or phone support for high-ticket clients. This ensures that they feel supported throughout their journey.

3. Build Value with Bonuses and Add-Ons

Enhancing your offer with bonuses and add-ons can significantly increase the perceived value. These extras should be relevant to the core solution and help the buyer achieve their goals faster or more easily.

Ideas for bonuses:

- **Bonus training sessions or courses**: Provide additional content that complements the core offer, such as advanced training or specialized modules that help clients reach their goals more effectively.
- **Exclusive resources**: Offer downloadable templates, workbooks, or guides that simplify the implementation of your solution.
- **Accountability check-ins**: Include regular progress check-ins (e.g., weekly or monthly calls) to help clients stay on track and ensure they're implementing the solution correctly.

Conclusion

Identifying your audience's most urgent pain points is the foundation of a successful high-ticket offer. By understanding the emotional drivers behind these problems, researching your audience's challenges, and prioritizing high-impact, high-value issues, you can craft a solution that people are eager to buy. Your solution should focus on delivering clear, measurable outcomes, providing personalized support, and offering additional value through bonuses and tailored components. By addressing the right pain points with a comprehensive solution, you'll create an irresistible offer that leads to rapid sales and significant financial success.

Chapter 8: Crafting a High-Impact Product

Creating a digital product or service in less than a day is not only possible, but it's also a smart way to generate quick revenue. Whether it's an ebook, online course, workshop, or consulting service, a high-impact product doesn't need to take months to develop. By focusing on solving a specific problem and delivering immediate value, you can craft a digital product that buyers are eager to purchase in a short timeframe.

In this chapter, we will walk through the step-by-step process of creating a high-impact digital product or service in less than a day. We'll explore how to identify your target audience's most pressing needs, select the right product format, outline your content, and use tools to produce and deliver your product quickly. With the right strategy, you can build a product that's ready to sell and capable of generating significant revenue within 24 hours.

Step 1: Choosing the Right Product Format

The first step in creating a digital product quickly is selecting the right format. The format you choose should align with your strengths, the needs of your audience, and the urgency of the problem you're solving. Certain digital product formats are easier to create in a short time frame while still delivering high value.

1. Digital Product Formats That Can Be Created Quickly

Here are several digital product formats that can be developed in less than a day:

- **Ebook or Guide**: An ebook is a written document, typically 10-30 pages, that provides in-depth information on a specific topic. Ebooks are fast to create if you already have content from blog posts, articles, or past presentations that can be repurposed.

- ◦ **Example**: "10 Proven Strategies to Double Your Online Sales in 30 Days."
- **Webinar or Workshop**: A live or pre-recorded workshop or webinar can be produced quickly, especially if you're an expert in the subject matter. You can structure the content as a 60-90 minute training session with slides and actionable advice.
  - ◦ **Example**: "How to Build a 6-Figure Coaching Business: A Step-by-Step Workshop."
- **Templates or Checklists**: Templates or checklists are downloadable resources that provide users with a framework for completing a task. They're fast to create and easy to scale since they require minimal ongoing effort.
  - ◦ **Example**: "Ultimate Marketing Funnel Template for Coaches and Consultants."
- **Mini-Course**: A mini-course consists of a few video or audio lessons (typically 3-5) that teach a specific skill or concept. Since mini-courses focus on narrow topics, they're faster to produce than full-length courses.
  - ◦ **Example**: "3-Day Facebook Ads Bootcamp for Beginners."
- **Consulting or Coaching Package**: Offering a one-time consulting session or coaching package doesn't require you to create a physical product. Instead, you're selling your time and expertise. You can structure your offer around a single session or a short series of coaching calls.
  - ◦ **Example**: "1-Hour Strategy Call: Get Expert Feedback on Your Sales Funnel."

2. Selecting the Best Format for Your Audience and Expertise

To decide on the best product format, consider the following:

- **What problem are you solving?** Different formats lend themselves to different problems. For example, a checklist might be ideal for simplifying a complex process, while a webinar may be better for explaining a multi-step strategy.

- **What is your audience's preferred learning style?** Some people prefer to read, others to watch videos, and others to take action with hands-on materials. If your audience is full of visual learners, a webinar might be ideal; if they prefer actionable tools, a checklist could work better.
- **What can you produce quickly and with quality?** Consider your strengths. If you're great at explaining concepts on camera, create a webinar or mini-course. If you're an expert writer, focus on crafting a guide or ebook.

Once you've selected the format that aligns with your expertise and audience needs, you can move on to the next step: outlining your content.

Step 2: Outlining Your Product or Service

Creating a clear and concise outline is crucial to building your product quickly. A well-structured outline ensures that you don't waste time figuring out what to include or how to organize your content. It also helps you stay focused on delivering the highest value in the shortest time.

1. Identify the Core Outcome

Every high-impact product should focus on solving one specific problem or delivering one clear outcome. This helps ensure that the product is focused, actionable, and provides immediate value.

To identify the core outcome, ask yourself:

- **What is the one main result I want my audience to achieve after using this product or service?**
- **How can I help them achieve this result quickly and effectively?**

For example, if you're creating an ebook on sales strategies, the core outcome might be: "By the end of this ebook, you will know how to implement five proven sales strategies that increase your online revenue in 30 days."

2. Break Down the Steps or Lessons

Once you've identified the outcome, break it down into a step-by-step process or key lessons. Each step should build on the previous one, leading the customer toward the final outcome.

For example, if you're creating a mini-course, you might outline the following lessons:

1. **Lesson 1: Understanding the Basics of Sales Psychology**
2. **Lesson 2: Crafting an Irresistible Offer**
3. **Lesson 3: Using Proven Sales Funnels to Drive Conversions**
4. **Lesson 4: Optimizing Your Marketing Campaigns for Results**
5. **Lesson 5: Tracking and Scaling Your Sales System**

Each step or lesson should be focused and actionable. Avoid trying to cover too much at once—your goal is to deliver a clear result quickly, not overwhelm your audience with excessive information.

3. Include Actionable Elements

To make your product high-impact, include elements that encourage the audience to take immediate action. Actionable elements help people implement what they've learned, which increases the perceived value of your product and leads to better results for your customers.

Ways to include actionable elements:

- **Checklists**: After each step, include a checklist that the audience can use to make sure they've implemented the strategy correctly.
- **Templates**: Provide templates that make it easy for the audience to execute your instructions (e.g., email templates, landing page templates, or marketing scripts).

- **Workbooks**: Add a workbook or worksheets that prompt the audience to apply what they've learned to their own situation. For example, a workbook could ask questions like, "How will you use Strategy X in your business this week?"

By including actionable elements, you increase engagement and ensure that your product delivers practical value.

Step 3: Creating the Product Quickly and Efficiently

With your product format and outline in place, the next step is to produce the content. While creating a digital product in less than a day requires speed, it doesn't mean sacrificing quality. The key is to focus on producing high-value content without getting bogged down in unnecessary details.

1. Repurpose Existing Content

If you've been producing content for a while—whether through blog posts, videos, webinars, or social media—you likely have existing materials that can be repurposed into a digital product. Repurposing content allows you to create something new without starting from scratch, saving you time and effort.

How to repurpose content:

- **Compile blog posts into an ebook**: If you've written several blog posts on a related topic, compile them into a cohesive ebook or guide. You can update the content, add an introduction and conclusion, and package it as a premium product.
- **Turn a webinar into a mini-course**: If you've previously hosted a webinar, break it down into short lessons and add accompanying materials (e.g., slides, worksheets) to create a mini-course.
- **Convert a podcast into a written guide**: If you've recorded podcasts or interviews, transcribe the audio and organize it into a written guide or ebook. You can edit the transcription for clarity and add any additional insights.

Repurposing content is one of the fastest ways to produce a digital product that still delivers high value.

2. Use Tools to Streamline Creation

There are many tools available that make it easy to create and deliver digital products quickly. Here are some of the most useful tools for different product formats:

- **Ebook Creation**: Use tools like **Google Docs** or **Canva** to create a visually appealing ebook or guide. Canva offers pre-designed templates that make formatting quick and easy.
- **Webinars or Workshops**: Use **Zoom** or **Google Meet** to record a live or pre-recorded webinar. You can then host the video on platforms like **Teachable** or **Kajabi** for easy access.
- **Mini-Course**: For a mini-course, use platforms like **Thinkific, Podia**, or **Teachable** to upload video lessons, quizzes, and course materials. These platforms make it easy to organize your content and deliver it to customers seamlessly.
- **Templates and Checklists**: Create downloadable templates or checklists in tools like **Google Sheets**, **Microsoft Word**, or **Canva**. These tools allow you to design and format resources that can be easily shared and downloaded by your audience.

Using the right tools will help you streamline the production process and create a professional-looking product in less time.

3. Focus on MVP (Minimum Viable Product)

When creating a product in less than a day, it's important to focus on the **Minimum Viable Product** (MVP). This means delivering the core value of your product without getting caught up in perfectionism or unnecessary details. Your goal is to provide a functional product that solves a specific problem—then you can refine or expand it over time based on customer feedback.

To focus on the MVP:

- **Stick to your outline**: Don't try to add extra lessons, bonuses, or features at the last minute. Stay focused on delivering the core content you outlined in Step 2.
- **Avoid over-polishing**: Your product should be professional, but it doesn't need to be perfect. For example, your webinar doesn't need Hollywood-level production value; as long as it's clear, concise, and actionable, it will deliver the value your audience is looking for.
- **Launch first, improve later**: If you discover areas for improvement, you can always create an updated version of the product later. Your priority should be launching the MVP to start generating revenue, rather than delaying the launch for perfection.

Step 4: Delivering and Monetizing Your Product

Once your product is ready, the final step is to deliver it to your audience and start generating sales. How you deliver your product will depend on the format you've chosen, but the key is to make the process smooth, professional, and user-friendly.

1. Choose a Platform for Delivery

Choose a platform that makes it easy for your audience to access your product or service. Here are some options based on product format:

- **Ebooks or Guides**: Use **Gumroad**, **SendOwl**, or **Amazon Kindle** to sell and deliver your ebook digitally. These platforms handle the payment process and provide instant download links to buyers.
- **Webinars or Workshops**: If you're offering a live webinar, use **Zoom** or **WebinarJam** for hosting. If it's pre-recorded, upload the video to platforms like **Teachable** or **Kajabi** for on-demand access.
- **Mini-Courses**: Platforms like **Thinkific**, **Kajabi**, or **Podia** are ideal for delivering mini-courses. They provide a professional

course layout, allow you to upload video lessons and worksheets, and make it easy for customers to navigate the content.

- **Consulting or Coaching Packages**: Use **Calendly** or **Acuity Scheduling** to book one-on-one coaching or consulting calls. These tools allow clients to schedule sessions directly on your calendar and send automatic reminders.

2. Price Your Product for Quick Sales

To generate sales quickly, price your product appropriately based on the value it provides and the urgency of the problem it solves. High-ticket offers (such as consulting or coaching) should be priced based on the outcome and transformation they provide, while lower-ticket items (such as ebooks or templates) can be priced to encourage impulse buys.

Pricing strategies:

- **Ebooks and Guides**: Typically priced between $10 and $50, depending on the depth of the content and the problem it solves.
- **Workshops and Webinars**: Live workshops can be priced between $50 and $500, depending on the level of interaction and expertise provided. Pre-recorded webinars are often priced between $30 and $100.
- **Mini-Courses**: Priced between $100 and $500, depending on the number of lessons, bonuses, and level of access to you as the instructor.
- **Consulting or Coaching Packages**: Depending on the level of personalization and expertise, these can be priced anywhere from $500 to $5,000 or more for high-ticket clients.

3. Drive Immediate Traffic to Your Product

To generate $100,000 in 24 hours, you'll need to drive immediate traffic to your product as soon as it's live. Leverage your existing audience, paid advertising, and partnerships to create a sense of urgency and drive fast sales.

Strategies for driving traffic:

- **Email marketing**: Send a series of emails to your list announcing the launch of your product, including a time-sensitive offer or discount to encourage fast purchases.
- **Paid advertising**: Run Facebook, Instagram, or Google Ads targeting your ideal customers. Use urgency-focused ad copy that highlights the immediate benefits of your product.
- **Partner promotions**: Collaborate with influencers, affiliates, or partners who can promote your product to their audience in exchange for a commission on sales.

Conclusion

Creating a high-impact digital product or service in less than a day is a powerful way to generate rapid revenue and meet urgent market demands. By choosing the right product format, outlining your content for quick production, and focusing on delivering the core outcome, you can craft a product that provides immediate value to your audience. With the right tools and strategies for repurposing content, streamlining production, and delivering your product, you can go from idea to sales in under 24 hours, positioning yourself for fast financial success.

Chapter 9: Packaging Your Offer for Maximum Appeal

Packaging your offer effectively is crucial to justifying a premium price and maximizing its appeal to potential buyers. The way you present and position your product or service can make all the difference in whether it's seen as a high-value, must-have solution or just another commodity in the marketplace. In this chapter, we'll explore proven techniques to package your digital product or service in a way that creates perceived value, builds trust, and encourages buyers to pay premium prices for the solution you're offering.

We'll cover everything from creating compelling branding and visuals, to structuring bonuses and guarantees that enhance the value of your offer, to positioning it as a solution worth the investment.

Step 1: Understanding the Importance of Perceived Value

Perceived value is the level of worth that a potential customer assigns to your product based on how it is presented. It doesn't matter how great your product is if it isn't packaged in a way that communicates its value effectively. The higher the perceived value, the more justified your premium pricing will be, and the more likely your audience will be to invest.

1. The Psychology of Premium Pricing

When a product or service is priced higher, buyers automatically associate it with higher quality and greater value. This psychological association is especially true for high-ticket offers, where the price itself often signals exclusivity, expertise, and transformative results. However, premium pricing must be accompanied by an experience and product that justifies the cost—this is where packaging comes in.

Key factors influencing perceived value:

- **Exclusivity**: Premium-priced products often feel more exclusive, offering something that can't be found in lower-priced alternatives.

- **Authority and Expertise**: Higher-priced offers signal that the creator is an expert in their field, capable of delivering superior results.
- **Luxury and Quality**: A well-packaged offer conveys quality and luxury, even if the actual product is digital. Buyers are willing to pay more for an experience that feels refined and valuable.

By understanding the psychology behind premium pricing, you can structure your offer to highlight its worth and justify its higher price point.

2. Why Packaging Matters

The packaging of your offer—both visual and structural—is how you communicate its value. Proper packaging tells your audience that this is not just a product or service; it's a solution that will deliver real results and provide a superior experience.

The presentation of your offer can include:

- **Design and branding**: The aesthetics of your sales page, product visuals, and promotional materials can significantly impact how your audience perceives your offer. Clean, professional, and luxurious design choices can elevate the perceived value of even the most basic product.
- **Content structure**: How you describe your offer, the bonuses you include, and the overall layout of your product details contribute to how buyers evaluate its worth.
- **Emotional appeal**: Beyond features and benefits, your packaging should resonate with your audience emotionally. Show them how your offer will change their lives or businesses and make them feel empowered, relieved, or successful.

Now, let's move on to the specific techniques you can use to package your product for maximum appeal.

Step 2: Designing for a Premium Experience

The first element of packaging that buyers encounter is the design of your offer. The look and feel of your branding, sales pages, product visuals, and even the delivery platform all contribute to the buyer's perception of value. Premium design is critical when it comes to justifying a higher price point.

1. Invest in Professional Branding and Visuals

High-end products are almost always associated with high-quality branding. Professional design and visuals can make your offer look polished, credible, and worth the investment. On the other hand, a poorly designed sales page or product can detract from its perceived value, regardless of the quality of the content inside.

Tips for premium branding:

- **Consistent branding**: Use consistent colors, fonts, and logo placement across all your marketing materials and product pages. This cohesiveness creates a sense of professionalism and trust.
- **Sleek, minimalistic design**: High-end brands often use sleek, clean designs with plenty of white space, high-resolution images, and bold typography. Avoid cluttered designs or overly complex layouts, as they can confuse or overwhelm potential buyers.
- **High-quality product images and mockups**: For digital products, use high-quality mockups to represent your product visually. If you're selling an ebook, course, or membership, create 3D covers, mockup videos, or screenshots that showcase the product in a polished, professional way.

You don't need to be a design expert to create premium visuals—there are tools like **Canva**, **Adobe Spark**, or hiring freelancers from platforms like **Fiverr** or **99designs** that can elevate your branding.

2. Create a Compelling Offer Page

Your offer page is the centerpiece of your product packaging. It's where potential buyers make the decision to purchase, so it should be designed to highlight your product's benefits, features, and exclusivity. A well-designed offer page not only looks good but also guides the buyer through a persuasive journey that ends in a purchase.

Key elements of a high-converting offer page:

- **Headline and subheadline**: Your headline should grab attention immediately and convey the key benefit of your product. The subheadline can offer additional details about the transformation your product delivers.
  - Example: **"Transform Your Business in 30 Days with Proven Marketing Strategies"** (headline) | **"Exclusive training program that doubles your revenue through targeted marketing"** (subheadline).
- **Benefits over features**: Focus on the results buyers will experience rather than just listing the features of your product. Use bullet points or short paragraphs that highlight the transformation they'll get.
  - Example: **"Unlock the secrets to consistent sales growth, reduce your ad spend by 30%, and automate your client acquisition process."**
- **Premium testimonials**: Include high-quality testimonials from past clients or customers, preferably with video or images to enhance credibility. Focus on specific results and success stories that demonstrate the value of your offer.
  - Example: **"In just 90 days, I increased my revenue by 50% using these strategies. This program is worth every penny!"**
- **Visual appeal**: Use high-quality images, mockups, or videos to showcase your product. A visually appealing page reinforces the premium nature of your offer.

- **Call-to-action**: Use clear, persuasive calls-to-action (CTAs) that encourage immediate purchase. Button text like "Enroll Now" or "Get Instant Access" works better than generic text like "Submit" or "Buy."

Your offer page should not only highlight what makes your product unique but also create a seamless experience that encourages conversions.

Step 3: Structuring Bonuses for Added Value

One of the most effective ways to package your offer for maximum appeal is by including bonuses. Bonuses enhance the perceived value of your product, making buyers feel like they're getting more than they paid for. When done correctly, bonuses can tip the scales in favor of a purchase, especially for high-ticket offers.

1. Choose Bonuses That Complement Your Offer

The best bonuses are those that align with the core product and help the buyer achieve their desired outcome more quickly or easily. Your bonuses should feel like a natural extension of your main offer, not random add-ons. They should also reinforce the premium nature of your product by adding extra value.

Ideas for bonuses that complement digital products:

- **Exclusive content**: Provide access to additional content that isn't available anywhere else, such as advanced training modules, behind-the-scenes videos, or bonus chapters.
- **Templates and checklists**: Offer downloadable resources that simplify implementation, such as marketing templates, step-by-step checklists, or ready-made scripts.
- **Access to private communities**: Give buyers access to a VIP group (e.g., a Facebook group or Slack channel) where they can interact with you and other high-level customers.

- **Personalized coaching or consultations**: For high-ticket products, include one or two coaching or strategy calls where the buyer gets direct, one-on-one support to implement the solution.

By carefully selecting bonuses that add real value, you can increase the perceived worth of your offer and justify premium pricing.

2. Use Time-Sensitive Bonuses

Creating a sense of urgency with time-sensitive bonuses can push potential buyers off the fence and encourage them to purchase sooner rather than later. These are bonuses that are only available for a limited time, typically during the launch period or within the first 24 hours of the offer.

Examples of time-sensitive bonuses:

- **Early-bird discounts**: Offer a discounted price or additional bonus to people who purchase within the first 24-48 hours of the product launch.
- **Fast-action bonuses**: Provide extra bonuses (e.g., exclusive training, additional coaching, or VIP access) to the first X number of people who buy.

Time-sensitive bonuses not only add value but also create urgency, which can drive faster sales and reduce hesitation.

Step 4: Offering Guarantees to Build Trust

One of the biggest barriers to selling high-ticket products is buyer hesitation. People may worry about whether your product will deliver the promised results or if it's worth the investment. Offering a guarantee is a powerful way to remove this risk and build trust with your audience.

1. Craft a Compelling Guarantee

A guarantee reduces the perceived risk of buying your product by offering customers a way to get their money back if they're not satisfied. While many sellers fear offering guarantees, they can actually increase conversions by reassuring buyers that they're making a safe investment.

Types of guarantees:

- **Money-back guarantee**: Offer a full refund if the buyer isn't satisfied within a specific time frame (e.g., 30 days or 60 days). This is the most common type of guarantee and provides buyers with a safety net.
  - Example: **"If you don't see measurable results within 30 days, we'll give you a full refund—no questions asked."**
- **Results-based guarantee**: Instead of a time-based guarantee, you can offer a results-based guarantee, where you promise a specific outcome. This is most effective when you're confident that your product will deliver tangible results.
  - Example: **"If you don't double your leads within 60 days of following our program, we'll refund your investment."**
- **Try-before-you-buy guarantee**: Allow potential customers to try your product for free or at a reduced price before committing to the full investment. This type of guarantee builds trust by letting them experience the value before making a final decision.
  - Example: **"Try the first module for free! If you don't see immediate value, you can cancel with no obligation."**

A strong guarantee can tip the balance in your favor and increase sales by removing the buyer's sense of risk.

2. Be Specific and Transparent

A vague or overly complex guarantee can actually increase skepticism, so it's important to be specific and transparent about your terms. Make it clear what buyers need to do to claim the guarantee, and avoid using fine print or hidden conditions that could undermine trust.

A strong guarantee:

- **Clearly defines the time frame**: State exactly how long the buyer has to request a refund (e.g., 30 days, 60 days, or 90 days).
- **Explains the process**: Outline the steps for claiming the guarantee in simple, straightforward terms.
- **Reassures the buyer**: Use language that makes the buyer feel secure and confident in their purchase decision.

By offering a clear and compelling guarantee, you remove one of the biggest objections to purchasing a high-ticket product: the fear of losing money.

Step 5: Creating a Sense of Exclusivity

High-ticket offers often sell best when they feel exclusive. People are more willing to invest in something that feels limited, special, or not available to the masses. Packaging your offer in a way that highlights its exclusivity can create a sense of scarcity and urgency, which encourages faster decisions and justifies a premium price.

1. Limit Availability

Limiting the availability of your product or service creates scarcity, making potential buyers feel like they need to act quickly to secure their spot. This tactic is especially effective for high-ticket offers, as people perceive exclusivity as a sign of higher value.

Ways to create exclusivity:

- **Limited spots**: Cap the number of spots available for a course, coaching program, or consulting package. For example, "Only 10 spots available for this exclusive program."
- **Time-limited access**: Make your offer available for a limited time, after which it will close. For example, "Enrollment is only open for 5 days—after that, the doors will close until next year."
- **Invite-only access**: Position your offer as invitation-only, where only select individuals are invited to join based on specific criteria.

Scarcity can drive demand and create a sense of urgency that encourages people to act quickly before the opportunity is gone.

2. Position Your Offer as a VIP Experience

Another way to create exclusivity is to position your offer as a VIP or luxury experience. This signals to buyers that they're getting premium treatment, personal attention, and access to a high-end solution that isn't available to everyone.

Examples of VIP experiences:

- **One-on-one coaching or mentoring**: Offer a high-touch, personalized experience where buyers get direct access to you as the expert. This level of personal attention is often associated with premium pricing.
- **Private masterminds**: Create an exclusive mastermind group for high-level clients where they receive tailored guidance, networking opportunities, and insider knowledge.
- **VIP support**: Provide premium customer support, such as 24/7 access to a dedicated account manager or priority response times for any questions or concerns.

When buyers feel like they're part of an exclusive group or getting personalized VIP treatment, they are more willing to invest at higher price points.

Conclusion

Packaging your offer for maximum appeal is about more than just design—it's about creating an experience that justifies a premium price and makes your audience feel confident in their purchase decision. By investing in professional branding, crafting a compelling offer page, adding value through bonuses, offering clear guarantees, and positioning your offer as exclusive, you can significantly increase the perceived value of your product or service. These techniques will help you not only sell your product but also command higher prices, attract high-ticket buyers, and drive significant revenue in a short time frame.

Chapter 10: Creating a Winning Offer Stack

Creating a winning offer stack is an essential strategy for dramatically increasing the perceived value of your product or service. By carefully combining your core offer with highly desirable add-ons and bonuses, you can present a package that not only justifies a premium price but also makes the purchase feel like a no-brainer for potential buyers. The key is to ensure that every component in the stack provides tangible value and helps the customer achieve their desired outcome faster or more efficiently.

In this chapter, we will explore how to strategically design and structure your offer stack to maximize its appeal. You'll learn how to select the right add-ons, structure bonuses, and present your offer in a way that enhances its perceived value and drives conversions.

Step 1: Understanding the Purpose of an Offer Stack

The concept of an **offer stack** is simple: instead of selling a single product or service, you bundle your main offer with additional bonuses and add-ons to increase its overall value. This method not only helps justify a higher price but also enhances the buyer's experience by offering more comprehensive solutions to their needs.

1. The Psychology Behind an Offer Stack

At its core, an offer stack taps into a fundamental consumer psychology: the perception of value. When customers are presented with an offer that includes multiple valuable elements, they are more likely to feel they are getting a great deal. By stacking your offer, you're providing a complete solution rather than just a single product, making the purchase more appealing.

- **Perceived Value**: The more bonuses and add-ons you include (as long as they're relevant and valuable), the more your product will be perceived as worth the investment.

- **Reducing Buyer Hesitation**: When you offer multiple resources that cater to different pain points or concerns, you reduce the buyer's hesitation by covering all their potential objections.
- **Creating Excitement**: A well-structured offer stack creates excitement and anticipation because customers feel like they're getting "more than expected."

2. The Role of Bonuses in Increasing Value

Bonuses play a critical role in an offer stack by adding extra layers of value. They can address specific pain points, simplify the implementation of the main product, or enhance the customer's experience. The goal is to provide bonuses that complement the core offer, making the buyer feel they are getting a complete, high-value package that solves multiple problems.

Step 2: Selecting the Right Add-Ons and Bonuses

Not all add-ons or bonuses are created equal. The most effective bonuses are those that either accelerate the buyer's success, make the implementation of the core product easier, or provide extra resources that enhance the overall solution. Your offer stack should be curated to include only bonuses that add real value to the customer experience.

1. Complementary Add-Ons That Amplify the Core Offer

The first step in creating a winning offer stack is selecting bonuses that align with your main product and enhance its core value. These bonuses should solve related problems or help the buyer implement the solution faster or more effectively.

Types of Complementary Add-Ons:

- **Guides and Templates**: Provide done-for-you guides or templates that simplify the implementation of your product. For example, if your core product is a digital marketing course, offer a bonus "Email Campaign Template" that saves customers time.
- **Supplementary Training**: Include bonus training modules that go beyond the core product and teach advanced strategies or

techniques. For example, an additional module on "Advanced Facebook Ad Retargeting" would enhance a general Facebook advertising course.

- **Exclusive Tools or Resources**: Provide exclusive access to tools or software that make it easier for the customer to achieve the desired outcome. For example, offering access to a keyword research tool would enhance a course on SEO strategies.

These types of bonuses directly improve the customer's ability to achieve results from your core product, thereby increasing the perceived value of your offer.

2. Adding Bonuses That Accelerate Results

People love getting faster results. If you can offer bonuses that help your customers achieve their goals more quickly, your offer will become much more attractive. These fast-track bonuses reduce the time and effort it takes for the customer to experience the transformation promised by your main product.

Examples of Accelerated Results Bonuses:

- **Quick-Start Guides**: A simplified version of your main product that helps customers get started immediately. For example, a "5-Step Quick Start Guide" to running profitable ads could be an ideal add-on for a comprehensive marketing course.
- **Fast-Action Coaching Calls**: Offer a limited number of one-on-one or group coaching calls where customers can get personalized advice on implementing the product faster. This adds a personal touch and helps clients avoid mistakes that might slow down their progress.
- **Accountability Checklists**: Create checklists or planners that keep customers on track to achieve their goals within a specific timeframe. This ensures they stay focused and move quickly through the steps of your program.

By adding bonuses that shorten the path to success, you make your offer more valuable and desirable to buyers looking for fast results.

3. Providing Bonuses That Simplify Implementation

Complexity can be a barrier to purchase, especially for high-ticket offers. By including bonuses that simplify the process, you can make your offer much more appealing to customers who may be intimidated by the perceived difficulty of implementing your solution.

Examples of Simplification Bonuses:

- **Step-by-Step Implementation Guides**: Break down the steps of your core product into an easy-to-follow guide that reduces overwhelm and ensures the customer knows exactly what to do next.
    - Example: "The Complete 30-Day Social Media Strategy Implementation Plan" to accompany a social media marketing course.
- **Done-for-You Resources**: Provide ready-made resources that save time and effort. These could include templates, spreadsheets, or scripts that customers can plug into their business immediately.
    - Example: "Plug-and-Play Webinar Funnel Template" for a course on building profitable webinars.
- **Workbooks and Checklists**: Offer printable or digital workbooks that guide customers through each stage of implementing the product.
    - Example: "Weekly Goal-Setting Workbook" for a business coaching program.

Simplification bonuses reduce friction in the buyer's mind, making it easier for them to see how your product will be valuable to them and how they can implement it without feeling overwhelmed.

4. Bonus Content That Adds Depth

You can enhance the perceived value of your offer by adding bonus content that dives deeper into specific topics or provides advanced strategies. This gives the buyer access to premium information that they wouldn't get anywhere else, making your offer more attractive.

Examples of Value-Adding Bonus Content:

- **Advanced Training Modules**: Offer bonus training on advanced techniques or strategies that are not covered in the core product. This gives the buyer a sense of exclusivity and access to higher-level insights.
  - Example: "Mastering Advanced LinkedIn Outreach" as a bonus for a general networking or business development course.
- **Case Studies and Behind-the-Scenes Content**: Provide detailed case studies or behind-the-scenes insights that show the practical application of your product. Customers love seeing real-world examples of success.
  - Example: "How I Scaled My Business from 6 to 7 Figures Using These Exact Strategies" for a business growth program.
- **Exclusive Interviews**: Include interviews with industry experts or thought leaders that give customers access to insider knowledge and strategies.
  - Example: "Exclusive Interview with a 7-Figure Entrepreneur on Building a Scalable Online Business."

Bonus content adds value by providing customers with additional learning opportunities and actionable insights, which helps justify a higher price point.

Step 3: Structuring Your Offer Stack

The way you structure and present your offer stack is key to maximizing its perceived value. A well-presented offer stack not only highlights the individual bonuses but also shows how each component contributes to the overall transformation your product promises.

1. Start with the Core Product

The first step is to present your core product clearly and compellingly. This is the foundation of your offer, so you need to ensure the customer understands the main value it provides and the transformation they will experience by using it.

Tips for Presenting the Core Product:

- **Focus on Results**: Clearly articulate the end result that customers will achieve by using your product. Use result-oriented language to explain the transformation.
  - Example: "By the end of this course, you'll have a fully optimized sales funnel that consistently generates leads and revenue."
- **List Key Features and Benefits**: Highlight the most important features of the product, but always tie them back to how they benefit the customer. For example, "10 in-depth training modules" should be framed as "10 modules that teach you how to double your revenue in 90 days."

Once the core product is positioned as valuable, you can begin layering your bonuses to amplify the overall appeal.

2. Layer Bonuses for Maximum Impact

Introduce each bonus one at a time, building on the core product's value. Each bonus should feel like a natural addition that enhances the customer's ability to achieve their desired outcome faster, more easily, or more completely.

How to Layer Bonuses Effectively:

- **Bonus 1 (Most Relevant)**: Start with the most relevant bonus that directly complements the core product. This shows customers that the bonus is not just an add-on but an essential component that will help them succeed.
  - Example: For a business growth course, the first bonus could be "Done-for-You Sales Funnel Template," which ties directly into what the customer will learn in the course.
- **Bonus 2 (Accelerates Results)**: Introduce a bonus that helps the customer achieve results faster. This could be a quick-start guide, coaching session, or fast-action checklist.
  - Example: "1-Hour Coaching Call to Fast-Track Your First Sales Funnel."
- **Bonus 3 (Simplifies the Process)**: Offer a bonus that simplifies the implementation of your product. This reassures customers that they'll have all the tools they need to succeed without feeling overwhelmed.
  - Example: "Step-by-Step Funnel Implementation Workbook."
- **Bonus 4 (Exclusive Access)**: Finish with an exclusive bonus that makes the customer feel like they're getting VIP treatment. This could be access to a private community, exclusive content, or lifetime updates.
  - Example: "Lifetime Access to All Future Course Updates."

By layering the bonuses this way, you build excitement and create a feeling of abundance, making the overall package feel irresistible.

3. Use Value Anchoring to Highlight Worth

Value anchoring is a powerful tool that helps customers understand the true worth of your offer. By assigning a specific dollar value to each component of your offer stack, you can dramatically increase the perceived value and justify a higher price.

How to Use Value Anchoring:

- **Assign Dollar Values to Each Bonus**: Break down the individual value of each bonus and the core product. For example, "Done-for-You Sales Funnel Template ($297 value)," "1-Hour Coaching Call ($500 value)," etc.
- **Show Total Value vs. Price**: After presenting the individual components, total the value and compare it to the actual price of the offer. This makes the price feel like a steal.
  - Example: "The total value of this offer is $2,791, but today you can get everything for just $997."

This technique helps customers understand the full value of what they're getting and reinforces the idea that they're receiving an incredible deal.

Step 4: Adding Time-Sensitive Bonuses

Adding time-sensitive or limited-time bonuses is a powerful way to create urgency and encourage fast action. These bonuses are only available for a short period, motivating potential buyers to make a decision quickly.

1. Fast-Action Bonuses

Fast-action bonuses reward buyers who take immediate action. These can be extra resources, coaching calls, or additional content that incentivizes quick purchases.

Examples of Fast-Action Bonuses:

- **Extra Coaching Calls**: Offer additional one-on-one or group coaching calls for buyers who purchase within the first 24-48 hours.
  - Example: "The first 20 people to buy will receive an extra 1-hour private coaching call to accelerate their results."
- **Exclusive Webinars or Q&A Sessions**: Offer access to a live webinar or Q&A session where buyers can ask you questions directly.
  - Example: "Buy today and join an exclusive live Q&A with me next week."
- **Limited-Time Content**: Offer extra training modules or content that's only available for early buyers.
  - Example: "Get access to our exclusive 'Scaling with Paid Ads' module when you buy before Friday."

Fast-action bonuses create a sense of scarcity and urgency, driving more immediate conversions.

2. Time-Limited Discounts or Offers

Offering time-limited discounts or bonuses can increase urgency and push potential buyers off the fence. These could be special offers available only during the launch window or bonuses that expire after a specific date.

Examples of Time-Limited Offers:

- **Discounts for Early Buyers**: Offer a discounted price for buyers who purchase during the launch period.
  - Example: "Enroll now and save $500—this offer ends in 48 hours."
- **Bonus Content for Launch Buyers**: Offer extra content or resources for buyers who purchase during the initial launch.
  - Example: "Buy before the end of the week and get exclusive access to our 'Advanced Copywriting Techniques' module."

Time-sensitive bonuses not only drive faster decisions but also create excitement and anticipation around your product launch.

Step 5: Delivering the Offer Stack with Excellence

Delivering your offer stack effectively is just as important as creating it. Once a customer has purchased your product, the onboarding and delivery process should match the premium nature of your offer, ensuring that they feel valued and supported.

1. Smooth Delivery Systems

Choose a delivery system that provides a seamless and professional experience for your customers. Whether it's an online course platform, membership site, or email sequence, the delivery process should be easy to navigate and provide immediate access to the purchased materials.

Popular Delivery Platforms:

- **Teachable**: Ideal for delivering online courses with video lessons, downloadable resources, and quizzes.
- **Kajabi**: A comprehensive platform for courses, memberships, and digital products.
- **Gumroad**: Simple and effective for delivering digital downloads like ebooks, templates, and checklists.

2. VIP Onboarding Experience

For high-ticket products, create a VIP onboarding process that makes customers feel special and supported from the start. This could include personalized welcome emails, instructions on how to use the product, and an invitation to a private community or bonus training session.

Ideas for VIP Onboarding:

- **Welcome Email Sequence**: Send a series of emails that guide the customer through the product, explain the bonuses they've received, and offer additional tips for success.

- **Exclusive Community Access**: If you offer access to a private group (e.g., a Facebook group or Slack channel), make sure to invite customers as part of the onboarding process, reinforcing the value of being part of an exclusive group.
- **Personalized Support**: Offer premium customer support, such as priority email or chat access, to ensure buyers have a smooth and satisfying experience with your product.

A great delivery experience sets the tone for a long-term relationship with your customer and increases the likelihood of positive testimonials and future purchases.

Conclusion

Creating a winning offer stack is all about providing a comprehensive solution that dramatically increases the perceived value of your core product or service. By selecting bonuses that complement the main offer, accelerate results, simplify implementation, and add depth, you can create an irresistible package that justifies a premium price. Structuring your offer stack carefully, using value anchoring, and adding time-sensitive bonuses will help you create urgency and maximize conversions. Finally, delivering the offer with excellence ensures a smooth customer experience, leading to satisfied buyers and long-term success.

Part 3: Preparing the Sales Process

Chapter 11: Fast-Tracking Your Sales Funnel

A **sales funnel** is a crucial component of any marketing strategy, and if you want to generate $100,000 in 24 hours, you need to fast-track the process of building a high-converting sales funnel. A well-designed sales funnel guides potential customers through the buyer's journey, from initial awareness to the final purchase, and maximizes conversions at every stage. While creating a sales funnel might seem like a time-consuming task, this chapter will teach you how to quickly design and implement an effective sales funnel that can drive rapid sales without sacrificing quality.

We will explore each stage of the funnel—from lead generation to closing the sale—and provide actionable tips on how to optimize each step for maximum conversions. By the end of this chapter, you'll know how to create a high-converting sales funnel in a short amount of time, positioning yourself to hit your revenue goals faster.

Step 1: Understanding the Stages of a Sales Funnel

Before diving into the creation process, it's important to understand the different stages of a sales funnel. A typical sales funnel consists of four main stages: **awareness**, **interest**, **decision**, and **action**. At each stage, your goal is to move potential customers closer to purchasing, while addressing their needs and concerns.

1. Awareness (Top of the Funnel)

At the awareness stage, potential customers are just learning about your brand or product. They may not even be aware of their specific problem yet. The goal here is to attract as many people as possible to your funnel, primarily through content that educates or entertains.

Key Objectives at the Awareness Stage:

- **Attract Attention**: Use channels like social media, paid ads, blog posts, or webinars to capture the attention of your target audience.
- **Build Trust**: Provide valuable content that helps your audience understand their problem and positions you as the solution.

2. Interest (Middle of the Funnel)

Once your audience is aware of their problem and your product or service, the next stage is to build interest. At this stage, potential customers are considering solutions, and your goal is to showcase the value of your offer.

Key Objectives at the Interest Stage:

- **Engage and Educate**: Use content that dives deeper into the solution your product offers. This could be through webinars, case studies, or email marketing.
- **Nurture Relationships**: Continue to build trust by providing more value through email sequences or free resources like guides or e-books.

3. Decision (Bottom of the Funnel)

At the decision stage, potential customers are ready to make a purchase decision. This is where you need to present your offer in a compelling way, overcoming any remaining objections and showing the customer why they should choose you over competitors.

Key Objectives at the Decision Stage:

- **Present Your Offer**: Highlight the features, benefits, and value of your product or service.
- **Overcome Objections**: Address common objections like price, time, or risk with clear messaging, guarantees, and testimonials.

4. Action (Conversion Stage)

The final stage of the funnel is where potential customers take action—whether that's making a purchase, signing up for a service, or booking a call. This is where your funnel must make it as easy as possible for them to say "yes."

Key Objectives at the Action Stage:

- **Create Urgency**: Use limited-time offers, bonuses, or fast-action incentives to encourage quick decisions.
- **Streamline the Checkout Process**: Ensure that your checkout or payment system is simple, secure, and mobile-friendly to reduce friction.

Step 2: Creating a High-Converting Lead Magnet

The first step in any sales funnel is to attract leads. A **lead magnet** is a valuable piece of content or resource that you offer in exchange for a potential customer's contact information, usually their email address. The goal of a lead magnet is to capture leads who are interested in your product or service and move them into your sales funnel.

1. Choosing the Right Lead Magnet

To create a high-converting lead magnet quickly, choose a resource that directly addresses a pain point your audience is experiencing. The lead magnet should provide immediate value, but it should also be simple enough to create in a short amount of time.

Examples of High-Converting Lead Magnets:

- **E-books or Guides**: Create a short guide or e-book that provides actionable advice or solves a specific problem. For example, "The Ultimate Guide to Scaling Your Online Business."
- **Checklists**: Offer a checklist that simplifies a process for your audience. For example, "10-Step Checklist for Launching a Successful Facebook Ad Campaign."
- **Webinars or Mini-Courses**: Host a free webinar or mini-course that delivers valuable content. For example, "How to Generate $100,000 in 24 Hours: A Step-by-Step Webinar."
- **Templates**: Provide downloadable templates or scripts that make it easier for your audience to implement your solution. For example, "Done-for-You Sales Funnel Template."

2. Designing a Simple Opt-In Page

Once you've created your lead magnet, you need an opt-in page where potential customers can enter their email address to access the resource. The opt-in page should be clean, simple, and focused on the benefits of your lead magnet.

Key Elements of a High-Converting Opt-In Page:

- **Clear Headline**: Your headline should communicate the value of the lead magnet in one concise sentence. For example, "Download the Free Guide to Doubling Your Online Revenue in 30 Days."
- **Benefit-Oriented Copy**: Briefly explain how the lead magnet will help solve the user's problem or improve their situation. Focus on benefits, not just features.
- **Simple Form**: Only ask for essential information, usually just a name and email address, to reduce friction and increase conversions.
- **Compelling Call to Action**: Use action-oriented language for your call to action (CTA), such as "Get Instant Access," rather than generic terms like "Submit."

3. Automating Lead Nurturing with Email Sequences

Once someone opts in for your lead magnet, the next step is to nurture them with an email sequence that moves them through your funnel. This sequence should build trust, provide additional value, and guide the lead toward making a purchase.

Components of an Effective Email Sequence:

- **Welcome Email**: Immediately send a welcome email that delivers the lead magnet and introduces your brand. This email should be friendly and informative, setting the stage for future communication.

- **Value Emails**: Over the next few days, send emails that offer additional value related to the lead magnet. This could be in the form of blog posts, videos, or case studies that further educate the lead and demonstrate your expertise.
- **Offer Introduction**: Once you've built trust, introduce your main offer. Highlight the core benefits, and explain how your product or service solves their problem.
- **Urgency and Close**: As you near the end of your email sequence, create urgency by offering limited-time bonuses, discounts, or fast-action incentives to encourage quick decisions.

Step 3: Creating a High-Converting Sales Page

The sales page is where leads make the decision to purchase your product or service. A high-converting sales page is crucial to the success of your funnel, as it directly impacts whether leads turn into paying customers.

1. Writing a Compelling Headline

The headline is the first thing visitors see when they land on your sales page, so it needs to grab their attention and clearly communicate the value of your offer.

Tips for Writing a Strong Sales Page Headline:

- **Focus on the Transformation**: Highlight the main benefit or result that customers will achieve by using your product. For example, "Double Your Revenue in 60 Days with Our Proven Business Scaling System."
- **Use Specific, Measurable Outcomes**: Specificity helps build credibility. For example, "How I Generated $100,000 in 24 Hours Using This 5-Step Sales Funnel."
- **Make It Attention-Grabbing**: Use powerful language that makes readers want to learn more. Avoid generic or vague headlines like "Check Out Our Product."

2. Presenting the Benefits and Features

After your headline, your sales page needs to clearly outline the benefits and features of your product. Focus on how your product will solve the customer's problem or improve their life, and back this up with concrete details.

How to Present Benefits and Features:

- **Start with the Benefits**: Lead with the key benefits that your product offers. Explain how it will help the customer achieve their desired outcome. For example, "Our course will show you exactly how to automate your marketing funnels, saving you hours of manual work every week."
- **Explain Features Later**: Once you've outlined the benefits, explain the specific features of your product that make those benefits possible. For example, "10 in-depth video lessons covering everything from lead generation to scaling with paid ads."
- **Use Bullet Points**: Bullet points are easy to skim and help break up text. Use them to list out the most important benefits and features in a concise way.

3. Adding Social Proof and Testimonials

Social proof is one of the most powerful tools for increasing conversions. By including testimonials, case studies, or reviews from past customers, you build trust and demonstrate that your product has delivered results for others.

Effective Use of Social Proof:

- **Customer Testimonials**: Include quotes from real customers that describe their experience with your product and the results they've achieved. Video testimonials can be even more persuasive.
- **Case Studies**: Share detailed case studies that show how your product has helped specific customers achieve their goals. Include

measurable outcomes, such as "This client increased their monthly revenue by 30% after implementing our strategies."

- **Social Media Mentions**: If people have shared positive comments about your product on social media, feature those as additional proof of its effectiveness.

4. Overcoming Objections

Potential buyers may have objections or concerns that prevent them from making a purchase. A high-converting sales page addresses these objections directly, helping customers feel confident in their decision.

Common Objections and How to Overcome Them:

- **Price**: Offer a payment plan, emphasize the value of your product, and explain how the investment will pay off in the long run.
- **Time**: Reassure customers that your product is easy to implement or that it will save them time in the future.
- **Risk**: Provide a money-back guarantee or risk-free trial to reduce perceived risk and build trust.

Step 4: Optimizing Your Checkout Process

The final step in fast-tracking your sales funnel is optimizing the checkout process. Even if your sales page is converting well, a complicated or confusing checkout process can cause potential buyers to abandon their purchase.

1. Simplify the Checkout Form

A streamlined checkout form reduces friction and makes it easier for customers to complete their purchase. Only ask for the essential information, and keep the number of steps to a minimum.

How to Simplify Your Checkout Process:

- **Ask for Minimal Information**: Only request information that is absolutely necessary for the purchase (name, email, payment details). Avoid asking for unnecessary details.

- **Use One-Page Checkout**: If possible, use a single-page checkout form to minimize the number of clicks and steps involved in the process.
- **Include Multiple Payment Options**: Offer a variety of payment methods, such as credit card, PayPal, or digital wallets, to accommodate different preferences.

2. Create Urgency at Checkout

To encourage customers to complete their purchase quickly, create a sense of urgency at checkout by offering time-sensitive bonuses, discounts, or fast-action incentives.

Ideas for Creating Urgency:

- **Countdown Timers**: Include a countdown timer on the checkout page that shows how long the customer has to claim a special offer or discount.
    - Example: "Buy within the next 10 minutes to receive a free bonus module!"
- **Limited-Time Discounts**: Offer a discount or price reduction that expires shortly after the customer lands on the checkout page.
    - Example: "Get 10% off your purchase if you complete checkout in the next hour."
- **Fast-Action Bonuses**: Provide an extra incentive for customers who complete their purchase quickly, such as a bonus course or coaching call.

Step 5: Analyzing and Optimizing Your Sales Funnel

Once your funnel is live, it's important to track its performance and make improvements as needed. Regularly analyzing the data from each stage of your funnel will help you identify areas for optimization and ensure that you're maximizing conversions.

1. Track Key Metrics

Key performance indicators (KPIs) will help you measure the effectiveness of your funnel and pinpoint any weak spots. Some of the most important metrics to track include:

- **Click-Through Rate (CTR)**: Measure the percentage of people who click on your ads, emails, or landing page links to enter your funnel.
- **Conversion Rate**: Track the percentage of people who move from one stage of the funnel to the next (e.g., from lead magnet opt-in to sales page, or from sales page to purchase).
- **Cart Abandonment Rate**: Measure how many people add your product to their cart but fail to complete the purchase.
- **Customer Lifetime Value (CLV)**: Calculate the total revenue you can expect to earn from each customer over the long term.

2. Optimize Based on Data

Once you've gathered enough data, use it to identify areas of improvement and make adjustments to your funnel. For example:

- **Low CTR**: If your click-through rate is low, revisit your headlines, ad copy, or lead magnet to make them more compelling.

- **Low Conversion Rate**: If people aren't converting on your sales page, consider tweaking the messaging, adding more social proof, or addressing common objections more thoroughly.
- **High Cart Abandonment**: If many people are abandoning their carts, streamline your checkout process, reduce friction, or add urgency.

Conclusion

Fast-tracking a high-converting sales funnel is key to achieving rapid revenue growth, especially when you're aiming for ambitious financial goals like generating $100,000 in 24 hours. By understanding the stages of a funnel, creating a compelling lead magnet, designing an effective sales page, and optimizing your checkout process, you can build a funnel that maximizes conversions in a short amount of time. Additionally, continuous optimization through data analysis will ensure that your funnel remains effective and profitable over the long term. With these strategies, you're well on your way to creating a sales funnel that drives fast, substantial results.

Chapter 12: The Power of Persuasive Copywriting

The art of **persuasive copywriting** is one of the most essential skills in building a high-converting sales funnel and driving fast sales. The words you use in your marketing materials, emails, and sales pages have the power to compel potential customers to take immediate action—or to click away. Writing copy that compels action requires a deep understanding of your audience's desires, pain points, and motivations, as well as the ability to present your offer in a way that feels irresistible.

In this chapter, we will explore the principles of persuasive copywriting and how to craft messages that move your audience through the buyer's journey, from awareness to conversion. You'll learn how to tap into your audience's emotions, use psychological triggers, and structure your copy to lead readers to take immediate action. By the end of this chapter, you'll be equipped with the tools you need to write high-impact, high-converting copy for any part of your sales funnel.

Step 1: Understanding the Psychology Behind Persuasion

Effective copywriting is deeply rooted in human psychology. People make buying decisions based on a combination of logical and emotional factors, but emotion often takes the lead. To write persuasive copy, you need to tap into your audience's emotional triggers while also addressing their logical needs.

1. The Role of Emotion in Decision-Making

Research has shown that people buy based on **emotion** and then justify their purchase with **logic**. This means your copy needs to connect emotionally with your audience by addressing their deepest desires and pain points. Only after you've established an emotional connection should you provide logical reasons (features, benefits, data) to back up the purchase decision.

Key Emotions to Tap Into:

- **Fear**: People often take action to avoid pain or negative consequences. For example, fear of failure or fear of missing out (FOMO) are powerful motivators.
- **Desire**: People want to achieve their goals and aspirations. Tap into their desire for success, happiness, health, wealth, or status.
- **Curiosity**: Humans are naturally curious, and creating intrigue can drive action. Use headlines and hooks that spark curiosity, making people want to learn more.
- **Urgency**: A sense of urgency, such as a limited-time offer, creates a fear of missing out, which pushes people to act quickly.

By using emotion as a driver in your copy, you can create an immediate connection with your reader and increase the likelihood that they'll take the desired action.

2. Psychological Triggers That Compel Action

In addition to emotion, certain **psychological triggers** can dramatically increase the persuasive power of your copy. These triggers appeal to inherent human biases and behaviors, making it easier to persuade your audience to take action.

Effective Psychological Triggers:

- **Scarcity**: People are more likely to act when they believe a resource is limited. Using phrases like "limited-time offer" or "only 5 spots left" makes your offer feel exclusive and scarce, pushing people to act quickly.
- **Social Proof**: People trust the actions of others, especially in uncertain situations. Including testimonials, reviews, case studies, or statistics helps build credibility and persuades potential buyers that your product is trusted by others.

- **Reciprocity**: When you give something valuable for free, people feel compelled to return the favor. This is why lead magnets, free trials, or free content often lead to increased conversions.
- **Authority**: People are more likely to trust and follow recommendations from an expert or authority figure. Positioning yourself as an expert in your niche builds trust and increases the persuasive power of your copy.
- **Urgency**: Creating a sense of urgency (e.g., limited-time bonuses, countdown timers) compels people to act immediately rather than delaying their decision.

Understanding these triggers and incorporating them into your copy will make your message more persuasive and effective at driving conversions.

Step 2: Crafting Attention-Grabbing Headlines

The **headline** is arguably the most important part of any copy. Whether it's the subject line of an email, the heading on a sales page, or the title of a blog post, the headline is what grabs attention and pulls readers in. Without a strong headline, even the most compelling offer may go unnoticed.

1. The Formula for High-Converting Headlines

A great headline needs to do three things:

1. **Grab attention**: The headline should immediately catch the reader's eye and make them want to keep reading.
2. **Create curiosity or promise value**: The headline should make a clear promise of a benefit or arouse curiosity about what the reader will learn.
3. **Speak to the audience's pain point or desire**: The headline should address the reader's core problem or aspiration, showing that you understand their needs.

Proven Headline Formulas:

- **Benefit-Driven Headline**: Highlight a clear benefit or result the reader will get from your product.
  - Example: "Double Your Sales in 30 Days with This Simple Marketing Strategy."
- **Question Headline**: Ask a question that addresses a pain point or curiosity.
  - Example: "Are You Losing Sales Because of These Common Marketing Mistakes?"
- **How-To Headline**: Show the reader how to achieve a specific goal.
  - Example: "How to Build a 6-Figure Business from Scratch in 90 Days."
- **Numbered List Headline**: People love lists because they promise easy-to-digest content.
  - Example: "5 Proven Strategies to Skyrocket Your Online Sales."
- **Curiosity-Based Headline**: Tease the reader with something unexpected or intriguing.
  - Example: "The Secret Formula Top Entrepreneurs Use to Generate Millions (and You Can Too)."

2. Using Subheadlines to Build Interest

Once you've grabbed attention with the headline, a **subheadline** can be used to build interest and provide more context. The subheadline should elaborate on the promise made in the headline and give the reader a reason to keep reading.

Effective Subheadline Strategies:

- **Expand on the Benefit**: Further explain the result or benefit promised in the headline.
    - Example: "Discover the step-by-step system that has helped hundreds of entrepreneurs scale their businesses without spending thousands on ads."
- **Address Objections**: Use the subheadline to reassure the reader and address potential concerns.
    - Example: "No prior experience needed. This system works for anyone, whether you're just starting out or already in business."

Step 3: Writing Persuasive Body Copy

The body copy is where you go beyond the headline and subheadline to persuade your reader to take action. Whether you're writing a sales page, an email, or an ad, the body copy should guide the reader through a logical progression from understanding their problem to believing that your solution is the answer.

1. Lead with Empathy and Understanding

Before presenting your solution, it's essential to show your audience that you understand their pain points, desires, and challenges. Empathy builds trust and demonstrates that you are in tune with their needs. The more the reader feels like you understand their situation, the more likely they are to listen to your offer.

Empathy-Driven Copy Example:

- "If you've ever struggled to attract clients online, you're not alone. Most entrepreneurs spend months trying to grow their business, only to feel frustrated by slow progress and inconsistent income. I've been there too."

By acknowledging the reader's problem, you build rapport and create a natural transition into offering a solution.

2. Present the Solution as the Answer to Their Problem

Once you've connected with the reader on an emotional level, it's time to introduce your product or service as the solution to their problem. You need to position your offer as the ideal, must-have solution that delivers the results they're looking for.

How to Position Your Solution:

- **Explain how it solves their problem**: Be specific about how your product addresses the pain points you mentioned earlier.
  - Example: "This course will teach you a proven, step-by-step system for generating high-quality leads without spending hours on social media or thousands on ads."
- **Highlight the transformation**: Focus on the transformation that your product will deliver, not just its features.
  - Example: "Imagine waking up to a full inbox of new client inquiries and knowing you've got a predictable system in place to consistently grow your business."

3. Use Benefits to Drive Action

While it's important to explain the features of your product, people don't buy features—they buy **benefits**. Features describe what your product does, while benefits explain how those features improve the customer's life or solve their problem.

Feature vs. Benefit Example:

- **Feature**: "This software includes an automated email follow-up system."
- **Benefit**: "This software will save you hours of manual work by automatically following up with leads, so you never miss out on a potential sale."

By focusing on benefits, you help the reader understand how your product will make their life better, which is a key motivator for action.

4. Overcome Objections and Build Trust

Even if your audience is interested in your offer, they may still have doubts or objections that prevent them from taking action. It's essential to address these objections head-on in your copy to build trust and remove any barriers to purchase.

Common Objections to Address:

- **Price**: If price is a concern, explain the value of the product and how the investment will pay off.
  - Example: "This system has helped hundreds of businesses generate thousands in revenue. The investment you make today could easily pay for itself with just a few new clients."
- **Time**: Reassure the reader that the product is easy to implement or that the results will justify the time investment.
  - Example: "Our course is designed to be completed in just 30 minutes a day, so you can see results without sacrificing time with your family or other business priorities."
- **Skepticism**: Use testimonials, case studies, and guarantees to build trust and credibility.
  - Example: "See what our customers are saying: 'I was skeptical at first, but within 30 days, I doubled my income using this system.'"

By anticipating objections and offering reassurance, you make it easier for the reader to feel confident about making a purchase.

Step 4: Using Compelling Calls to Action (CTAs)

Your copy can be persuasive, but without a clear and compelling **call to action (CTA)**, your audience may not know what to do next. The CTA is where you tell the reader exactly what action to take, whether it's buying a product, signing up for a webinar, or downloading a lead magnet.

1. Make the CTA Clear and Action-Oriented

The CTA should be direct, clear, and action-oriented. It should tell the reader exactly what to do next in a way that leaves no room for confusion.

Effective CTA Phrases:

- "Get Instant Access Now"
- "Start Your Free Trial"
- "Download the Guide Today"
- "Join the Program Now"

Avoid vague or passive language like "Submit" or "Click Here." Your CTA should feel active and create a sense of urgency.

2. Add a Sense of Urgency or Scarcity

To further drive action, add urgency or scarcity to your CTA. This could be a time-sensitive discount, a limited number of spots, or a bonus that expires soon. Urgency compels people to act immediately rather than putting off their decision.

Examples of Urgent CTAs:

- "Claim Your Spot Now—Only 10 Spots Left!"
- "Get 30% Off Today—Offer Ends at Midnight"
- "Join Now and Receive a Free Bonus—Limited Time Only"

Urgency helps overcome procrastination, encouraging potential customers to make a decision quickly.

Step 5: Testing and Optimizing Your Copy

Copywriting is as much an art as it is a science, and even the most persuasive copy can benefit from testing and optimization. By testing different variations of your copy, headlines, CTAs, and offers, you can continuously improve your results and drive higher conversions.

1. A/B Testing Headlines and CTAs

One of the most effective ways to optimize your copy is through **A/B testing**, where you compare two versions of the same element to see which performs better. Headlines and CTAs are two of the most critical elements to test, as small changes can significantly impact conversions.

How to Run A/B Tests:

- **Headlines**: Test different headlines to see which one drives more engagement and conversions. For example, you might test a benefit-driven headline against a curiosity-based headline to see which resonates more with your audience.
- **CTAs**: Test different CTA phrases and placements to see which ones drive the most action. You might experiment with "Get Instant Access Now" vs. "Download the Guide Today" or place the CTA in different sections of the page.

By running A/B tests, you can continuously refine your copy to improve performance and maximize conversions.

2. Analyzing Copy Performance

In addition to A/B testing, it's important to track key metrics to measure the effectiveness of your copy. Metrics like open rates (for email subject lines), click-through rates, conversion rates, and time on page can provide valuable insights into what's working and what needs improvement.

Metrics to Track:

- **Open Rates**: Measure the effectiveness of your email subject lines.
- **Click-Through Rates (CTR)**: Track how many people click on links in your emails, ads, or web pages.
- **Conversion Rates**: Measure how many people take the desired action (e.g., making a purchase, signing up for a webinar).
- **Time on Page**: Analyze how long readers are staying on your page to determine if your copy is engaging enough.

By regularly analyzing these metrics, you can identify areas for improvement and make data-driven decisions to enhance your copy's effectiveness.

Conclusion

The power of persuasive copywriting cannot be overstated when it comes to driving immediate action and fast sales. By understanding the psychology of persuasion, crafting attention-grabbing headlines, writing compelling body copy, and using effective calls to action, you can create copy that moves readers from curiosity to conversion. Additionally, by testing and optimizing your copy over time, you'll continually improve your results, driving more sales and increasing your revenue. With the strategies outlined in this chapter, you'll be able to write copy that compels immediate action and propels your business toward its financial goals.

Chapter 13: Pricing Strategy for Maximum Profits

Setting the right price for your product or service is one of the most crucial decisions you'll make when aiming to achieve maximum profits. Price too high, and you risk scaring off potential customers; price too low, and you could undermine the perceived value of your offer or fail to hit your revenue goals. The key to a successful pricing strategy is striking a balance between profitability and conversion rates. In this chapter, we'll dive deep into the psychology of pricing, how to structure your pricing tiers, and the tactics you can use to price your products in a way that maximizes both sales and revenue.

By the end of this chapter, you'll have a clear understanding of how to set the right price to achieve your financial goals—whether it's generating $100,000 in 24 hours or consistently earning high profits—while ensuring that your offer remains attractive to your target audience.

Step 1: Understanding Pricing Psychology

Pricing is not just about numbers—it's about perception. The way you price your product significantly affects how your audience perceives its value, quality, and exclusivity. Understanding the psychology behind pricing will allow you to price your product in a way that maximizes perceived value while encouraging customers to take action.

1. The Relationship Between Price and Perceived Value

One of the most powerful psychological drivers in pricing is the idea that higher prices are often associated with higher quality. Consumers tend to equate price with value, meaning that a higher-priced product is often perceived as more valuable or effective, even if that's not necessarily true. On the other hand, products that are priced too low can be seen as inferior or not worth the investment.

Key Insights:

- **Higher Prices = Higher Perceived Value**: When you price your product higher, it often signals exclusivity, premium quality, and a more significant transformation. This is particularly important for high-ticket offers like coaching programs, courses, or consulting services.
- **Lower Prices Can Undermine Value**: If you price your product too low, especially in industries where premium pricing is expected, it can lead to skepticism about the quality or effectiveness of your offer.

2. The Power of "Charm Pricing"

"Charm pricing" refers to the practice of pricing products just below a whole number (e.g., $99 instead of $100). Research has shown that charm pricing can significantly boost sales, as consumers tend to perceive prices like $99.99 as significantly lower than $100, even though the difference is minimal.

Charm Pricing in Action:

- **$997 vs. $1,000**: While the price difference is only $3, pricing a product at $997 instead of $1,000 can make it feel more affordable and attractive to potential buyers.
- **$49 vs. $50**: Even with smaller numbers, pricing just below the nearest whole number can improve conversion rates without drastically affecting profit margins.

Step 2: Setting Pricing Goals Based on Revenue Targets

Before deciding on a price point, it's important to reverse-engineer your pricing strategy based on your revenue goals. Whether your goal is to generate $100,000 in 24 hours or build a long-term sustainable income stream, understanding how your price affects your ability to hit those targets is crucial.

1. Reverse-Engineering Your Revenue Goal

Start by determining your revenue goal and then break it down into the number of units or clients you need to sell to hit that target. This will help you determine the best price range for your offer.

Formula:

Price×Number of Sales=Revenue Goal\text{Price} \times \text{Number of Sales} = \text{Revenue Goal}Price×Number of Sales=Revenue Goal

Example 1:

Revenue Goal: $100,000 in 24 hours

If you price your product at $1,000, you would need to sell 100 units to hit your goal:

1,000×100=100,0001,000 \times 100 = 100,0001,000×100=100,000

Example 2:

Revenue Goal: $100,000 in 24 hours

If you price your product at $2,500, you would only need to sell 40 units to hit your goal:

2,500×40=100,0002,500 \times 40 = 100,0002,500×40=100,000

2. Balancing Price with Volume

While higher prices require fewer sales to reach your revenue goal, you also need to consider your target audience's ability and willingness to pay. If your audience is more price-sensitive, pricing too high could limit conversions, making it harder to reach your goal. On the other hand, pricing too low may require a volume of sales that is unrealistic for your funnel.

Balancing Price and Conversion:

- **High Price, Lower Volume**: If you're offering a premium product, service, or experience, you can price higher and focus on selling to a smaller number of highly qualified leads. This is a common strategy for coaching programs, consulting services, or high-end digital products.

- **Lower Price, Higher Volume**: If your product is designed for a wider audience, you may choose a lower price point to attract more customers. This works well for digital products like e-books, templates, or courses where you can scale easily.

Step 3: Choosing the Right Pricing Model

Different pricing models work better for different types of products, services, and audiences. Selecting the right pricing model for your offer can significantly impact both conversions and your overall revenue.

1. One-Time Payment vs. Subscription Model

Depending on your product or service, you may opt for a **one-time payment** or a **subscription-based model**.

- **One-Time Payment**: A single payment gives the customer lifetime access to the product or service. This model works well for courses, coaching programs, and digital products.
    - **Pros**: Immediate revenue, no ongoing commitment for the customer.
    - **Cons**: Limited lifetime customer value unless you sell additional products or upgrades.
- **Subscription Model**: Customers pay on a recurring basis (monthly, yearly) for ongoing access to your product or service. This model is great for memberships, SaaS products, and services that provide continuous value.
    - **Pros**: Predictable recurring revenue, higher customer lifetime value.
    - **Cons**: Requires consistent value delivery to retain subscribers.

Example:

- If you're selling a course, you could offer a one-time payment of $997 or a subscription model where customers pay $97 per month for 12 months.

2. Tiered Pricing and Package Options

Offering **tiered pricing** or **package options** can help you capture a wider range of customers while still maximizing your revenue. With tiered pricing, you offer multiple versions of your product or service at different price points, allowing customers to choose the option that best fits their needs and budget.

Common Tiered Pricing Structures:

- **Basic, Standard, Premium**: Each tier offers more features, access, or support. For example, the basic package may include just the course, while the premium package includes coaching calls and exclusive content.
- **One-Time Payment vs. Payment Plan**: Offering a payment plan can make high-ticket offers more accessible to customers who can't afford a large upfront payment.

Example:

- **Basic Package**: $997—Access to the course and all modules.
- **Standard Package**: $1,497—Includes course access plus one coaching call.
- **Premium Package**: $2,497—Includes course access, three coaching calls, and access to a private mastermind group.

3. Bundling and Upsells

Bundling allows you to increase the perceived value of your offer by packaging multiple products or services together. This is particularly effective if you have complementary products that your customers would benefit from purchasing together.

Upselling is the process of offering an additional, higher-priced product or service after the initial purchase. This strategy helps increase the average order value (AOV) and maximizes revenue from each customer.

Examples of Bundles and Upsells:

- **Product Bundle**: Bundle an e-book, course, and template pack for a higher price than each would cost individually. For example, instead of selling the course for $997, bundle it with a related template pack for $1,197.
- **Upsell**: After a customer purchases your main product, offer them an upsell like a one-on-one coaching session, an advanced course, or exclusive access to a membership.

By bundling complementary products and using upsells, you can significantly boost your overall revenue without needing to generate more leads or customers.

Step 4: Pricing Strategies to Boost Conversions

While your pricing model and tiers are important, there are additional strategies you can use to make your pricing more appealing and increase conversions. These tactics create urgency, reduce perceived risk, and incentivize fast action.

1. Use Time-Limited Discounts and Promotions

One of the most effective ways to drive immediate action is by offering **limited-time discounts** or **promotions**. These create urgency, pushing potential customers to make a decision quickly rather than delaying their purchase.

Examples of Time-Limited Promotions:

- **Launch Discount**: Offer a special discount for customers who purchase during your launch period. For example, "Get 20% off if you enroll in the next 48 hours."
- **Fast-Action Bonus**: Provide an exclusive bonus to customers who take action quickly. For example, "The first 50 buyers get a free one-hour coaching session."

By creating a sense of urgency with time-sensitive promotions, you can increase the likelihood of immediate purchases and boost your overall conversion rate.

2. Offer Payment Plans

For high-ticket products, offering **payment plans** can help make your offer more accessible to a larger audience. A payment plan allows customers to spread the cost over several months, reducing the upfront financial burden.

Example of a Payment Plan:

- Instead of charging $2,000 upfront for a course, offer a payment plan of $200 per month for 12 months. While this increases the overall cost, the lower monthly payments make it easier for customers to commit.

Payment plans can help you close more sales, especially for high-ticket offers, while still allowing you to meet your revenue goals.

3. Add Guarantees to Reduce Risk

One of the most common objections customers have is the **risk** of investing in a product or service that may not deliver the promised results. Offering a **money-back guarantee** or a risk-free trial can help eliminate this concern, making customers feel more comfortable about their purchase.

Types of Guarantees:

- **30-Day Money-Back Guarantee**: If customers aren't satisfied within 30 days, they can request a full refund.
- **Results-Based Guarantee**: Guarantee that your product will deliver a specific result, or the customer can request a refund. For example, "If you don't see a 10% increase in revenue within 60 days, we'll give you your money back."
- **Risk-Free Trial**: Offer a free or low-cost trial period for customers to experience the product before committing to the full purchase.

By reducing perceived risk, you can increase buyer confidence and boost conversions, especially for higher-priced offers.

Step 5: Testing and Optimizing Your Pricing

Even the best pricing strategy can benefit from **testing and optimization**. By experimenting with different price points, payment structures, and promotions, you can identify the sweet spot that maximizes both conversions and profits.

1. A/B Testing Price Points

A/B testing allows you to compare two different price points to see which one results in more sales or higher revenue. For example, you could test pricing your product at $997 vs. $1,497 to see which option performs better.

How to Run a Price A/B Test:

- **Split Traffic**: Direct half of your traffic to a sales page with the lower price and the other half to a sales page with the higher price.
- **Compare Results**: Track key metrics like conversion rate, total revenue, and average order value (AOV) to determine which price point is more profitable.

By testing different price points, you can optimize your pricing strategy for maximum revenue.

2. Analyzing Customer Feedback

Customer feedback can provide valuable insights into how your audience perceives the value of your product and its price. Pay attention to customer feedback, surveys, and reviews to see if there are recurring themes about the price being too high, too low, or just right.

Key Questions to Ask Customers:

- "Did the price feel fair for the value you received?"
- "What made you hesitate before purchasing?"
- "Would you have been willing to pay more for additional features or support?"

By listening to your customers, you can fine-tune your pricing strategy to better align with their expectations and maximize conversions.

Conclusion

Pricing strategy plays a pivotal role in achieving your revenue goals, and setting the right price requires a deep understanding of your audience, product, and market. By leveraging pricing psychology, reverse-engineering your revenue goals, selecting the right pricing model, and using strategies like limited-time promotions, payment plans, and guarantees, you can create a pricing structure that maximizes both profits and conversions. Additionally, by continuously testing and optimizing your pricing, you can refine your strategy to ensure you're achieving the highest possible revenue while delivering maximum value to your customers.

With these strategies in place, you'll be well on your way to setting a price that supports your goal of generating $100,000 (or more) in a short period of time, while also building a sustainable and profitable business.

Chapter 14: Setting Up Instant Payment Systems

Setting up a quick and reliable payment system is one of the most critical aspects of your business, especially when aiming to generate $100,000 in 24 hours. Without a seamless payment process, even the best sales funnel or marketing campaign could fall short. Your customers need to feel confident that their payment details are secure, and you need to ensure that transactions are processed quickly and without error. In this chapter, we'll explore how to set up instant payment systems that facilitate smooth transactions, improve customer trust, and ensure that you're ready to handle large volumes of payments without disruptions.

By the end of this chapter, you'll know how to choose the best payment platforms, integrate them into your sales funnel, optimize the user experience, and ensure security and compliance, all while maintaining a fast and efficient payment process.

Step 1: Choosing the Right Payment Gateway

The first step in setting up a fast and reliable payment system is choosing the right **payment gateway**. A payment gateway is a service that authorizes and processes credit card or direct payments for online transactions. The gateway you choose can affect your transaction fees, processing times, customer trust, and overall user experience.

1. What to Look for in a Payment Gateway

When selecting a payment gateway, there are several key factors to consider:

- **Transaction Speed**: How quickly does the payment gateway process transactions and transfer funds to your account? Instant payment processing is ideal, especially when handling large volumes of sales.

- **Transaction Fees**: Most payment gateways charge a percentage per transaction, along with possible fixed fees. You'll want to choose a gateway that offers competitive rates while also providing high-quality service.

- **Security**: Security is non-negotiable. The payment gateway must offer top-notch encryption, fraud detection, and compliance with **PCI-DSS (Payment Card Industry Data Security Standard)** requirements.
- **Global Payments**: If you sell internationally, make sure the payment gateway supports multiple currencies and accepts a wide range of payment methods (e.g., credit cards, debit cards, PayPal, Apple Pay, etc.).
- **User Experience**: The checkout process should be seamless and easy to use for your customers. A complicated or clunky payment experience can lead to cart abandonment.
- **Mobile Compatibility**: Ensure the payment gateway works well on mobile devices since a growing percentage of users make purchases on their smartphones.

2. Top Payment Gateways to Consider

Here are some of the most popular and trusted payment gateways that you can consider based on your business needs:

- **PayPal**: One of the most widely used payment gateways, PayPal offers a fast and secure payment option. It's easy to integrate with most e-commerce platforms and is familiar to customers worldwide.
  - **Pros**: Global acceptance, supports multiple currencies, and offers PayPal Credit for buyers.
  - **Cons**: Higher transaction fees (typically 2.9% + $0.30 per transaction).
- **Stripe**: Stripe is known for its developer-friendly API and seamless integrations. It's a favorite among businesses that need custom payment setups or want to integrate with multiple platforms.

- ◦ **Pros**: Supports a wide range of payment methods, including credit cards, digital wallets, and ACH transfers. It also offers instant payouts to your bank account.
  - ◦ **Cons**: Requires some technical expertise for setup.
- **Square**: Square is an excellent option for businesses that sell both online and in person. It offers a free point-of-sale (POS) system and supports mobile payments.
  - ◦ **Pros**: Easy to use, integrated with POS systems, and offers a flat-rate transaction fee of 2.6% + $0.10.
  - ◦ **Cons**: Limited international support (available only in a few countries).
- **Shopify Payments**: If you're using Shopify to host your store, Shopify Payments is the platform's built-in payment processor. It's easy to use and integrates seamlessly with Shopify's checkout system.
  - ◦ **Pros**: No additional transaction fees for Shopify users, multiple payment methods supported.
  - ◦ **Cons**: Only available to Shopify store owners.
- **Authorize.Net**: A reliable and secure payment gateway that supports a wide range of payment methods. It's ideal for businesses that require extensive security and fraud detection features.
  - ◦ **Pros**: Advanced fraud detection tools, supports recurring billing, and multi-currency transactions.
  - ◦ **Cons**: Higher setup and monthly fees.

Each of these payment gateways has unique advantages, so it's important to choose the one that aligns best with your business model, customer base, and geographical reach.

Step 2: Integrating Payment Systems into Your Sales Funnel

Once you've chosen your payment gateway, the next step is to **integrate it into your sales funnel**. A seamless payment experience is critical for reducing friction, minimizing cart abandonment, and ensuring that transactions are completed smoothly.

1. Optimizing the Checkout Experience

Your checkout page is where your customers make their final decision to purchase, and any friction in this process can result in lost sales. A well-optimized checkout process should be fast, intuitive, and provide clear guidance throughout the transaction.

Best Practices for Checkout Optimization:

- **Use a Single-Page Checkout**: If possible, design a single-page checkout experience to minimize the number of steps required to complete the purchase. Every extra step in the process increases the risk of cart abandonment.
- **Auto-Fill and Auto-Detect**: Enable auto-fill options for forms to speed up the checkout process. For example, auto-detect the country and credit card type based on the first few digits entered by the customer.
- **Clear Call-to-Action (CTA)**: Your payment page should have a prominent, clear, and action-oriented CTA button. Instead of "Submit," use more engaging language like "Complete Purchase Now."
- **Guest Checkout Option**: Not all customers want to create an account. Offer a guest checkout option to simplify the process for those who prefer to complete the purchase without registering.
- **Mobile Optimization**: Ensure that the checkout page is mobile-responsive. With mobile commerce on the rise, you must provide a smooth experience for mobile users.

2. Setting Up Payment Pages and Buy Buttons

For many digital products or high-ticket offers, you'll need to set up **dedicated payment pages** or use **buy buttons** to allow for quick transactions. These payment pages can be integrated into your landing pages, sales pages, or email sequences, allowing customers to make purchases with minimal friction.

Creating High-Converting Payment Pages:

- **Minimal Design, Maximum Clarity**: Keep the design of your payment page simple and distraction-free. The focus should be entirely on completing the transaction.
- **Highlight Benefits Near the Payment Form**: Include a brief reminder of the key benefits or bonuses the customer is receiving, reinforcing why they are making the purchase.
- **Security Badges and Payment Logos**: Display security badges (e.g., SSL certificates) and accepted payment method logos (e.g., Visa, MasterCard, PayPal) to build trust and reassure customers that their payment is safe.
- **Include Payment Options**: Ensure that you offer multiple payment options (e.g., credit cards, digital wallets, PayPal) to accommodate different customer preferences.

Buy Buttons: If you're using platforms like Shopify or Teachable, you can create **buy buttons** that can be embedded on various pages or within email campaigns. These buttons streamline the buying process and take the customer directly to the checkout page.

Example of a Simple Buy Button:

"Buy Now for $997"

When clicked, the button takes the user directly to the checkout page, reducing friction and improving conversion rates.

Step 3: Offering Multiple Payment Options

Giving your customers flexibility in how they pay can significantly increase your conversions. Offering multiple payment options ensures that more people can complete their purchase, regardless of their preferred payment method.

1. Accepting Credit and Debit Cards

At a minimum, your payment system should support major credit and debit cards (Visa, MasterCard, American Express, etc.). Credit and debit cards are the most commonly used payment methods for online transactions and should be the foundation of your payment options.

2. Supporting Digital Wallets

Digital wallets like **Apple Pay**, **Google Pay**, and **PayPal** offer customers a faster and more secure way to complete their purchases, especially on mobile devices. Many customers prefer these options because they allow for one-click payments without needing to enter card details.

Benefits of Digital Wallets:

- **Faster Checkout**: Digital wallets allow for one-click checkout, reducing the number of steps required to complete a transaction.
- **Increased Trust**: Many customers feel more secure using a trusted digital wallet service like PayPal or Apple Pay, especially when purchasing from a new or unfamiliar brand.
- **Mobile Optimization**: Digital wallets are particularly effective for mobile users, as they don't require lengthy form-filling.

3. Offering Payment Plans or Financing

For high-ticket items, offering **payment plans** or **financing options** can make your product more accessible to a wider audience. This allows customers to spread their payments over several months, reducing the upfront financial burden.

Payment Plan Options:

- **Installment Plans**: Allow customers to break the total cost into equal monthly payments. For example, instead of paying $1,000 upfront, a customer could pay $250 per month for four months.
- **Third-Party Financing**: Services like **Klarna**, **Afterpay**, or **PayPal Credit** allow customers to finance their purchase, making larger payments more manageable.

Offering flexible payment options not only increases your conversion rates but can also make high-ticket offers more appealing to customers who may otherwise hesitate to invest in a larger purchase.

Step 4: Ensuring Payment Security and Compliance

Security is one of the most important aspects of your payment system. Customers need to feel confident that their payment details are protected, and you must ensure that your payment system complies with all necessary regulations, such as **PCI-DSS** (Payment Card Industry Data Security Standard).

1. Choosing a PCI-Compliant Gateway

The easiest way to ensure compliance is by choosing a **PCI-compliant** payment gateway. Most major gateways, such as Stripe, PayPal, and Authorize.Net, are PCI-compliant by default, meaning they meet the strict security standards required to handle and process payment information.

What is PCI Compliance?

PCI compliance refers to a set of security standards designed to protect customer payment data. If you process, store, or transmit credit card data, you must adhere to these standards.

2. Using SSL Certificates for Secure Transactions

Ensure that your website and payment pages are secured with **SSL encryption**. SSL (Secure Sockets Layer) certificates encrypt sensitive data (like credit card information) during transmission, making it difficult for hackers to intercept or steal it.

How to Tell if Your Website is SSL-Encrypted:

- Look for the **padlock symbol** in the address bar.
- Your website URL should begin with **https://** instead of **http://**.

SSL encryption not only protects your customers but also builds trust, as most savvy buyers now expect websites to display the padlock symbol when making online purchases.

3. Implementing Fraud Detection Tools

Payment fraud is a significant concern for online businesses. To minimize the risk of fraudulent transactions, use your payment gateway's built-in **fraud detection tools**. Most gateways offer advanced fraud protection, including:

- **Address Verification Systems (AVS)**: This checks the billing address provided by the customer against the address on file with the credit card company.
- **Card Verification Code (CVC) Requirements**: Always require customers to enter the three- or four-digit CVC code from their credit card.
- **Velocity Checks**: This prevents multiple transactions from being processed in quick succession from the same IP address, reducing the likelihood of fraud attempts.

By implementing these security measures, you can protect your business from chargebacks and fraudulent activity while maintaining customer trust.

Step 5: Testing and Monitoring Your Payment System

Once your payment system is set up, it's crucial to **test** and **monitor** it regularly to ensure smooth transactions and address any issues before they affect your customers.

1. Testing the Payment Process

Before launching your product or service, run test transactions to ensure everything works correctly. This includes:

- Testing multiple payment methods (e.g., credit cards, PayPal, digital wallets).
- Verifying that payments are processed smoothly and funds are deposited into your account without delay.
- Checking that email confirmations and receipts are sent to customers after purchase.

Most payment gateways provide **sandbox environments** that allow you to test transactions without processing real payments.

2. Monitoring Transactions and Addressing Issues

After your payment system goes live, monitor transactions regularly to identify and resolve any potential issues, such as:

- **Declined Transactions**: Identify any patterns of declined transactions and address possible reasons, such as incorrect card details or insufficient funds.
- **Cart Abandonment**: Use tools like **Google Analytics** or **Hotjar** to track cart abandonment rates. If you notice a high abandonment rate, consider optimizing the checkout process or offering cart recovery emails.
- **Customer Support for Payment Issues**: Provide responsive customer support to help customers who encounter issues with payments. Offering live chat or email support can help resolve problems quickly and prevent lost sales.

Conclusion

Setting up instant payment systems is a critical step in creating a seamless buying experience and ensuring that your business can handle high volumes of transactions, especially when working toward ambitious financial goals like generating $100,000 in 24 hours. By choosing the right payment gateway, optimizing the checkout process, offering flexible payment options, and ensuring top-notch security, you can create a payment system that boosts conversions, builds trust with your customers, and facilitates smooth transactions. With the right setup, your payment process will be an asset, helping you achieve your revenue goals while providing a positive, hassle-free experience for your customers.

Chapter 15: Upselling and Cross-Selling for Additional Revenue

Upselling and cross-selling are two of the most effective strategies for maximizing the lifetime value of your customers and significantly increasing your profits. By offering additional products, services, or upgrades during or after a purchase, you can boost your revenue without needing to acquire new customers. In fact, the probability of selling to an existing customer is far higher than selling to a new prospect, making upselling and cross-selling essential techniques for any business aiming to achieve rapid financial success.

In this chapter, we'll explore how to use upsells and cross-sells to increase your average order value (AOV), the psychology behind successful upselling and cross-selling, and actionable strategies to implement these techniques in your sales funnel. By the end of this chapter, you'll have a clear blueprint for maximizing revenue from every customer who interacts with your business.

Step 1: Understanding the Difference Between Upselling and Cross-Selling

Before diving into the strategies, it's important to understand the distinction between **upselling** and **cross-selling**, as each serves a different purpose in increasing customer value.

1. What is Upselling?

Upselling is the practice of encouraging customers to purchase a more expensive or premium version of the product they are already considering or have already bought. This could be an upgrade to a higher-tier product, additional features, or a larger quantity.

Examples of Upselling:

- **Higher-tier product**: If a customer is about to buy a course for $500, you offer them the premium version of the course with additional coaching for $1,000.
- **Upgrading the product**: A customer purchasing a basic software package can be upsold to the pro version with more features.
- **Increasing quantity**: If a customer is buying one product, you can offer a discount for purchasing in bulk (e.g., "Buy two and save 20%!").

The goal of upselling is to provide a better, more valuable solution to the customer while increasing the overall value of the sale.

2. What is Cross-Selling?

Cross-selling is the practice of offering complementary or related products alongside the customer's current purchase. These additional products enhance or complement the original purchase, giving the customer a more comprehensive solution.

Examples of Cross-Selling:

- **Related products**: A customer buying a camera could be offered camera accessories such as lenses, tripods, or memory cards.
- **Service add-ons**: A customer purchasing a web design package might be cross-sold hosting services or SEO optimization tools.
- **Bundling products**: Offering a bundle of related products at a discounted rate. For example, "Add this guidebook and templates to your course purchase for only $50 more!"

The goal of cross-selling is to offer customers more value by providing complementary products that enhance their experience, while increasing the total order value.

Step 2: The Psychology Behind Upselling and Cross-Selling

Both upselling and cross-selling tap into key psychological triggers that make them highly effective at increasing sales. By understanding these triggers, you can craft offers that feel like natural, valuable extensions of the customer's initial purchase rather than hard sales tactics.

1. Building on Buyer Momentum

After a customer has made the decision to buy, they are already in a **buying mindset**. At this point, they've overcome any initial objections, decided that your product will solve their problem, and are emotionally invested in the purchase. This makes them more open to additional offers, especially if those offers enhance the value of their purchase.

By presenting an upsell or cross-sell at this moment, you're capitalizing on the momentum of the buyer's decision. They're already committed to spending money, so the idea of spending a little more to get a better product or experience is less of a hurdle.

2. Offering Immediate Value

The key to successful upselling and cross-selling is ensuring that the additional offer provides **immediate value**. Customers are more likely to accept an upsell or cross-sell if they can quickly see how it benefits them. Whether it's saving time, increasing convenience, or improving the results they'll achieve with the product, the value must be clear.

Example of Immediate Value:

- **Upsell**: If a customer is purchasing an online course, offering them an upgrade to a package that includes one-on-one coaching will immediately make the purchase feel more personal and impactful.
- **Cross-sell**: If a customer is buying a marketing automation tool, cross-selling them templates or pre-designed workflows will help them implement the tool more quickly and easily.

3. Reducing Decision Fatigue

Offering a limited number of well-targeted upsells or cross-sells helps reduce **decision fatigue**, making it easier for customers to say "yes." When presented with too many choices, customers may feel overwhelmed and be less likely to make additional purchases. Focus on a few carefully selected offers that are directly related to the customer's main purchase.

By simplifying the decision-making process and presenting highly relevant, valuable options, you increase the likelihood of a successful upsell or cross-sell.

Step 3: Implementing Upselling Strategies

Upselling can significantly increase your average order value, especially when it's done strategically. Below are several techniques to implement upselling in a way that feels natural and valuable to your customers.

1. Offer Tiered Versions of Your Product

One of the simplest upsell strategies is to offer **tiered versions** of your product or service. This allows customers to choose between a basic, standard, and premium version of your offer, with each tier offering more features or value at a higher price point.

Example:

- **Basic Tier**: Access to the core product (e.g., online course) for $500.
- **Standard Tier**: Core product plus additional resources (e.g., workbooks, templates) for $750.
- **Premium Tier**: Core product, additional resources, and personalized support (e.g., one-on-one coaching) for $1,500.

By presenting these options, you give customers the opportunity to self-select the level of value they want. Many will opt for the higher-priced tiers if they perceive the additional features as worth the investment.

2. Use "Order Bumps" at Checkout

An **order bump** is a highly effective upsell technique that offers a small, relevant upgrade or add-on during the checkout process. The order bump is typically displayed right on the checkout page, making it easy for customers to add the upsell with a single click.

Examples of Order Bumps:

- **Digital Products**: "Add the Advanced Marketing Strategy Workbook to your order for just $37."
- **Services**: "Upgrade to VIP support and get priority access to customer service for just $47."

Order bumps are low-friction upsells because they don't require the customer to rethink their purchase. They're already in the process of checking out, and adding a small, valuable offer at this stage feels like a natural extension of their decision.

3. Time-Limited Upsell Offers

Another way to increase the effectiveness of your upsell strategy is to offer **time-limited upsells** that are only available immediately after the initial purchase. This creates urgency and pushes the customer to act quickly, as they know the offer will expire soon.

Examples of Time-Limited Upsells:

- "Upgrade to the premium version within the next 24 hours and get a 20% discount!"
- "Add a private coaching session to your order for a one-time offer of $97, available only at checkout."

The time-sensitive nature of the upsell encourages customers to take action now, rather than delaying or second-guessing their decision.

Step 4: Implementing Cross-Selling Strategies

Cross-selling allows you to offer additional products that complement the customer's original purchase, enhancing their experience while increasing your revenue. Below are several strategies for cross-selling effectively.

1. Offer Complementary Products

The most straightforward way to cross-sell is to offer **complementary products** that align with the customer's original purchase. These products should solve related problems or help the customer achieve better results with their main purchase.

Examples of Complementary Cross-Sells:

- A customer buying a camera could be cross-sold a camera bag, tripod, or extra battery.
- A customer purchasing an online course could be cross-sold a companion e-book, templates, or software tools that make the course easier to implement.

By offering products that enhance the customer's original purchase, you provide additional value while increasing the overall sale amount.

2. Bundle Products Together

Bundling is a great way to increase the perceived value of your offer and encourage customers to purchase multiple products at once. With **product bundles**, you combine related items and offer them at a discounted price compared to purchasing each item individually.

Examples of Product Bundling:

- **Digital Product Bundle**: Bundle an online course, e-book, and template package together for one price. For example, "Get the Course, Workbook, and Template Pack for just $597 (Save $150)!"

- **Physical Product Bundle**: Bundle related products, such as offering a skincare set that includes a cleanser, toner, and moisturizer at a discounted rate.

Product bundles not only increase the average order value but also make the purchase feel like a better deal for the customer, as they are receiving more value for their money.

3. Cross-Sell via Post-Purchase Emails

The relationship with your customer doesn't end once they make a purchase. In fact, the post-purchase period is an excellent opportunity for cross-selling additional products through **post-purchase email sequences**. These emails should focus on enhancing the customer's experience with their original purchase by offering complementary products or services.

Examples of Post-Purchase Cross-Sells:

- **Email Follow-Up**: "Now that you've enrolled in our course, would you like to add private coaching sessions to your learning experience?"
- **Upsell for Product Enhancements**: "Thanks for purchasing our marketing automation tool! Upgrade to the pro version to unlock advanced features and maximize your results."

Post-purchase emails allow you to stay engaged with your customers while offering additional value, leading to repeat sales and higher customer lifetime value.

Step 5: Optimizing Upsell and Cross-Sell Performance

Even the best upselling and cross-selling strategies can benefit from continuous **testing** and **optimization**. By tracking key metrics and experimenting with different offers, you can refine your approach to maximize revenue from every customer.

1. Track Key Metrics

To measure the success of your upsell and cross-sell efforts, track the following metrics:

- **Upsell Take Rate**: The percentage of customers who accept an upsell offer.
- **Cross-Sell Take Rate**: The percentage of customers who add a cross-sell product to their order.
- **Average Order Value (AOV)**: How much each customer spends on average, including upsells and cross-sells.
- **Customer Lifetime Value (CLV)**: The total revenue you can expect to earn from a customer over their lifetime, including repeat purchases and upsells.

By tracking these metrics, you'll gain insights into which upsell and cross-sell offers are most effective, allowing you to adjust your strategies accordingly.

2. A/B Test Upsell and Cross-Sell Offers

A/B testing allows you to experiment with different upsell and cross-sell offers to see which ones drive the best results. For example, you could test offering a premium upsell vs. a mid-tier upsell or compare different cross-sell products to see which combination increases average order value the most.

Examples of A/B Testing:

- **Test Different Upsell Offers**: Test offering a one-time discount on an upsell vs. offering an additional bonus for upgrading.
- **Test Order Bump Placement**: Experiment with placing the order bump on the checkout page vs. placing it earlier in the funnel to see which placement leads to higher conversions.

By regularly testing and optimizing your upsell and cross-sell offers, you'll continually improve your revenue without having to rely on acquiring new customers.

Conclusion

Upselling and cross-selling are powerful tools that allow you to increase revenue from each customer while providing additional value to enhance their experience. By offering premium upgrades, complementary products, and time-sensitive offers, you can maximize your average order value and customer lifetime value. Additionally, by implementing these strategies at various touchpoints throughout the customer journey—during checkout, through post-purchase emails, and via product bundles—you'll be able to increase profits without adding significant marketing costs.

The key to successful upselling and cross-selling lies in understanding your customers' needs and offering solutions that feel natural and valuable. With the right approach, you can dramatically boost your bottom line while delivering a superior experience to your customers, helping you achieve your revenue goals faster and more efficiently.

Part 4: Traffic Generation

Chapter 16: The Power of Paid Ads

Paid advertising is one of the fastest and most effective ways to generate immediate traffic and achieve rapid sales. When used strategically, platforms like **Facebook**, **Google**, and **Instagram** can put your product or service in front of millions of potential customers, driving traffic to your website or sales page almost instantly. However, running successful paid ad campaigns requires more than just boosting posts or creating ads at random. It involves careful targeting, compelling ad creative, and optimizing your budget to ensure a positive return on investment (ROI).

In this chapter, we'll explore how to use Facebook, Google, and Instagram ads to generate high-quality traffic quickly, while maintaining control over your budget and maximizing conversions. You'll learn the best practices for crafting compelling ad copy, choosing the right audience, and running campaigns that can help you reach your goal of generating $100,000 in 24 hours or achieving sustainable growth over the long term.

Step 1: Understanding the Role of Paid Ads in Your Sales Funnel

Before diving into the specifics of each platform, it's important to understand how paid ads fit into your overall **sales funnel**. Paid ads are most effective when they're designed to drive traffic to different stages of the funnel, from awareness to conversion.

1. Top-of-Funnel (Awareness)

At the top of the funnel, the goal is to generate awareness and attract new potential customers. At this stage, you're introducing people to your brand, product, or service, and educating them about the solution you offer.

Key Objectives at the Awareness Stage:

- Drive traffic to educational content (e.g., blog posts, videos, lead magnets).

- Build brand recognition and trust through engaging ad creatives.
- Start capturing leads through free resources or email opt-ins.

2. Middle-of-Funnel (Consideration)

In the middle of the funnel, your audience is already aware of your product or service and is considering making a purchase. The focus here is to provide more value and help potential customers understand why your offer is the right solution for them.

Key Objectives at the Consideration Stage:

- Use retargeting ads to re-engage people who have visited your website but haven't made a purchase.
- Offer more in-depth content, such as case studies, testimonials, or product demos.
- Drive traffic to your sales pages or webinars where potential customers can learn more.

3. Bottom-of-Funnel (Conversion)

At the bottom of the funnel, your prospects are ready to make a purchase, and your ads should be focused on closing the deal. This is where you present your main offer, showcase the benefits, and eliminate any objections.

Key Objectives at the Conversion Stage:

- Drive traffic to a checkout page or sales page.
- Use time-limited offers or discounts to create urgency.
- Use retargeting ads to close the sale for people who have added items to their cart but haven't completed the purchase.

By aligning your paid ads with each stage of the funnel, you'll be able to guide potential customers from awareness to conversion, all while optimizing your ad spend for maximum return.

Step 2: Using Facebook Ads for Targeted Traffic

Facebook remains one of the most powerful advertising platforms, thanks to its advanced targeting options and massive user base. With over 2.9 billion active users, Facebook offers advertisers the ability to reach a highly specific audience based on demographics, interests, behaviors, and more.

1. Setting Up a Facebook Ad Campaign

To create a successful Facebook ad campaign, you'll need to follow a few key steps:

Step 1: Define Your Objective Facebook Ads Manager allows you to choose from a variety of campaign objectives, such as brand awareness, traffic, lead generation, or conversions. For most direct-response campaigns aimed at generating immediate revenue, you'll want to select the **Conversions** objective. This will optimize your ads to reach people who are most likely to take a specific action, such as making a purchase.

Step 2: Audience Targeting One of the strengths of Facebook advertising is its advanced audience targeting. You can target your ads based on:

- **Demographics**: Age, gender, location, job title, education level.
- **Interests**: Hobbies, behaviors, and activities, such as "entrepreneurship," "health and fitness," or "online shopping."
- **Custom Audiences**: You can upload a list of existing customers or leads, or create a custom audience based on website visitors or people who have engaged with your content.
- **Lookalike Audiences**: Facebook allows you to create lookalike audiences, which are groups of people who share similar characteristics with your existing customers, making it easier to find new, high-quality leads.

Step 3: Ad Creative and Copy Your ad creative (images, videos, or carousel ads) should be visually engaging and aligned with your brand. For copy, use persuasive, benefit-driven language that speaks to the pain points and desires of your target audience. Make your call to action (CTA) clear and compelling, whether it's "Shop Now," "Sign Up," or "Get Your Free Guide."

Step 4: Budget and Bidding Start by setting a daily or lifetime budget for your campaign. Facebook will distribute your budget over the course of the campaign, optimizing for the best results. You can also choose between **automatic bidding** (where Facebook sets the bid to maximize your results) or **manual bidding** (where you set your maximum bid amount).

2. Facebook Ad Types to Use

Facebook offers a variety of ad formats, and choosing the right one depends on your campaign goals:

- **Single Image Ads**: These are straightforward ads featuring one image or graphic, often used for product promotions or brand awareness.
- **Video Ads**: Video is highly engaging and effective for storytelling or demonstrating the benefits of your product. Keep videos short and to the point, ideally under 30 seconds.
- **Carousel Ads**: These allow you to showcase multiple images or videos in a single ad, making them ideal for displaying product features, customer testimonials, or case studies.
- **Lead Ads**: These are designed to capture leads directly within Facebook, without requiring users to leave the platform. They're perfect for collecting email addresses in exchange for a free resource or offer.

3. Retargeting with Facebook Ads

One of the most powerful features of Facebook ads is **retargeting**. This allows you to show ads to people who have previously interacted with your business but didn't convert. Retargeting ads are highly effective at moving prospects through the funnel, as they've already shown interest in your product.

Examples of Retargeting Strategies:

- **Cart Abandonment Ads**: Show ads to people who added products to their cart but didn't complete the purchase. Offer a discount or incentive to close the sale.
- **Content Engagement Retargeting**: Retarget people who have watched a video, clicked on an ad, or visited your website. Use these ads to push them closer to conversion by offering a special deal or bonus.

Step 3: Leveraging Google Ads for High-Intent Traffic

Google Ads is another powerful platform, particularly for targeting people who are actively searching for solutions to their problems. By running ads on Google's search network, you can capture high-intent traffic—people who are already looking for products or services like yours.

1. Google Search Ads

Google Search Ads are text-based ads that appear at the top of search results pages when users enter specific keywords. These ads are ideal for capturing high-intent traffic since they target people actively searching for the products or services you offer.

Step 1: Keyword Research The first step in running Google Search Ads is to perform **keyword research**. Use tools like **Google Keyword Planner, Ubersuggest,** or **SEMrush** to find relevant keywords that people are searching for in your niche. Focus on keywords that have a high search volume and intent to buy, but avoid overly competitive terms that may drive up your cost per click (CPC).

Step 2: Write High-Converting Ad Copy Your Google ads need to be clear, concise, and highly relevant to the search terms you're targeting. Include the following elements in your ad copy:

- **Headline**: Use keywords that match the user's search query and clearly state the benefit of your product or service.
  - Example: "Buy High-Quality Office Chairs – Free Shipping!"
- **Description**: Expand on your offer, highlighting key benefits, features, or discounts.
  - Example: "Ergonomic office chairs designed for comfort and productivity. Shop today and get 10% off!"
- **Call to Action (CTA)**: End with a strong CTA that encourages immediate action, such as "Shop Now" or "Learn More."

Step 3: Bidding and Budgeting Set a daily budget based on your goals and decide whether to use **manual bidding** (where you set the maximum amount you're willing to pay per click) or **automated bidding** (where Google optimizes your bids for conversions). Focus on bidding for high-intent keywords that are more likely to result in sales.

2. Google Display Ads

Google Display Ads are visual ads that appear across Google's vast network of websites, apps, and YouTube. While search ads target high-intent users, display ads are better for building brand awareness and retargeting potential customers who have already interacted with your brand.

Using Display Ads for Retargeting:

- **Remarketing Lists**: Create remarketing lists that target users who have visited your website, watched a video on YouTube, or engaged with your app.
- **Display Ad Creative**: Use eye-catching images, graphics, or videos in your display ads. Make sure the ad is visually appealing and reinforces the message of your original offer.

Step 4: Instagram Ads for Visual Storytelling

Instagram, owned by Facebook, is a visually driven platform with over 1 billion active users, making it an excellent choice for businesses with strong visual branding. Instagram ads are ideal for e-commerce products, lifestyle brands, and any business that can tell a compelling story through visuals.

1. Setting Up Instagram Ads

Instagram ads can be run directly through **Facebook Ads Manager**, allowing you to take advantage of Facebook's robust targeting options. The key difference is that Instagram ads rely heavily on **high-quality visuals** to capture attention.

Ad Types on Instagram:

- **Image Ads**: Single image ads that feature striking visuals and concise copy. Use these ads to showcase products or services in action.
- **Video Ads**: Short videos (up to 60 seconds) that tell a story or demonstrate how your product works. These are particularly effective for engaging audiences with storytelling.
- **Carousel Ads**: Allow users to swipe through multiple images or videos. Ideal for showcasing a range of products, customer testimonials, or key features.
- **Instagram Stories Ads**: Full-screen ads that appear in between Instagram Stories. These ads are highly immersive and should be designed to feel natural within the flow of Instagram Stories content.

2. Instagram Ad Best Practices

When running Instagram ads, focus on creating ads that are **native** to the platform and **engaging** to your target audience. Instagram users respond best to content that feels organic rather than overly promotional.

Best Practices:

- **Use High-Quality Visuals**: Whether it's a photo or video, the quality of your visuals can make or break your ad. Invest in professional images or videos that reflect your brand's aesthetic and stand out in a user's feed.
- **Keep Copy Short and Sweet**: Instagram is a highly visual platform, so keep your ad copy short, benefit-driven, and easy to read. Use emojis sparingly to add personality.
- **Engage with Stories**: Instagram Stories ads offer a highly engaging, full-screen experience. Use Stories ads to create urgency, showcase limited-time offers, or provide a behind-the-scenes look at your product or service.

Step 5: Optimizing and Scaling Paid Ad Campaigns

Once your ads are live, the work doesn't stop. Continuous **monitoring** and **optimization** are key to ensuring your paid ad campaigns are successful and profitable.

1. Monitor Key Metrics

Keep a close eye on the following metrics to gauge the performance of your campaigns:

- **Click-Through Rate (CTR)**: Measures how often people who see your ad click on it. A low CTR could mean your ad isn't relevant to your audience or that your creative needs improvement.
- **Cost Per Click (CPC)**: The amount you pay each time someone clicks on your ad. Aim to keep this as low as possible while maintaining high-quality traffic.
- **Conversion Rate**: The percentage of people who click on your ad and complete a desired action, such as making a purchase or signing up for your email list.

- **Return on Ad Spend (ROAS)**: Measures the revenue generated for every dollar spent on ads. A ROAS above 1 means you're generating more revenue than you're spending, while a ROAS below 1 indicates you're losing money on the campaign.

2. A/B Test Your Ads

A/B testing is crucial for identifying which ad elements work best. Test different variables, such as:

- **Ad Creative**: Compare different images, videos, or carousels to see which drives more engagement.
- **Ad Copy**: Test variations in headlines, descriptions, and CTAs to find the most compelling message.
- **Targeting**: Experiment with different audience segments to identify the most responsive and profitable groups.
- **Placements**: Try running ads on different placements, such as Facebook Feed, Instagram Stories, or Google Display Network, to see which platform delivers the best results.

3. Scale Winning Campaigns

Once you've identified a winning ad campaign, it's time to **scale**. Increase your budget gradually to ensure that the performance remains consistent. Monitor your metrics closely to ensure that as you scale, your ROI stays positive.

Scaling Strategies:

- **Increase Ad Spend**: Gradually increase your daily budget for high-performing campaigns to reach a larger audience.
- **Expand Targeting**: Use lookalike audiences or broader interest targeting to expand the reach of your ads while still targeting relevant users.
- **Test New Creatives**: Even as you scale, continue testing new ad creatives to prevent ad fatigue and keep your audience engaged.

Conclusion

Paid ads are a powerful tool for driving immediate traffic and generating fast sales, whether you're using Facebook, Google, or Instagram. By aligning your ads with your sales funnel, targeting the right audiences, and creating compelling ad creatives, you can attract high-quality traffic and guide them toward conversion. With continuous monitoring, testing, and optimization, you can ensure that your paid ad campaigns are profitable and scalable, helping you reach ambitious revenue goals like $100,000 in 24 hours. By mastering the art of paid advertising, you'll be equipped to turn traffic into conversions and maximize the return on your ad spend.

Chapter 17: Influencer and Partner Marketing

In today's digital landscape, one of the fastest and most effective ways to drive massive traffic and generate immediate sales is through **influencer and partner marketing**. These strategies allow you to tap into the established audiences and credibility of other individuals or brands, giving your product or service instant exposure to highly engaged communities. By collaborating with influencers and strategic partners, you can not only reach a wider audience but also build trust quickly—two key components for achieving rapid growth.

In this chapter, we'll explore how to leverage influencer marketing and strategic partnerships to drive massive traffic and increase your sales. You'll learn how to find the right influencers, establish meaningful partnerships, and create campaigns that align with your business goals, helping you reach your financial objectives in record time.

Step 1: Understanding the Power of Influencer Marketing

Influencer marketing involves partnering with individuals who have a large and engaged following on social media, blogs, or other digital platforms. These influencers have built trust with their audience, making their endorsements highly valuable. When an influencer promotes your product, they essentially vouch for your brand, leading to increased credibility, traffic, and sales.

1. Why Influencer Marketing Works

The effectiveness of influencer marketing lies in the **relationship** between influencers and their audience. Followers trust the recommendations of influencers they follow because these individuals are perceived as authentic and relatable, unlike traditional ads, which can feel impersonal.

Key Reasons Influencer Marketing Works:

- **Trust and Authenticity**: Followers view influencers as experts or role models, and their recommendations often carry more weight than paid ads or direct marketing.
- **Targeted Audiences**: Influencers usually cater to niche audiences, allowing you to target specific demographics that are likely to be interested in your product.
- **Social Proof**: When an influencer endorses your product, it acts as social proof, showing that someone their audience trusts believes in your offering.

2. Types of Influencers

Influencers come in different sizes, each with unique advantages depending on your goals and budget. These include:

- **Mega-Influencers**: Celebrities or public figures with millions of followers. While they can offer massive reach, they typically charge high fees, and their audiences can be broad and less targeted.
- **Macro-Influencers**: Influencers with followers ranging from 100,000 to 1 million. They often have high engagement and reach but at a more affordable rate than mega-influencers.
- **Micro-Influencers**: Influencers with 10,000 to 100,000 followers. These influencers have highly engaged niche audiences, making them ideal for targeted campaigns with more authenticity.
- **Nano-Influencers**: Influencers with 1,000 to 10,000 followers. Though smaller, their followers tend to be highly loyal and engaged, and they offer affordable or even free collaboration opportunities.

For most businesses looking to generate sales quickly, **macro- and micro-influencers** often provide the best balance of reach, engagement, and affordability.

Step 2: Finding the Right Influencers for Your Brand

Not all influencers are a good fit for every brand. The success of an influencer marketing campaign largely depends on finding influencers whose audience aligns with your target market and whose content resonates with your brand values.

1. Define Your Audience

Before you start reaching out to influencers, you need to have a clear understanding of your **target audience**. What are their demographics, interests, and pain points? Knowing your audience will help you identify the influencers who speak to the people most likely to be interested in your product.

Key Audience Considerations:

- **Age and Gender**: Make sure the influencer's audience aligns with your target demographics.
- **Interests and Hobbies**: Look for influencers who cover topics related to your industry. For example, if you sell fitness equipment, target influencers in the health and fitness space.
- **Location**: If your product or service is region-specific, ensure the influencer's audience is concentrated in that location.

2. Tools for Finding Influencers

There are several tools available to help you identify and connect with influencers who are a good fit for your brand. Some of the most popular include:

- **Instagram Search and Hashtags**: Start by searching for influencers on Instagram using industry-related hashtags. For example, if you're in the fashion space, hashtags like #fashionblogger or #streetstyle can help you find relevant influencers.

- **YouTube**: Many influencers create long-form content on YouTube, offering a great platform for product reviews, tutorials, and demonstrations. Search for content creators in your niche and check the engagement on their videos.
- **Influencer Platforms**: Services like **Upfluence**, **BuzzSumo**, **AspireIQ**, and **Grin** help you discover influencers, analyze their audience metrics, and manage collaborations.

3. Evaluating Influencers

Once you've identified potential influencers, evaluate their suitability based on a few key factors:

- **Engagement Rate**: An influencer's engagement rate is often more important than their follower count. Look for influencers with high likes, comments, shares, and meaningful interactions on their posts.
- **Content Quality**: Assess the quality of their content. Does it align with your brand's tone and aesthetic? Authentic, high-quality content is more likely to resonate with their audience.
- **Audience Fit**: Use tools like **HypeAuditor** or **Social Blade** to analyze the influencer's audience demographics. Make sure the audience is a good match for your product, including factors like location, age, and interests.

Step 3: Crafting Influencer Campaigns that Drive Results

Once you've selected your influencers, the next step is to craft campaigns that are engaging, authentic, and designed to drive traffic and conversions.

1. Set Clear Goals and KPIs

Before launching any influencer campaign, define your objectives and the key performance indicators (KPIs) that will measure success. Are you aiming to generate sales, increase brand awareness, or build your email list? Your goals will determine how you structure the campaign.

Common Influencer Campaign Goals:

- **Direct Sales**: Provide influencers with an exclusive discount code or affiliate link to track sales generated from their promotion.
- **Traffic**: Drive traffic to your website or landing page using a custom URL in the influencer's bio or post.
- **Lead Generation**: Use influencers to promote a free lead magnet (e.g., eBook, webinar) to collect email addresses.

KPIs to Track:

- **Engagement Rate**: Measure likes, comments, shares, and clicks.
- **Traffic**: Use tools like **Google Analytics** to track how much traffic is driven from the influencer's content.
- **Conversion Rate**: Measure how many users who clicked on the influencer's content completed a purchase or signed up for your offer.

2. Types of Influencer Content

There are several types of content that influencers can create to promote your product, each offering different levels of engagement and effectiveness.

- **Sponsored Posts**: A sponsored post is a simple, one-off piece of content where the influencer promotes your product directly. This could be a photo, video, or Instagram story showcasing the product.
- **Product Reviews**: Product reviews provide more in-depth insights, as influencers share their personal experiences using your product. These are highly effective for building trust and credibility.

- **Giveaways and Contests**: Hosting a giveaway or contest with an influencer is a great way to generate engagement and increase visibility. Followers are often required to follow your brand, tag friends, or visit your website to participate.
- **Takeovers**: With an Instagram or YouTube takeover, the influencer temporarily takes control of your brand's account and creates content for your followers. This can help boost engagement and build a stronger connection between the influencer and your audience.

3. Ensuring Authenticity

The most successful influencer campaigns are those that feel **authentic** and natural. Influencers who are given creative freedom to promote your product in their own voice and style tend to achieve better results than overly scripted promotions.

Best Practices for Authenticity:

- **Allow Creative Freedom**: Give influencers guidelines but allow them to create content in their own style. Their followers trust their voice, so authenticity is key.
- **Be Transparent About Sponsorships**: Ensure that all influencer posts clearly disclose their relationship with your brand to comply with FTC regulations.
- **Focus on Storytelling**: Encourage influencers to share personal stories about how they use your product or how it has benefited them, making the promotion feel more genuine.

Step 4: Leveraging Strategic Partnerships for Massive Exposure

While influencer marketing focuses on individuals, **partner marketing** involves forming alliances with other businesses or brands that share your target audience but are not direct competitors. These partnerships can help you tap into new markets, expand your reach, and drive traffic quickly.

1. Types of Strategic Partnerships

There are several types of partnerships that can help you grow your business:

- **Joint Ventures (JVs)**: A joint venture is when two businesses collaborate on a project, product launch, or marketing campaign. Both partners promote the campaign to their respective audiences, expanding the reach of both brands.
  - Example: A fitness company could partner with a health food brand to create a joint bundle offer or promote a co-branded webinar on nutrition and exercise.
- **Affiliate Partnerships**: With affiliate partnerships, you allow other businesses or influencers to promote your product in exchange for a commission on sales. This is a low-risk way to grow your business, as you only pay for results.
  - Example: A software company could partner with industry bloggers, offering them a percentage of sales generated from their referral links.
- **Co-Branding**: Co-branding involves two brands collaborating on a product or service that features both names. This strategy is great for boosting credibility and tapping into new customer segments.
  - Example: A fashion brand and a designer could create a limited-edition clothing line together, with both brands promoting the product.

2. Finding the Right Partners

The key to successful partnerships is finding brands or businesses that complement yours without directly competing. These partners should have access to your target market and share similar brand values.

Steps to Finding Partners:

- **Research Non-Competing Brands**: Look for businesses that cater to the same audience but offer different products or services. For example, if you sell home decor, consider partnering with a brand that sells kitchenware or furniture.
- **Use Networking Tools**: Platforms like **LinkedIn**, industry forums, and networking events can help you identify potential partners. Reach out with a proposal that highlights the mutual benefits of collaboration.
- **Check Partner Fit**: Ensure that your potential partner's audience, branding, and values align with yours. Both businesses should benefit from the collaboration and add value to their customers.

3. Structuring Successful Partner Campaigns

Once you've identified potential partners, it's essential to structure the campaign in a way that maximizes value for both parties. The partnership should benefit both businesses equally, whether through increased exposure, revenue, or lead generation.

Steps to Structuring a Partner Campaign:

- **Define Mutual Goals**: Set clear objectives for the partnership, whether it's increasing sales, driving traffic, or growing email lists. Both partners should benefit equally from the campaign.
- **Offer Incentives**: Create incentives for both parties to promote the campaign actively. This could include revenue sharing, cross-promotions, or exclusive discounts for each partner's audience.
- **Use Tracking Links**: Use unique tracking links to monitor the performance of each partner's contributions and measure the success of the campaign. This will help you track conversions, traffic, and ROI.

Step 5: Measuring the Success of Influencer and Partner Campaigns

To ensure your influencer and partner marketing efforts are delivering results, it's crucial to measure the performance of each campaign and make adjustments as needed.

1. Tracking Metrics for Influencer Campaigns

For influencer marketing, track the following metrics to assess the success of each campaign:

- **Engagement**: Measure likes, comments, shares, and other interactions on the influencer's post. High engagement rates indicate that the content resonates with their audience.
- **Traffic**: Use tools like **Google Analytics** or custom URLs to track how much traffic the influencer is driving to your website or landing page.
- **Conversions**: If your goal is to generate sales, track how many users who clicked on the influencer's link completed a purchase. Use promo codes or affiliate links to attribute sales accurately.

2. Tracking Metrics for Partner Campaigns

For partner marketing campaigns, you'll want to track similar metrics to ensure the collaboration is driving results for both parties:

- **Referral Traffic**: Measure how much traffic is being generated from your partner's promotions.
- **Lead Generation**: If the campaign focuses on growing your email list or generating leads, track the number of new subscribers or leads generated from the partner's audience.
- **Sales and Revenue**: Track how many sales or subscriptions are directly attributable to the partner campaign. If you're using affiliate links, ensure that each partner's contributions are properly tracked and rewarded.

3. Optimize and Scale

Based on the performance data you collect, optimize your campaigns for better results. Identify which influencers or partners drive the highest ROI and consider scaling those relationships with ongoing collaborations. Similarly, pause or adjust campaigns that aren't delivering the expected results.

Conclusion

Influencer and partner marketing offer powerful ways to drive massive traffic and achieve rapid sales growth by leveraging the trust, credibility, and reach of established audiences. By finding the right influencers and partners, crafting authentic and engaging campaigns, and tracking your results, you can quickly scale your business and reach ambitious revenue goals like generating $100,000 in 24 hours.

Both influencer and partner marketing allow you to tap into new audiences and build trust faster than many traditional marketing methods, giving you a competitive advantage in today's crowded digital landscape. With the right strategy and execution, these methods can become essential tools in your arsenal for rapid business growth and long-term success.

Chapter 18: Affiliate Marketing Blitz

Affiliate marketing is one of the fastest ways to expand your reach, generate massive traffic, and skyrocket your sales, all while leveraging the efforts of others. By building an **affiliate army**, you can have an entire network of people promoting your product or service for you, earning a commission for every sale they drive. This creates a **win-win** scenario where affiliates benefit financially, and you gain access to new audiences and sales without increasing your marketing costs.

In this chapter, we will cover how to set up an affiliate program, recruit high-performing affiliates quickly, and scale your affiliate marketing efforts to drive significant traffic and revenue. You'll learn the strategies and tools necessary to build a large, motivated affiliate team that can help you generate $100,000 (or more) in 24 hours.

Step 1: Understanding the Power of Affiliate Marketing

Affiliate marketing is a **performance-based** strategy where you reward affiliates (partners) for bringing you sales, leads, or traffic. Affiliates earn a percentage of every sale they drive, providing them with a financial incentive to promote your product or service.

1. Why Affiliate Marketing is Effective

Affiliate marketing is powerful for several reasons:

- **Cost-Effective**: You only pay when you make a sale. This makes affiliate marketing a low-risk, high-reward strategy compared to traditional ads, where you pay upfront without guaranteed results.
- **Scalable**: With affiliate marketing, there's no limit to how many affiliates you can recruit. Each affiliate brings their own audience, allowing you to scale quickly and efficiently.
- **Leverages Existing Networks**: Affiliates already have established relationships with their audience, making it easier for them to promote your offer. This built-in trust makes their recommendations more likely to convert into sales.

2. Types of Affiliate Marketing Models

There are several affiliate models, and the right one for you depends on your business and goals. The most common models include:

- **Pay-Per-Sale**: Affiliates earn a commission for every sale they generate. This is the most popular model for eCommerce and digital products.
- **Pay-Per-Lead**: Affiliates earn a commission for driving leads, such as sign-ups for a free trial, webinar registration, or email opt-in.
- **Pay-Per-Click**: Affiliates earn a commission based on the number of clicks they send to your website, regardless of whether the user converts. This model is less common for sales-focused affiliate programs but can work for driving traffic.

For most businesses aiming to generate sales quickly, the **pay-per-sale** model is the best fit, as it directly rewards affiliates for revenue generated.

Step 2: Setting Up a High-Converting Affiliate Program

A successful affiliate marketing campaign starts with a well-structured affiliate program that incentivizes affiliates to promote your offer. The key is to create a program that's **easy to join, easy to understand, and attractive enough** for affiliates to want to participate.

1. Choose the Right Affiliate Platform

To launch your affiliate program quickly, you'll need an affiliate management platform that tracks affiliate performance, processes payments, and provides promotional tools. There are several affiliate platforms to choose from, each offering various features to support your program.

Popular Affiliate Platforms:

- **ClickBank**: ClickBank is one of the largest affiliate marketplaces, ideal for digital products. It offers a robust tracking system, easy payouts, and access to a large network of potential affiliates.
- **ShareASale**: Known for its transparency and ease of use, ShareASale is a popular choice for businesses looking to attract a wide range of affiliates. It supports both physical and digital products.
- **CJ Affiliate**: Formerly Commission Junction, CJ Affiliate is a trusted network that provides access to top-tier affiliates and advertisers. It's ideal for businesses looking to scale quickly with high-quality partners.
- **Rakuten Marketing**: This network is favored by large brands and offers a high level of affiliate support and tracking.
- **Teachable**: If you're selling online courses, Teachable allows you to create an affiliate program directly within the platform, making it easy to track and pay affiliates for course sales.

2. Offer Competitive Commissions

To attract top affiliates, you need to offer competitive commissions that make it worth their time to promote your product. The commission rate should balance profitability with the ability to incentivize affiliates.

Typical Commission Ranges:

- **Digital Products**: Commissions for digital products are often higher, ranging from **30% to 50%**, since the margins are typically larger.
- **Physical Products**: For physical products, commissions are usually lower, between **5% and 20%**, depending on profit margins and industry standards.

- **Subscription Services**: For subscription-based services, you can offer recurring commissions, where affiliates earn a percentage of the subscription fee for the lifetime of the customer. This is highly attractive to affiliates as it provides them with long-term income.

Example: If you're selling a digital course for $500, offering a **40% commission** would give affiliates $200 per sale, which is an attractive incentive for them to actively promote your course.

3. Create Attractive Incentives and Bonuses

In addition to commissions, consider offering **bonuses and incentives** for affiliates who exceed certain sales targets. This can motivate your affiliates to promote your product more aggressively, especially during launches or promotions.

Examples of Affiliate Incentives:

- **Performance Bonuses**: Offer a cash bonus or increased commission rate to affiliates who reach certain sales milestones. For example, "Earn an extra $500 if you generate 50 sales in the next 30 days."
- **Tiered Commission Structure**: Increase commission rates based on performance. For example, affiliates start with a 30% commission and can earn up to 50% as they generate more sales.
- **Contests and Leaderboards**: Run affiliate contests with prizes for top performers, such as cash rewards, tech gadgets, or vacation packages.

Step 3: Recruiting High-Performing Affiliates Quickly

To launch an **affiliate marketing blitz** and drive traffic quickly, you'll need to recruit a large number of affiliates in a short period. The key is to target affiliates who already have a relevant audience and are motivated to promote your offer.

1. Target Existing Customers and Partners

One of the easiest ways to build your affiliate army quickly is by recruiting **existing customers** and **business partners**. These individuals are already familiar with your product and may be willing to promote it in exchange for commissions.

Steps to Recruit Existing Customers:

- **Email Campaign**: Send an email to your existing customer base inviting them to join your affiliate program. Highlight the benefits of becoming an affiliate, such as earning commissions and sharing a product they already love.
- **Referral Incentives**: Offer referral incentives for customers who recommend your affiliate program to others. This can help you grow your affiliate network organically.

Example Email Script: "Hey [Customer Name],
We're excited to announce the launch of our affiliate program! If you love our products, you can now earn up to 40% commission by promoting them to your friends, family, or audience. Sign up here to get started and start earning today!"

2. Leverage Influencer Networks

Influencers who already promote products in your niche can be powerful affiliates. By offering influencers a commission-based partnership, you incentivize them to promote your offer more frequently, knowing they'll earn a percentage of each sale.

Steps to Recruit Influencers as Affiliates:

- **Direct Outreach**: Reach out to influencers in your industry, offering them an affiliate partnership with attractive commission rates. Explain how promoting your product aligns with their content and benefits their audience.

- **Affiliate Marketplaces**: Join affiliate marketplaces like **Click-Bank** or **ShareASale**, where influencers and content creators often search for new affiliate opportunities.
- **Influencer Platforms**: Use platforms like **Upfluence** or **AspireIQ** to identify influencers who are open to affiliate partnerships. These platforms allow you to filter influencers by niche, engagement rate, and audience size.

Example Outreach Message: "Hi [Influencer Name],
I'm [Your Name] from [Your Brand]. We love your content on [relevant niche] and think our product, [Product Name], would be a perfect fit for your audience. We'd love to partner with you as an affiliate and offer a 40% commission on every sale you generate. Let me know if you're interested, and I'd be happy to share more details!"

3. Recruit Bloggers and Content Creators

Bloggers and content creators are often looking for new products and services to recommend to their audience. By recruiting bloggers as affiliates, you can reach highly targeted audiences who trust the recommendations of the content creators they follow.

Steps to Recruit Bloggers:

- **Guest Blogging and Reviews**: Reach out to bloggers in your niche and offer them the opportunity to review your product or feature it in their content. If they agree to the collaboration, sign them up as affiliates so they can earn commissions from any sales they generate.
- **Affiliate Networks for Bloggers**: Platforms like **FlexOffers**, **Rakuten Marketing**, and **CJ Affiliate** cater specifically to bloggers and website owners who promote affiliate products. Join these networks to connect with relevant bloggers.

- **SEO and Content Marketing**: Identify blogs that rank well for keywords related to your product. Reach out to these blogs, offering them a partnership where they can earn affiliate commissions by featuring your product in their content.

Step 4: Providing Affiliates with the Tools and Resources for Success

Once you've recruited affiliates, you need to provide them with the tools and resources they need to promote your product effectively. The easier you make it for affiliates to promote your offer, the more likely they are to drive traffic and sales.

1. Create an Affiliate Dashboard

Your affiliate platform should offer an easy-to-use dashboard where affiliates can:

- **Access Tracking Links**: Provide unique tracking links for affiliates to ensure they receive credit for each sale they generate.
- **Monitor Performance**: Affiliates should be able to see their sales, commissions, and other performance metrics in real-time.
- **Receive Payouts**: Ensure that your affiliate platform processes payouts automatically, either monthly or after affiliates reach a minimum payout threshold.

2. Offer Ready-Made Marketing Materials

Help affiliates promote your product by providing them with ready-made marketing materials that they can use across their channels. This can include:

- **Email Templates**: Pre-written email sequences that affiliates can send to their email lists.
- **Social Media Posts**: Provide high-quality images, captions, and hashtags that affiliates can post on platforms like Instagram, Facebook, and Twitter.

- **Banner Ads**: Create banner ads in various sizes that affiliates can display on their websites or blogs.
- **Product Descriptions**: Provide a list of product benefits, features, and selling points that affiliates can use when promoting your offer.

By providing affiliates with professional, high-converting assets, you make it easier for them to promote your product and drive sales.

3. Offer Ongoing Support and Communication

Affiliates are more likely to be active and successful if they feel supported. Set up an affiliate support system that includes:

- **Regular Communication**: Send monthly or bi-weekly newsletters to affiliates with updates, tips, and insights on how to improve their performance.
- **Dedicated Support**: Have a dedicated support team or contact person who can answer affiliate questions and provide guidance on promotion strategies.
- **Training Resources**: Offer webinars, videos, or guides that teach affiliates how to market your product effectively. This could include training on email marketing, paid ads, or content creation.

Step 5: Scaling and Optimizing Your Affiliate Program

Once your affiliate program is up and running, focus on **scaling** and **optimizing** it to increase sales and maximize your affiliate marketing ROI.

1. Encourage Active Affiliates

Not all affiliates will actively promote your product, so it's important to identify and nurture those who are generating sales. Offer additional incentives to high-performing affiliates to keep them engaged and motivated.

Strategies to Encourage Active Affiliates:

- **Performance Bonuses**: Reward top-performing affiliates with bonuses, such as cash prizes or higher commission rates.
- **Affiliate Contests**: Run contests to encourage affiliates to generate more sales in a set time frame. Offer prizes to the top three affiliates based on sales volume or traffic driven.
- **Featured Affiliates**: Spotlight your top affiliates in newsletters or on your website to give them recognition and encourage others to follow suit.

2. Analyze Performance and Make Adjustments

Monitor the performance of your affiliate program regularly to identify what's working and what isn't. Key metrics to track include:

- **Affiliate Sales**: How many sales are being generated by affiliates, and which affiliates are contributing the most?
- **Conversion Rates**: Are affiliate traffic sources converting at a high rate? If not, consider providing additional training or better promotional materials.
- **Average Order Value (AOV)**: Look at the average order value from affiliate sales to ensure that the program is contributing meaningfully to your bottom line.

Use these insights to refine your program. For example, if certain affiliates aren't performing well, reach out to them with personalized advice on how to improve. If a specific type of affiliate (e.g., bloggers) performs better than others, focus on recruiting more affiliates from that group.

Conclusion

Affiliate marketing is one of the most powerful and scalable strategies for generating massive traffic and sales in a short period. By building an **affiliate army**, you can leverage the networks, trust, and influence of others to promote your product or service, allowing you to reach audiences far beyond your own. The key to success lies in setting up a well-structured, high-converting affiliate program, offering competitive commissions and incentives, and providing affiliates with the resources they need to effectively promote your offer.

The **affiliate marketing blitz** approach allows you to quickly recruit motivated partners, such as existing customers, influencers, bloggers, and content creators, who can start driving traffic immediately. By offering attractive commissions, running contests or performance bonuses, and ensuring your affiliates have the tools and support they need, you can mobilize a large network of marketers eager to help you hit ambitious revenue targets, such as generating $100,000 in 24 hours.

To ensure long-term success, continue nurturing relationships with your top-performing affiliates, optimizing your commission structure, and expanding your network. With the right strategies in place, affiliate marketing can become a reliable, high-impact channel that consistently drives revenue growth, helping you scale your business quickly and efficiently.

Chapter 19: Leveraging Email Lists and Communities

Email marketing and online communities are two of the most powerful tools for generating massive buzz around your product or service. Both channels provide direct access to highly engaged audiences who are already interested in your offerings or in the niche you serve. Whether you're aiming to launch a product, promote a sale, or build long-term relationships, tapping into your email list and relevant online communities can help you drive significant traffic and boost conversions quickly.

In this chapter, we'll explore how to leverage **email marketing** and **online communities** to create buzz, build excitement, and drive rapid sales. You'll learn the best strategies for crafting compelling email campaigns, building and nurturing your email list, and engaging with online communities to achieve your goal of generating $100,000 (or more) in a short time frame.

Step 1: The Power of Email Marketing

Email marketing remains one of the most effective and reliable marketing channels, providing the highest return on investment (ROI) of any digital marketing method. Unlike social media, where algorithms control visibility, email marketing allows you to send targeted, personalized messages directly to your subscribers' inboxes.

1. Why Email Marketing Works

Email marketing is so effective because it gives you **direct access** to your audience, allowing you to communicate one-on-one with people who have already shown interest in your business. The familiarity and trust that come from being in someone's inbox make email a powerful tool for nurturing relationships and driving conversions.

Key Benefits of Email Marketing:

- **High Engagement**: Email is a personal form of communication. People are more likely to engage with emails than with social media ads or posts.
- **Ownership**: You own your email list, meaning you're not at the mercy of algorithm changes on platforms like Facebook or Instagram.
- **Segmentation and Personalization**: With email marketing, you can segment your audience based on behavior, interests, and demographics, sending highly relevant messages that increase the likelihood of conversions.
- **Automation**: You can set up automated email sequences that work around the clock, nurturing leads and driving sales while you focus on other areas of your business.

2. Building and Growing Your Email List

To successfully leverage email marketing, you need a robust email list filled with people who are interested in your product or service. The larger and more engaged your email list, the more powerful your email marketing efforts will be.

Strategies for Growing Your Email List:

- **Lead Magnets**: Offer a valuable free resource, such as an eBook, checklist, or webinar, in exchange for email addresses. Lead magnets should solve a specific problem or provide actionable insights that align with your product or service.
  - Example: "Download our free guide to mastering email marketing and start growing your business today!"
- **Exit-Intent Popups**: Use exit-intent popups on your website to capture visitors before they leave. These popups offer a com-

pelling incentive, such as a discount or free resource, to encourage visitors to subscribe.

- **Content Upgrades**: Offer additional exclusive content within your blog posts or articles, known as a **content upgrade**, to entice readers to sign up. For example, you could offer a downloadable version of the post with extra insights or templates.
- **Contests and Giveaways**: Run a contest or giveaway where people must enter their email address to participate. This can quickly build your email list while creating excitement around your brand.

3. Segmenting Your Email List for Maximum Impact

Segmentation is the process of dividing your email list into smaller groups based on specific criteria. Segmentation allows you to send **targeted messages** that resonate with different audience segments, making your email campaigns more effective.

Ways to Segment Your Email List:

- **Demographics**: Segment by age, location, gender, or other relevant demographics.
- **Behavior**: Segment based on how subscribers have interacted with your emails, website, or products. For example, you could create a segment for people who have viewed a specific product but haven't purchased it yet.
- **Customer Journey**: Group subscribers by their position in the sales funnel. New leads might receive educational content, while repeat customers might get exclusive offers or loyalty rewards.

By segmenting your list, you can craft highly personalized email campaigns that speak directly to each audience's needs, increasing open rates, click-through rates, and conversions.

Step 2: Crafting High-Converting Email Campaigns

To maximize the potential of email marketing, you need to create **compelling, value-driven email campaigns** that not only capture attention but also encourage immediate action.

1. The Anatomy of a High-Converting Email

A successful email is composed of several key elements that work together to engage the reader and drive conversions.

Key Elements of a High-Converting Email:

- **Subject Line**: The subject line is the first thing your subscribers see and determines whether they open your email. It should be attention-grabbing, relevant, and create curiosity or urgency.
    - Example: "Don't Miss Out: Limited-Time Offer Inside!"
- **Preheader Text**: This is the preview text that appears next to the subject line in the inbox. Use it to reinforce your subject line and provide a sneak peek of what's inside.
    - Example: "Get 30% off your next purchase—only available for the next 24 hours!"
- **Personalization**: Personalize your emails by using the recipient's name or tailoring the content to their interests. Personalized emails have higher open rates and conversion rates.
    - Example: "Hey [Name], we thought you'd love this special offer on [Product Name]!"
- **Compelling Copy**: Keep your email copy concise, clear, and focused on the benefits of your offer. Highlight why the reader should take action now and how it will solve their problem.
- **Call to Action (CTA)**: Every email should have a clear, compelling CTA that directs the reader toward the desired action, whether it's making a purchase, signing up for a webinar, or downloading a resource.
    - Example: "Claim your 30% discount now—offer ends tonight!"

- **Visuals**: Use high-quality images or graphics to make your email visually appealing. Ensure that any images used are relevant to your message and enhance the overall content.
- **Mobile Optimization**: Ensure your emails are mobile-friendly. With more than half of all emails being opened on mobile devices, it's crucial that your emails are easy to read and interact with on small screens.

2. Types of Email Campaigns to Generate Buzz

There are several types of email campaigns you can use to create buzz and drive traffic quickly. Each serves a specific purpose depending on where your subscribers are in the customer journey.

Types of Email Campaigns:

- **Product Launch Emails**: Build anticipation for your new product with a series of emails leading up to the launch. Tease features, offer sneak peeks, and create urgency with a limited-time offer.
- **Flash Sale Emails**: Announce a flash sale or limited-time promotion to create urgency and encourage immediate action. Use countdown timers and bold CTAs to drive conversions.
- **Welcome Series**: Send a sequence of emails to new subscribers, introducing them to your brand and building a relationship. Offer valuable content and special deals to convert them into customers.
- **Abandoned Cart Emails**: Remind subscribers who added items to their cart but didn't complete the purchase. Offer a discount or incentive to encourage them to finalize their purchase.
    - Example: "Forgot something? Complete your order now and get 10% off!"
- **Re-engagement Campaigns**: Re-engage inactive subscribers with a special offer or personalized message to bring them back into the fold. Show that you value them and offer an exclusive deal.

     ◦ Example: "We miss you! Here's a special 20% off just for you."

By mixing these campaign types, you can create an ongoing flow of engagement, driving consistent traffic and sales while keeping your audience excited about your offers.

Step 3: Leveraging Online Communities for Massive Buzz

Online communities—whether on social media platforms, forums, or private groups—offer a powerful way to generate buzz and drive traffic. These communities are often made up of passionate individuals who trust the opinions of other members, making them highly engaged and open to recommendations.

1. Finding the Right Online Communities

To maximize the effectiveness of community engagement, you need to find the **right communities** where your target audience spends their time. The key is to identify groups that are aligned with your niche and are highly active.

Popular Online Communities:

- **Facebook Groups**: Facebook Groups are one of the most active and engaged online communities, with millions of groups covering every niche imaginable. Search for groups related to your industry or product.
  - ◦ Example: If you sell fitness products, join fitness and wellness groups where people are already discussing relevant topics.
- **Reddit**: Reddit is a massive online community divided into **subreddits**, each focused on a specific interest or topic. Find subreddits related to your niche and participate in the discussions.
  - ◦ Example: If you sell tech products, join subreddits like **r/technology** or **r/gadgets** to engage with users interested in tech.

- **Quora**: Quora is a question-and-answer platform where people ask for recommendations, advice, and insights. By answering questions related to your niche, you can establish authority and drive traffic to your website.
- **Niche Forums**: Many industries have specific forums where professionals and enthusiasts gather to discuss relevant topics. These are often tight-knit communities where recommendations are highly valued.

2. Engaging with Online Communities Effectively

The key to success in online communities is to engage in a way that is **authentic** and adds value. Instead of immediately promoting your product, build trust by providing helpful insights, answering questions, and sharing valuable content. Once you've established credibility, you can introduce your product or service in a way that feels natural.

Best Practices for Engaging in Online Communities:

- **Contribute Value First**: Before promoting your product, spend time engaging with the community by answering questions, offering advice, and sharing relevant content. Establish yourself as a helpful and knowledgeable member.
- **Avoid Spammy Promotion**: Communities are quick to shut down users who post blatant promotions. Instead, subtly mention your product in the context of a discussion, such as recommending it when someone asks for solutions to a problem.
- **Share Exclusive Offers**: Offer community members something special, such as a discount or early access to your product. This makes them feel valued and increases the likelihood that they'll engage with your offer.
- **Build Relationships**: Consistently engage with community members to build relationships and trust. Over time, these members will become advocates for your brand, promoting your product organically within the community.

3. Hosting Webinars and Live Events in Communities

Hosting **live events**, such as webinars, Q&A sessions, or live product demos, is a powerful way to engage with online communities and generate excitement. These events allow you to showcase your expertise, demonstrate your product, and answer questions in real-time.

Steps to Hosting a Successful Webinar or Live Event:

- **Choose a Topic**: Select a topic that resonates with the community's interests and aligns with your product or service. The topic should provide immediate value and solve a problem for attendees.
- **Promote the Event**: Share the event details in relevant online communities and invite members to join. Make sure to emphasize the value they'll get from attending, such as learning new strategies or receiving exclusive offers.
- **Engage with Attendees**: During the event, encourage participants to ask questions, share their thoughts, and engage with you. This builds rapport and keeps the event interactive.
- **Offer a Special Deal**: At the end of the event, offer attendees a special promotion or discount for your product. This creates urgency and encourages immediate action.

Step 4: Combining Email Marketing and Community Engagement for Maximum Impact

The most effective way to generate massive buzz is by **combining email marketing with community engagement**. By leveraging your email list to drive traffic to online communities (or vice versa), you can create a loop of engagement that builds excitement and increases conversions.

1. Promote Community Content in Emails

Use your email list to promote content from your online communities, such as upcoming webinars, discussions, or product-related threads. This encourages your subscribers to join the conversation, adding to the buzz around your product.

Example:

"Join our exclusive Q&A session in the [Community Name] Facebook Group! We'll be answering all your burning questions and offering a special deal just for attendees."

2. Use Communities to Build Your Email List

Online communities can also serve as a powerful tool for growing your email list. When you engage in a community, offer a **lead magnet** or free resource that requires users to sign up with their email address. This allows you to capture the attention of engaged community members and bring them into your email marketing ecosystem.

Example:

"If you found this tip helpful, download our free [niche-specific guide] for even more strategies! Just enter your email here, and we'll send it right over."

Conclusion

Email marketing and online communities are essential tools for generating massive buzz and driving rapid traffic to your offers. By building and nurturing a well-segmented email list, crafting compelling email campaigns, and engaging authentically with online communities, you can create an ecosystem that drives excitement, trust, and conversions.

The key to success lies in understanding the unique dynamics of each channel—email lists allow for direct and personal communication, while online communities provide organic engagement and social proof. By leveraging the strengths of both, you can create a powerful marketing engine that not only generates immediate sales but also builds long-term relationships with your audience. Whether you're aiming to hit a revenue milestone like $100,000 in 24 hours or seeking sustained growth, these strategies will help you maximize the potential of email marketing and community engagement.

Chapter 20: The 24-Hour Social Media Strategy

Social media has revolutionized how businesses interact with their audiences and promote their products, offering instant access to millions of potential customers. If you're aiming to generate $100,000 in 24 hours, leveraging the viral power of platforms like **Twitter**, **TikTok**, and **Instagram** is essential. These platforms allow you to create real-time buzz, engage with your audience directly, and tap into viral trends that can catapult your offer to a massive audience in a short time frame.

In this chapter, we'll explore how to craft a **24-hour social media strategy** designed to go viral. You'll learn how to create attention-grabbing content, tap into trending topics, and engage with influencers to generate massive awareness, traffic, and sales—all within a single day.

Step 1: Understanding the Viral Nature of Social Media

To succeed in creating a viral social media campaign, it's crucial to understand the dynamics that drive **virality**. Viral content spreads rapidly because it resonates with people on an emotional level, encourages them to share it with their network, and aligns with current trends.

1. What Makes Content Go Viral?

Virality is not random—it follows specific patterns. Content that goes viral typically has one or more of the following characteristics:

- **Emotional Impact**: Viral content often evokes strong emotions, whether it's excitement, humor, inspiration, or even outrage. When people feel something deeply, they're more likely to share it.
  - Example: A humorous TikTok video that makes viewers laugh or an inspiring Instagram post that motivates followers to take action.

- **Relatability**: People share content that they can relate to or that represents their identity, beliefs, or aspirations. Relatable content feels personal and often leads to more engagement.
    - Example: A meme on Twitter about the challenges of entrepreneurship that resonates with small business owners.
- **Timeliness**: Content that taps into current events or trends has a much higher chance of going viral. Social media platforms are fast-moving, and aligning your content with trending topics or hashtags can give it a boost.
    - Example: A TikTok video using a trending sound or challenge, or a Twitter post referencing a hot topic in the news.
- **High Shareability**: Content that's easy to share, whether it's a meme, short video, or infographic, is more likely to spread quickly. Shareability comes from content that is concise, visually appealing, and easy to understand.
    - Example: Instagram posts with clear visuals and short, impactful messages, or Twitter threads with bite-sized, actionable tips.

2. The Role of Algorithms

Every social media platform uses algorithms to determine which content is shown to users. Understanding these algorithms can help you optimize your content to reach a larger audience.

- **Twitter**: Twitter's algorithm prioritizes content that garners high engagement (likes, retweets, comments) in a short period. Tweets with hashtags, media (images or videos), and mentions of trending topics perform better.
- **Instagram**: Instagram favors content that generates immediate engagement (likes, comments, saves, shares) and interaction through direct messages. Stories, Reels, and carousel posts can increase visibility.

- **TikTok**: TikTok's algorithm is built to surface highly engaging content to a broad audience quickly. Videos that gain rapid likes, comments, and shares can be pushed to the **For You Page (FYP)**, where they can reach millions.

By creating content designed to maximize engagement, you can take advantage of these algorithms to push your posts into the viral sphere.

Step 2: Crafting Attention-Grabbing Content

To go viral within 24 hours, your content needs to be eye-catching, emotionally compelling, and designed to encourage immediate interaction. Each social media platform has different strengths and content formats, so it's important to tailor your approach to each.

1. Twitter: Short, Punchy, and Timely

Twitter is built for **real-time conversation** and is ideal for creating a buzz quickly. The key to success on Twitter is brevity—each tweet must capture attention in just a few seconds.

Strategies for Going Viral on Twitter:

- **Craft Engaging Tweets**: Keep your tweets short, focused, and punchy. Ask a question, make a bold statement, or share a hot take that sparks conversation. Use eye-catching images, GIFs, or videos to increase engagement.
  - Example: "Want to make $100,000 in 24 hours? Here's how I did it. ◈ [link]"
- **Leverage Trending Hashtags**: Use trending hashtags relevant to your niche or product. This helps your content reach a broader audience, as people searching for those hashtags are more likely to see your tweet.
  - Example: "#EntrepreneurLife can be tough, but with the right strategy, you can hit $100,000 in 24 hours. Let's talk about how. ◈ #MarketingTips"
- **Create Twitter Threads**: Threads are a powerful way to dive deeper into a topic while keeping each tweet concise. Each tweet

in the thread should add value and encourage readers to continue reading and engaging.

- ◦ Example: "THREAD: How I generated $100,000 in 24 hours using these 5 simple strategies. [Tweet 2] First, identify a niche with urgent demand..."

Engagement Boosters:

- **Ask Questions**: Encourage followers to reply by asking open-ended questions related to your product or industry.
- **Polls**: Create polls to encourage interaction and generate engagement, which can push your tweet to more users.
- **Tag Influencers**: Mention or tag influencers in your industry to increase the chances of getting retweets or comments from them, which amplifies your reach.

2. TikTok: Entertaining, Engaging, and Trend-Driven

TikTok is a platform built on short-form video content and thrives on trends. To go viral on TikTok, you need to create content that is visually appealing, quick, and tied to popular trends or challenges.

Strategies for Going Viral on TikTok:

- **Use Trending Sounds and Hashtags**: TikTok's virality is driven by trends, especially sounds and challenges. Find trending sounds that align with your content and create videos using those sounds. Similarly, use trending hashtags to increase the likelihood of your content being surfaced on the For You Page (FYP).
  - ◦ Example: Use a trending song to create a video showcasing your product, coupled with a popular challenge, such as showing the "before" and "after" of using your service.
- **Keep Videos Short and Punchy**: The most successful TikTok videos are between 15-30 seconds long. Capture attention within

the first few seconds by using fast-paced editing, bold text over-lays, or an engaging hook.

- ◦ Example: Start your video with a bold claim: "Want to make $100,000 in 24 hours? Here's how…"

- **Behind-the-Scenes and Storytelling**: TikTok users love authentic, behind-the-scenes content. Show the process behind your business, product creation, or success story, and invite users into your world.

- ◦ Example: Share a behind-the-scenes look at your product launch or an unfiltered day in the life of running your business.

Engagement Boosters:

- **Call to Action**: End your video with a clear call to action (CTA), such as "Follow for more tips," "Share with a friend," or "Click the link in bio."
- **Duet and Stitch**: Engage with other creators' content by using TikTok's **Duet** and **Stitch** features. This allows you to add your perspective or reaction to trending content, increasing the chances of reaching a broader audience.

3. Instagram: Visual Storytelling and Engagement

Instagram offers several content formats—**Stories**, **Reels**, **carousel posts**, and **IGTV**—making it a versatile platform for engaging with your audience in different ways. To go viral, focus on creating highly shareable content that resonates with your target audience.

Strategies for Going Viral on Instagram:

- **Create Reels**: Instagram Reels are short, engaging videos that often have a higher chance of going viral compared to regular posts. Similar to TikTok, Reels should be fun, entertaining, and aligned with trending music or challenges.

- Example: Create a Reel showing a quick tip or tutorial related to your product or service. Use music that's currently trending on Instagram to increase visibility.
- **Carousel Posts**: Carousel posts allow you to share multiple images or slides in a single post, encouraging users to swipe through and engage with your content. Use these to tell a story, share tips, or break down a concept.
  - Example: "5 Steps to Generate $100,000 in 24 Hours: Swipe to learn the secrets."
- **Instagram Stories**: Stories provide an informal way to engage with your audience through polls, Q&As, and behind-the-scenes content. Use interactive elements like stickers, countdown timers, and swipe-up links to drive engagement and traffic.
  - Example: Use a countdown sticker to build anticipation for a flash sale or product launch.

Engagement Boosters:

- **Host Giveaways**: Run an Instagram giveaway where users must follow your account, tag friends, and share your post to enter. Giveaways generate massive engagement, as users are incentivized to share your content with their network.
  - Example: "◈ Giveaway Alert! ◈ Win [Product Name]! To enter: 1) Follow us, 2) Tag 2 friends, 3) Share this post to your story."
- **User-Generated Content**: Encourage your followers to create content featuring your product or service, and repost it on your profile. This builds social proof and increases engagement as users see their content featured.
  - Example: "Tag us in your [Product Name] photos for a chance to be featured!"

Step 3: Engaging with Influencers and Communities

Engaging with influencers and online communities is a powerful way to amplify your social media strategy and tap into new audiences. Influencers, especially micro-influencers, often have highly engaged followers who trust their recommendations, making them ideal partners for creating viral buzz.

1. Collaborating with Influencers

Influencers can help you reach your target audience quickly and authentically. By partnering with influencers who align with your brand, you can leverage their credibility to promote your product to their followers.

Steps to Collaborate with Influencers:

- **Identify Relevant Influencers**: Look for influencers who have an engaged following within your niche. Micro-influencers (with 10,000 to 100,000 followers) often have higher engagement rates and are more affordable than larger influencers.
- **Offer a Clear Value Proposition**: When reaching out to influencers, be clear about how the partnership will benefit them. Offer compensation, free products, or a commission for each sale they drive.
- **Create Co-Branded Content**: Collaborate with influencers to create authentic content, such as product reviews, tutorials, or challenges. The more organic the promotion feels, the more likely their followers are to engage with it.
  - Example: Partner with an Instagram fitness influencer to showcase your fitness product in a workout routine.

2. Engaging with Online Communities

Online communities, such as Facebook Groups, Reddit, and niche forums, are excellent places to build relationships and drive traffic. By actively participating in these communities, you can position yourself as an authority and create buzz around your product.

Steps to Engage with Communities:

- **Contribute Value First**: Before promoting your product, spend time offering valuable insights and advice in the community. Establish yourself as a helpful and trustworthy member.
- **Share Exclusive Offers**: Once you've built trust, share exclusive offers, discounts, or special content with the community. Make sure your promotion feels like a benefit to the group rather than a sales pitch.
  - Example: "As a thank you to this group, we're offering an exclusive 20% off discount for the next 24 hours."

Step 4: Running Paid Social Media Campaigns for Immediate Traffic

While organic strategies can drive significant traffic, **paid social media advertising** is an excellent way to generate immediate, scalable traffic to your offer. Platforms like Facebook, Instagram, Twitter, and TikTok offer highly targeted advertising options that allow you to reach a precise audience quickly.

1. Facebook and Instagram Ads

Facebook and Instagram's advertising platforms are interconnected, allowing you to run ads across both platforms simultaneously. You can target users based on demographics, interests, behaviors, and custom audiences (such as your email list or website visitors).

Best Practices for Paid Ads on Facebook and Instagram:

- **Targeting**: Use Facebook's advanced targeting options to reach your ideal audience. You can also use **Lookalike Audiences** to find people similar to your existing customers.
- **Ad Creatives**: Create eye-catching, high-quality images or videos with a clear call-to-action. Use Instagram Stories Ads and carousel ads to engage users visually.
- **Retargeting**: Use retargeting ads to reach users who have previously interacted with your content, visited your website, or abandoned their cart. Retargeting ads have higher conversion rates because the audience is already familiar with your brand.

2. TikTok Ads

TikTok's advertising platform allows you to target users based on demographics, interests, and behaviors. The platform is ideal for creating highly engaging, visually-driven ads that feel native to the platform.

Best Practices for TikTok Ads:

- **In-Feed Ads**: These ads appear in users' feeds and feel similar to organic TikTok videos. Keep them short, engaging, and aligned with popular trends or challenges.
- **Hashtag Challenges**: Run a branded hashtag challenge that encourages users to create content around your product. This is an excellent way to increase brand awareness and create user-generated content.
- **TopView Ads**: These ads appear when users first open the TikTok app, giving you premium visibility for your promotion.

Step 5: Analyzing and Optimizing Your Social Media Strategy

Once your social media strategy is live, it's crucial to track your performance in real-time and adjust your tactics based on what's working. Each platform provides insights and analytics that help you understand which posts are driving engagement, traffic, and sales.

1. Key Metrics to Track

- **Engagement Rate**: Track likes, comments, shares, and saves to gauge how well your content is resonating with your audience.
- **Click-Through Rate (CTR)**: Monitor the number of clicks your posts, ads, or bio links generate. A high CTR indicates that your content is successfully driving traffic to your offer.
- **Conversion Rate**: Measure the percentage of social media users who make a purchase after clicking through to your site.
- **Virality Metrics**: Look at how often your content is shared or reposted. The more people share your content, the more likely it is to go viral.

2. Optimizing Based on Performance

- **Double Down on What's Working**: If a certain type of post (e.g., Reels, Twitter threads, or TikTok challenges) is performing well, create more of that content to maintain momentum.
- **Adjust Low-Performing Content**: If certain posts or ads aren't getting engagement, experiment with different formats, messaging, or visuals to improve performance.
- **Engage with Your Audience**: Respond to comments, questions, and messages in real-time to increase engagement and build relationships with your audience.

Conclusion

Social media platforms like Twitter, TikTok, and Instagram offer unparalleled opportunities to generate buzz and drive sales quickly, especially when you aim to achieve ambitious revenue goals like $100,000 in 24 hours. By crafting attention-grabbing content, leveraging viral trends, engaging with influencers and communities, and running targeted paid ads, you can create a **24-hour social media strategy** that maximizes your reach and engagement.

The key to success lies in creating content that resonates with your audience, taking advantage of platform algorithms, and maintaining consistent engagement throughout the campaign. With the right strategy in place, you'll be able to harness the viral power of social media to achieve massive results in a short amount of time, driving both traffic and sales to your offer.

Chapter 21: Creating Shareable, Viral Content

In the age of social media, creating content that people are eager to share is a cornerstone of viral marketing success. Whether you're aiming to drive sales, build brand awareness, or generate massive traffic in a short time, **shareable content** has the power to amplify your reach far beyond what paid ads or direct marketing can achieve. By crafting content that resonates emotionally, aligns with current trends, and encourages engagement, you can tap into your audience's natural inclination to share, helping your message spread organically.

In this chapter, we will explore proven techniques for creating **shareable, viral content** across different platforms. You'll learn how to harness the psychology of sharing, design content that connects with your audience, and use formats that encourage virality. By the end of this chapter, you'll have the tools to craft compelling content that people want to share with their networks, helping you achieve your revenue goals quickly.

Step 1: Understanding the Psychology Behind Sharing

Before diving into content creation, it's crucial to understand **why** people share content. Sharing is not random—people share for specific reasons, and tapping into these motivations can make your content more likely to go viral.

1. Why Do People Share?

People share content that aligns with their personal identity, makes them feel good, or helps them connect with others. Understanding these motivations allows you to create content that resonates on a deeper level and encourages people to hit the share button.

Key Motivations for Sharing Content:

- **Emotional Connection**: Content that evokes strong emotions—whether it's happiness, awe, fear, or even anger—drives people to share. When something stirs us emotionally, we're more likely to want others to experience it too.
  - Example: A heartwarming story of a business overcoming challenges during the pandemic could inspire people to share because it makes them feel hopeful.
- **Identity and Self-Expression**: People often share content that reflects their values, beliefs, or lifestyle. Sharing content is a way for people to express who they are or what they care about.
  - Example: A motivational post about entrepreneurship might be shared by business owners who want to signal their ambition and perseverance to their network.
- **Social Currency**: Sharing content that is interesting, novel, or insightful allows people to enhance their social status. When people share valuable or exclusive information, they appear knowledgeable or "in the know."
  - Example: A behind-the-scenes look at a groundbreaking new product can be shared as a way for people to show they have insider knowledge.
- **Helping Others**: People share content that they believe will benefit others, whether it's a how-to guide, an inspiring message, or a useful resource. Helping others by sharing valuable content reinforces social bonds and can lead to higher engagement.
  - Example: A practical guide on how to increase productivity might be shared by someone looking to help their friends or followers improve their work habits.

By creating content that taps into these motivations, you'll increase the likelihood that people will share it with their network.

2. The Role of Emotions in Shareability

Emotions are the driving force behind viral content. Studies have shown that **emotionally charged content** is more likely to be shared, especially when those emotions are positive or awe-inspiring.

Types of Emotions That Drive Shares:

- **Happiness and Joy**: Content that makes people smile or laugh tends to get shared widely. Humorous memes, uplifting stories, and feel-good videos often go viral because they bring joy to the audience.
- **Awe and Inspiration**: Inspirational content that showcases human achievement, beautiful visuals, or profound ideas creates a sense of awe, making it highly shareable.
- **Surprise or Shock**: Content that surprises or shocks people—whether through unexpected facts, controversial opinions, or eye-opening statistics—often gets shared because it challenges assumptions or provokes strong reactions.
- **Anger or Outrage**: While less positive, content that evokes anger or outrage can also go viral. Controversial topics that align with the audience's values may be shared as a way to express frustration or demand change.

Balancing emotional impact with the right message is key to making your content shareable. Positive emotions like joy, awe, and inspiration tend to result in more widespread and sustained sharing, whereas negative emotions like anger may drive initial shares but can also lead to polarizing responses.

Step 2: Designing Content That Connects with Your Audience

Once you understand the psychology behind sharing, the next step is to design content that **resonates** with your target audience. To do this, you must create content that aligns with their values, interests, and emotions while delivering a clear message.

1. Know Your Audience Inside and Out

The more you understand your audience, the easier it is to create content they'll want to share. Knowing your audience's demographics, interests, challenges, and aspirations allows you to tailor your content to their specific needs.

Questions to Help You Understand Your Audience:

- What are their biggest pain points or challenges?
- What inspires or motivates them?
- What type of content do they already engage with (e.g., videos, articles, memes)?
- Which platforms are they most active on (Instagram, TikTok, LinkedIn, etc.)?

Use these insights to create content that feels personal and relevant to your audience. For example, if you're targeting entrepreneurs, you might create content that speaks to their struggles with time management or the challenges of scaling a business.

2. Craft Engaging Stories

Storytelling is one of the most powerful tools for creating viral content. Stories make your message relatable, memorable, and emotionally impactful. When people see themselves in the stories you tell, they are more likely to share them with others.

Components of a Shareable Story:

- **Relatable Characters**: Use characters that your audience can identify with. This could be a customer, a business owner, or even yourself. Relatable characters create an emotional connection and make the story feel personal.
  - Example: A small business owner shares their journey of starting a company from scratch, overcoming setbacks, and finally achieving success.

- **Conflict and Resolution**: Every good story has a challenge that needs to be overcome. Highlight the obstacles your characters face and how they overcome them, creating a sense of accomplishment or triumph that inspires your audience.
    - Example: A brand story about how a company developed an innovative product despite industry skepticism can be highly motivating for budding entrepreneurs.
- **Emotional Appeal**: Focus on the emotional impact of your story. Whether it's joy, pride, empathy, or excitement, emotion will drive engagement and sharing.
    - Example: A campaign highlighting the efforts of healthcare workers during the pandemic could evoke emotions of gratitude and pride, encouraging people to share it as a tribute to frontline heroes.

3. Use Visuals to Capture Attention

In the fast-paced world of social media, visual content is key to grabbing attention. **Images, videos, and graphics** are far more engaging than text alone, and they often drive higher levels of interaction and sharing.

Best Practices for Visual Content:

- **High-Quality Images**: Use professional, high-quality images that are visually appealing and relevant to your message. Whether it's product photography, lifestyle shots, or custom graphics, quality visuals make your content more attractive to share.
- **Infographics**: Infographics are highly shareable because they distill complex information into easy-to-understand visuals. They are particularly effective for educational content, such as statistics, processes, or how-to guides.
    - Example: An infographic on "5 Steps to Starting a Successful Online Business" can be shared widely within entrepreneurial circles.

- **Short, Engaging Videos**: Videos tend to generate more engagement than static posts, especially on platforms like Instagram, TikTok, and YouTube. Keep your videos short and to the point (15-60 seconds), with a clear message and call to action.
  - Example: A quick video showing a product in action or a behind-the-scenes look at your business can spark interest and shares.
- **Text Overlays**: For both images and videos, use text overlays to highlight key messages or calls to action. This is especially effective for social platforms where users may scroll quickly and need a visual cue to stop and engage.
  - Example: "Limited Time Offer—Get 50% Off Today Only!"

Step 3: Creating Content Formats That Encourage Virality

Different content formats naturally lend themselves to sharing. Choosing the right format for your message can make a huge difference in how quickly your content spreads.

1. Memes and Humor

Memes are one of the most shareable forms of content on social media because they are **funny**, **relatable**, and often reflect current trends or cultural references. Memes tend to spread quickly, especially when they align with your audience's humor.

Best Practices for Creating Memes:

- **Keep It Simple**: Memes should be easy to understand at a glance. Use simple images, paired with short, witty text that conveys your message quickly.
  - Example: A meme about the struggles of working from home during a pandemic could resonate with remote workers and spread quickly.

- **Align with Current Trends**: Use memes to reference trending topics, pop culture, or recent events. By staying timely, you increase the chances of your content being shared.
  - Example: Creating a meme that uses a popular TV show reference (e.g., from *Stranger Things* or *Game of Thrones*) could resonate with fans of the show.
- **Relatability is Key**: Memes should reflect shared experiences, frustrations, or joys that your audience can relate to.
  - Example: A humorous meme about the difficulties of running a business could resonate with entrepreneurs and get shared widely within that community.

2. How-To Guides and Tutorials

People love sharing content that provides **value**, especially if it helps them solve a problem or learn something new. How-to guides and tutorials are excellent formats for providing actionable insights in a way that's easy to share.

Best Practices for Creating How-To Content:

- **Make It Simple**: Break down complex topics into simple, actionable steps that your audience can follow. Use clear language and visuals to guide them through the process.
  - Example: A video tutorial on "How to Create a Viral Instagram Reel in 5 Steps" could be highly shareable among marketers and content creators.
- **Use Listicles**: People love lists because they are easy to digest and share. Create content like "5 Tips to Improve Your Productivity" or "Top 10 Tools for Entrepreneurs," which can be shared on social media or as blog content.
- **Infographics**: As mentioned earlier, infographics are ideal for presenting how-to content in a visually engaging format. They simplify information and make it easy for users to share with others.

3. User-Generated Content (UGC)

One of the most effective ways to create viral content is by involving your audience directly through **user-generated content (UGC)**. When people feel like they're part of your content creation process, they're more likely to share it.

Ways to Encourage UGC:

- **Hashtag Challenges**: Launch a branded hashtag challenge, especially on platforms like TikTok or Instagram. Encourage your audience to create content around a specific theme or activity using your product or service, then share it using your branded hashtag.
    - Example: A fitness brand might create a #30DayFitnessChallenge and encourage users to post their progress with the hashtag. This generates massive engagement and creates a sense of community around your brand.
- **Photo or Video Contests**: Run a contest where users submit their photos or videos featuring your product, with the chance to win a prize. Repost the best submissions on your profile to encourage others to participate.
    - Example: A fashion brand might run a contest where users submit their best outfits styled with the brand's clothing, with the winning entry receiving a gift card or free products.
- **Customer Testimonials and Reviews**: Encourage your customers to share their experiences with your product or service. Testimonials, reviews, and unboxing videos can be reposted on your social media channels, creating a loop of user-generated content that others are likely to share.

Step 4: Encouraging Sharing with Clear CTAs and Incentives

Even if your content is engaging, you need to **actively encourage** people to share it. By including clear **calls to action (CTAs)** and offering incentives for sharing, you can increase the likelihood of your content spreading.

1. Include a Strong Call to Action (CTA)

Every piece of viral content should include a clear and compelling CTA that encourages your audience to take the next step—whether it's sharing, commenting, or visiting your website.

Effective CTAs for Viral Content:

- **Share This Post**: A simple yet direct call to action that reminds your audience to share the content with their network.
    - Example: "Found this helpful? Share it with a friend who needs to see this!"
- **Tag a Friend**: Asking users to tag their friends is a highly effective way to increase engagement and extend your reach.
    - Example: "Tag a friend who needs this in their life! ◈"
- **Join the Conversation**: Encourage users to leave a comment or join a discussion in the comments section. This not only drives engagement but also keeps your content active in social media algorithms.
    - Example: "What's your best productivity tip? Drop it in the comments!"

2. Offer Incentives for Sharing

People are more likely to share content when there's something in it for them. By offering incentives like discounts, free resources, or entry into a contest, you can motivate your audience to spread your content further.

Incentives for Sharing:

- **Discounts and Promo Codes**: Offer a special discount or promo code to users who share your content. This not only increases sharing but also drives conversions.
    - Example: "Share this post and get 20% off your next order! Use code: SHARE20 at checkout."
- **Contests and Giveaways**: Run a contest where users must share your content to enter. Make the prize appealing enough to encourage widespread participation.
    - Example: "Share this post and tag 3 friends for a chance to win a $100 gift card!"
- **Exclusive Access**: Offer users exclusive content, such as a free eBook, webinar, or early access to a product launch, in exchange for sharing your post.
    - Example: "Share this video and get early access to our upcoming product launch!"

Step 5: Optimizing Your Content for Each Platform

Different social media platforms have different content preferences, and optimizing your content for each platform can significantly increase its shareability.

1. Twitter

- **Short, Punchy Tweets**: Twitter thrives on brevity. Use concise, impactful language to capture attention in just a few words.
- **Hashtags**: Use trending and relevant hashtags to increase the visibility of your tweets.
- **Retweetable Content**: Create content that encourages retweets, such as polls, quotes, and thought-provoking questions.

2. Instagram

- **Visually Stunning Images**: Use high-quality, visually appealing images and videos that stand out in the feed.

- **Instagram Stories and Reels**: Create short, engaging content for Stories and Reels, as these formats are highly favored by Instagram's algorithm.
- **Interactive Elements**: Use polls, questions, and quizzes in Instagram Stories to encourage user interaction.

3. TikTok

- **Short, Engaging Videos**: Keep videos under 30 seconds to maximize watch time. Start with a hook in the first few seconds to grab attention.
- **Trending Sounds and Challenges**: Use popular sounds and participate in challenges to increase the likelihood of your content appearing on TikTok's For You Page.
- **Duet and Stitch**: Encourage users to create Duet or Stitch videos in response to your content, increasing engagement and shares.

Conclusion

Creating shareable, viral content is a blend of art and science. By understanding the psychology behind sharing, crafting content that resonates emotionally with your audience, and using the right formats for each platform, you can significantly increase the likelihood of your content going viral. Whether it's through humor, storytelling, or practical how-to guides, the key is to create content that people feel compelled to share because it adds value, resonates with their identity, or simply entertains them.

To amplify your results, always include clear calls to action and consider offering incentives for sharing. By leveraging these techniques, you can tap into the power of viral marketing, helping you reach new audiences, generate massive buzz, and drive significant traffic and sales within a short timeframe—such as hitting your goal of $100,000 in 24 hours.

Part 5: Launch Execution

Chapter 22: Launching with a Bang

A successful launch, especially when aiming to generate $100,000 in 24 hours, hinges on building **anticipation and hype** before the launch day. The more excitement you create, the more likely people will rush to take action the moment your offer goes live. A well-executed pre-launch strategy will engage your audience, prime them for the big day, and ensure that when the doors open, they're ready to buy.

In this chapter, we will walk through the exact steps to create a buzz-filled pre-launch campaign, from warming up your audience to leveraging multiple channels for maximum visibility. You'll learn how to create a sense of urgency, use teasers, and drive early interest that can catapult your sales on launch day. By the end of this chapter, you'll have a detailed blueprint to ensure your launch goes off with a bang, helping you achieve your revenue goals.

Step 1: Setting the Stage for a Successful Launch

The first step in building anticipation is laying a strong foundation. Before you can create hype, you need to define clear objectives, know your audience inside out, and have a detailed plan of action that spans the entire pre-launch period.

1. Define Your Launch Objectives

Before you start promoting your product, it's essential to be clear about your **launch goals**. While generating $100,000 in 24 hours may be the ultimate aim, you should also define specific objectives for each phase of your launch, including metrics for success.

Questions to Consider:

- How many units or products do you need to sell to meet your revenue target?
- What is your desired conversion rate for visitors who land on your sales page?

- How much engagement (email sign-ups, social media interactions, etc.) do you want during the pre-launch?

Setting clear objectives will guide your pre-launch activities and help you measure the success of your efforts.

2. Know Your Audience

Understanding your target audience is crucial to creating a launch that resonates. This involves knowing their pain points, desires, and buying behaviors. By identifying their needs, you can craft messaging that speaks directly to them and positions your offer as the perfect solution.

Key Audience Insights:

- **Pain Points**: What problems are your audience struggling with, and how does your product solve them?
- **Desires**: What goals or dreams does your audience have? How can your product help them achieve those desires?
- **Buying Triggers**: What motivates your audience to make a purchase? Is it urgency, scarcity, exclusivity, or the fear of missing out?

These insights will shape your messaging and help you create the emotional connection needed to drive engagement and conversions.

3. Map Out a Pre-Launch Timeline

Your pre-launch should be meticulously planned to ensure maximum impact. A typical pre-launch period lasts **2-4 weeks**, giving you enough time to build anticipation and engage with your audience without losing momentum.

Sample Pre-Launch Timeline:

- **Weeks 1-2**: Tease the launch with sneak peeks, early-bird offers, and content that builds curiosity.

- **Week 3**: Begin collecting email addresses or sign-ups for exclusive access or early-bird discounts.
- **Week 4 (Final Week)**: Ramp up urgency with countdowns, reminders, and limited-time bonuses. Ensure that by the time the product launches, your audience is primed to buy.

Step 2: Creating Buzz and Anticipation Before the Launch

Building anticipation before a launch is all about making your audience feel excited and eager to be among the first to experience your product. This is done through **strategic teasing**, creating a sense of exclusivity, and engaging your audience with valuable pre-launch content.

1. Tease Your Audience with Sneak Peeks

People love being in on a secret, and teasers create an element of **mystery** and **excitement** around your upcoming launch. By sharing small bits of information without revealing everything, you can pique your audience's curiosity and make them more interested in learning more.

Ways to Tease Your Audience:

- **Behind-the-Scenes Content**: Share behind-the-scenes photos, videos, or stories about the development of your product. This makes your audience feel like they're part of the process and builds a deeper connection with your brand.
  - Example: Post an Instagram Story showing the final stages of product design with a caption like, "We're almost ready... stay tuned for something big!"
- **Sneak Peeks**: Give your audience small glimpses of your product without revealing too much. For example, show a blurred or cropped image, or share a short video that teases the benefits of the product.
  - Example: "We've been working on something that's going to change the game... any guesses? ◇"
- **Teaser Trailers**: Create short teaser videos that highlight the main benefits of your product but leave viewers wanting more.

These videos should be short, visually appealing, and focus on building excitement.

- Example: A teaser video showing snippets of your product being used, paired with upbeat music and captions like "Coming Soon."

2. Build Exclusivity with Early Access Offers

One of the most effective ways to build anticipation is by offering **early access** to a select group of people. Exclusivity makes your audience feel special and valued, increasing their desire to be part of the launch. Offering something limited—whether it's early access, a special discount, or a bonus—creates urgency and drives early engagement.

Strategies for Creating Exclusivity:

- **VIP or Early-Bird Lists**: Create an early-bird sign-up list for people who want first access to your product. Offer an exclusive incentive for signing up, such as a discount, bonus, or limited-time offer.
    - Example: "Join our VIP list and get access to the launch 24 hours before anyone else—plus a special discount! Sign up now."
- **Limited Edition Products**: If possible, offer a limited-edition version of your product that's only available during the pre-launch period. This adds an extra layer of exclusivity and urgency.
    - Example: "Pre-order now and receive the limited-edition version of [Product Name], available only during this exclusive launch."
- **Secret Bonuses**: Offer a secret bonus to those who sign up early or engage with your pre-launch content. This could be an additional product, a guide, or a one-on-one consultation.
    - Example: "Sign up for early access and get a secret bonus when we launch! Limited to the first 100 people."

3. Create Valuable Pre-Launch Content

During the pre-launch period, it's important to engage your audience with content that educates, entertains, or inspires them. This content should build a connection between your audience and your product, addressing their pain points and showcasing how your product will solve their problems.

Ideas for Pre-Launch Content:

- **Educational Content**: Share blog posts, videos, or infographics that address common problems your audience faces and how your product solves them. By educating your audience, you're positioning your product as the go-to solution.
  - Example: A blog post titled "5 Reasons Why Most Entrepreneurs Fail in Their First Year (And How Our New Tool Can Help You Succeed)."

- **Case Studies or Testimonials**: Share case studies, testimonials, or user stories that highlight how your product has helped others. Social proof is a powerful way to build trust and anticipation.
  - Example: "Meet Sarah, who used [Product Name] to grow her business by 50% in just 3 months. Find out how she did it."

- **Countdown Emails and Social Posts**: Use countdowns to build excitement as the launch date approaches. Remind your audience how much time is left before they can get access to your offer.
  - Example: "Only 3 days left until we reveal our biggest product yet! Are you ready?"

Step 3: Engaging Your Audience on Multiple Channels

To create maximum buzz around your launch, it's essential to engage your audience across multiple channels—email, social media, and even paid advertising. Each channel plays a different role in your pre-launch strategy, and using them together helps ensure you reach as many people as possible.

1. Use Email Marketing to Build Anticipation

Email marketing is one of the most effective ways to build anticipation for your launch. By sending targeted, engaging emails leading up to your launch, you can nurture your audience, build excitement, and ensure they're ready to take action on launch day.

Email Pre-Launch Sequence:

- **Teaser Email**: Send an initial email teasing the upcoming launch, using subject lines that create curiosity. Include a call-to-action (CTA) encouraging readers to join your early-bird list or VIP access.
  - Example: "Something big is coming... and you won't want to miss it! Get early access here."
- **Value-Based Email**: Send emails that focus on providing value to your audience, such as educational content, case studies, or how your product solves their problems.
  - Example: "Here's how [Product Name] will save you hours each week (and help you grow your business faster)."
- **Countdown Email**: In the final week before your launch, send countdown emails reminding your audience how much time is left before the big day.
  - Example: "Only 3 days left until we launch! Don't miss your chance to get early access."

2. Leverage Social Media to Build Hype

Social media is an excellent platform for engaging your audience in real time and creating a viral buzz around your launch. By using a combination of organic posts, Stories, and paid ads, you can amplify your reach and ensure your audience is eagerly anticipating your launch.

Social Media Pre-Launch Strategy:

- **Teaser Posts**: Share teasers about your upcoming launch across Instagram, Twitter, Facebook, TikTok, and LinkedIn. Use captivating visuals, short videos, and behind-the-scenes content to generate excitement.
    - Example: A teaser video on Instagram showing a quick demo of the product with a caption like, "Get ready to experience something new... coming soon!"
- **Countdown Stories**: Use Instagram and Facebook Stories to share countdowns as your launch date approaches. Include interactive elements like polls, questions, or countdown stickers to engage your audience.
    - Example: "Only 5 days left! What feature are you most excited about? Tap to let us know!"
- **Influencer Partnerships**: Partner with influencers or brand advocates in your industry to create buzz. Ask them to share teasers, post about the launch, or even offer exclusive early access to their followers.
    - Example: "Excited to announce that I'll be teaming up with [Brand] for their upcoming launch. Stay tuned for exclusive access!"

3. Run Targeted Ads to Build Awareness

Running paid ads in the pre-launch phase can help you reach a broader audience and drive more sign-ups for early access or VIP offers. By targeting specific audiences on platforms like Facebook, Instagram, and Google, you can increase awareness and ensure a steady stream of interest leading up to your launch.

Best Practices for Pre-Launch Ads:

- **Target the Right Audience**: Use Facebook and Instagram's advanced targeting features to reach your ideal audience based on demographics, interests, and behaviors.

- Example: If you're launching a digital marketing tool, target business owners, marketers, and entrepreneurs.
- **Highlight Early Access or Bonuses**: Use ads to promote your early-bird list, exclusive offers, or bonuses for signing up before the launch.
  - Example: "Be the first to get access to [Product Name] when it launches—sign up for our VIP list today and receive a special bonus."
- **Retarget Interested Visitors**: If you've been building a pre-launch list, use retargeting ads to remind those who visited your landing page or engaged with your posts to sign up before the launch.
  - Example: "You showed interest in [Product Name]—don't miss out! Join our early-bird list for exclusive perks."

Step 4: Creating Urgency as the Launch Approaches

As you get closer to launch day, it's important to create a sense of **urgency** that motivates people to take action immediately. By emphasizing scarcity, deadlines, and limited-time offers, you can ensure that your audience is ready to act the moment your product goes live.

1. Use Countdown Timers

Countdown timers are a highly effective way to create urgency and remind your audience that time is running out. Use countdown timers in your emails, on your website, and in social media posts to build anticipation as the launch date approaches.

Example:

"Only 24 hours left until we launch! Don't miss your chance to be the first to get [Product Name]."

2. Emphasize Scarcity and Limited Availability

People are more likely to take action when they feel like they might miss out. By highlighting scarcity—whether it's limited product availability, time-limited bonuses, or early-bird pricing—you can drive urgency and compel your audience to buy on launch day.

Examples of Scarcity Tactics:

- **Limited-Quantity Offers**: "Only 100 units available at this special price—act fast before they're gone!"
- **Time-Limited Bonuses**: "Order within the first 24 hours and receive a free bonus gift!"
- **Exclusive Early-Bird Pricing**: "Sign up before launch day to lock in our early-bird pricing—only available for the first 48 hours."

Step 5: Coordinating a Seamless Launch Day

On launch day, everything should be ready to go, from your sales page to your checkout process to your customer support team. Your goal is to create a seamless experience for your audience, ensuring that they can take action quickly and easily.

1. Prepare Your Sales Page and Checkout

Your sales page is the heart of your launch, so make sure it's optimized for conversions and ready to handle a surge in traffic. Ensure that the page clearly communicates the benefits of your product, includes compelling testimonials or case studies, and features a strong call to action.

Sales Page Checklist:

- Clear and compelling headline
- Concise and benefit-driven copy
- Strong visuals (images or videos) that showcase your product
- Social proof (testimonials, reviews, case studies)
- Simple and visible call-to-action buttons ("Buy Now" or "Get Instant Access")
- Fast-loading checkout process

2. Be Ready for Real-Time Engagement

During the launch, it's important to engage with your audience in real time. Monitor your social media channels, respond to comments or questions, and provide customer support through live chat or email. Real-time engagement helps build trust and ensures a smooth buying experience.

Launch Day Engagement Tips:

- **Social Media Engagement**: Monitor your social media channels throughout the day, responding to comments, answering questions, and sharing updates.
- **Live Q&A or Webinar**: Host a live Q&A session or webinar on launch day to answer any last-minute questions and demonstrate the value of your product.
- **Customer Support**: Ensure your customer support team is on standby to assist with any issues or questions during the checkout process.

Conclusion

Launching with a bang requires careful planning, strategic engagement, and creating excitement that builds up to a crescendo on launch day. By teasing your audience, offering exclusive access, creating valuable content, and leveraging multiple channels, you can generate buzz and anticipation that leads to massive results. When combined with urgency tactics and a seamless launch experience, you'll be well-positioned to hit your goal of generating $100,000 in 24 hours.

With the steps outlined in this chapter, you'll have everything you need to build hype, engage your audience, and ensure that when the moment comes, your launch day goes off with a bang, delivering both immediate sales and long-term success.

Chapter 23: Running Flash Sales and Promotions

When it comes to generating rapid sales, few strategies are as effective as **flash sales** and **limited-time promotions**. By creating an environment of urgency, scarcity, and exclusivity, you tap into your audience's psychological fear of missing out (FOMO), which compels them to take action immediately. Running a well-executed flash sale with the right promotions can help you generate a massive influx of revenue in a short period—perfect for achieving ambitious goals like $100,000 in 24 hours.

In this chapter, we will explore the essential components of running **high-converting flash sales** and promotions, from creating a sense of urgency with countdown timers to structuring irresistible limited-time offers that drive conversions. You'll learn the psychology behind time-sensitive sales and discover how to maximize the impact of your promotions to increase sales and build long-term customer loyalty.

Step 1: Understanding the Power of Flash Sales and Promotions

Flash sales and limited-time promotions work because they play on two powerful psychological triggers: **urgency** and **scarcity**. When customers know they have a limited window to buy and that the product or deal may run out, they're more likely to act quickly.

1. Why Flash Sales Work

Flash sales create an intense buying environment where customers feel compelled to make a purchase decision immediately, often without the luxury of time for deliberation. Here's why flash sales are so effective:

- **Urgency**: The time-limited nature of flash sales encourages customers to act now rather than later. If they wait, they may miss out on the deal entirely.
  - Example: "This deal ends in 24 hours—don't miss your chance to save 50%!"

- **Scarcity**: When there's limited availability, people are driven by the fear of missing out on something valuable. Scarcity can be achieved through limited stock or a special offer that's only available for a short time.
  - Example: "Only 50 units left at this price! Act now before they're gone."
- **Impulse Buying**: Flash sales often trigger impulse purchases. When customers are presented with a high-value offer for a short time, they may make a purchase without fully thinking it through, simply to avoid missing out.
  - Example: A flash sale offering a massive discount on a popular product could prompt customers to buy without their usual hesitation.

By combining urgency, scarcity, and irresistible offers, flash sales can generate a significant spike in sales in a short amount of time.

Step 2: Planning Your Flash Sale Strategy

A successful flash sale requires thoughtful planning and precise execution. To make the most of your promotion, you need to define your objectives, choose the right products, and ensure that your offer is truly compelling.

1. Define Your Goals and Timeline

Before launching a flash sale, it's important to have a clear understanding of your objectives and how long the sale will last. Are you looking to boost revenue quickly, clear out old inventory, or acquire new customers? Your goal will influence the type of promotion you run and the messaging you use.

Common Flash Sale Goals:

- **Revenue Generation**: If your primary goal is to generate a large amount of revenue in a short time, focus on high-ticket items or bundling products together to increase the average order value.

- Example: "Get $500 off our premium product bundle—today only!"

- **Clearing Inventory**: If you have excess inventory or seasonal products that need to be moved, a flash sale can help clear stock quickly.
  - Example: "End-of-season clearance! Everything must go—up to 70% off for 48 hours only."
- **Customer Acquisition**: If your goal is to acquire new customers, consider offering a steep discount on your most popular or entry-level products to attract first-time buyers.
  - Example: "First-time customers: Get 40% off your first purchase—this weekend only!"

Next, determine the **duration** of your flash sale. Most flash sales last between 24-72 hours, though some businesses may opt for even shorter promotions (e.g., 12 or 6 hours) to create heightened urgency.

2. Choose the Right Products and Offers

Not all products are suited for flash sales. The key is to select products that are desirable to your target audience and can be positioned as **must-have** items. Additionally, you'll need to structure offers that feel compelling enough to trigger immediate action.

Choosing Products for a Flash Sale:

- **Best-Sellers**: Offering discounts on your best-selling products can drive significant interest and increase sales volume, as these are products that already resonate with your audience.
  - Example: "Our #1 best-seller is now 50% off for 24 hours!"
- **Exclusive or Limited-Edition Items**: Flash sales are perfect for promoting exclusive, limited-edition, or newly launched products. The combination of novelty and scarcity increases their appeal.
  - Example: "Limited-edition product launch—available only during this 24-hour flash sale."

- **Product Bundles**: Create bundles of complementary products to increase the perceived value of your offer. Bundles allow you to increase the average order value and clear inventory at the same time.
  - Example: "Get our complete skincare routine bundle for 40% off—today only."

Structuring Irresistible Offers:

- **Discount Percentage**: The bigger the discount, the more likely people are to take advantage of the offer. Discounts of 30% or higher are often the sweet spot for generating urgency.
  - Example: "Today only—get 50% off everything in our store!"
- **Buy-One-Get-One (BOGO) Offers**: BOGO promotions are highly effective because they give customers the sense of getting more for their money. This type of offer also encourages larger order quantities.
  - Example: "Buy one, get one free on all apparel—48 hours only!"
- **Free Shipping**: Offering free shipping during a flash sale can remove one of the biggest barriers to online purchases and further incentivize customers to buy.
  - Example: "Free shipping on all orders placed during our 24-hour flash sale."

Step 3: Building Urgency with Countdown Timers

One of the most powerful tools in any flash sale is the **countdown timer**. A visible timer reminds your audience that the clock is ticking, creating a sense of urgency that prompts them to act before time runs out.

1. **Using Countdown Timers on Your Website**

Adding a countdown timer to your website—especially on the product pages and checkout page—serves as a constant reminder that the sale won't last forever. The visual representation of time running out creates a psychological pressure to act now, before it's too late.

Best Practices for Countdown Timers:

- **Display Prominently**: Place the countdown timer in a prominent position at the top of your website, on the product page, or even in a banner that follows the user as they scroll. It should be impossible to miss.
    - Example: "Flash Sale Ends In: 4 hours, 23 minutes, 12 seconds."
- **Use Bold, High-Contrast Colors**: Make the timer stand out by using bold, high-contrast colors that catch the eye and draw attention. Red, orange, or bright yellow are effective choices for creating urgency.
- **Show Time Remaining at Checkout**: Reinforce urgency by displaying the countdown timer on the checkout page. This reminds customers that they need to complete their purchase quickly to lock in the deal.

2. Adding Countdown Timers to Emails and Ads

In addition to your website, you can add countdown timers to **emails** and **ads** to further build urgency and drive traffic to your flash sale. Email marketing is particularly effective during a flash sale because it allows you to reach customers directly and remind them about the limited-time offer.

Examples of Countdown Timers in Emails:

- **Pre-Launch Emails**: Send an email before the sale starts, with a countdown timer leading up to the launch. This builds excitement and ensures your audience is ready to take action as soon as the sale goes live.
  - Example: "The flash sale starts in 6 hours—get ready for 50% off all products!"
- **Mid-Sale Reminders**: Send emails throughout the flash sale, with countdown timers reminding customers how much time is left to take advantage of the offer.
  - Example: "Only 12 hours left to save—don't miss out!"
- **Last-Chance Emails**: As the sale comes to an end, send a final reminder email emphasizing the urgency with a timer showing the minutes or hours left.
  - Example: "Last chance! The sale ends in just 2 hours."

Countdown timers can also be integrated into social media ads, banner ads, and Google Ads to maximize visibility and drive urgency across multiple platforms.

Step 4: Promoting Your Flash Sale for Maximum Reach

To ensure your flash sale is a success, you need to promote it across multiple channels and create excitement before the sale even begins. A multi-channel promotional strategy will help you reach your existing audience and attract new customers who may not have been aware of your brand.

1. Email Marketing

Email marketing is a key driver of flash sale success because it allows you to reach your audience directly in their inbox, creating a personal connection and encouraging immediate action.

Flash Sale Email Sequence:

- **Teaser Email**: Send an email 24-48 hours before the sale begins to build anticipation. Use a subject line that piques curiosity, and encourage your subscribers to be on the lookout for the sale announcement.
    - Example: "Something BIG is coming... stay tuned for our flash sale!"
- **Launch Email**: As soon as the sale goes live, send an email announcing the sale with clear details about the offer and a strong call to action. Include a countdown timer to build urgency.
    - Example: "Our 24-hour flash sale is LIVE! Get 40% off everything in our store—shop now before it's gone."
- **Reminder Emails**: Throughout the sale, send reminder emails to keep the urgency high. Each email should emphasize how much time is left and highlight the benefits of acting now.
    - Example: "Only 6 hours left to save—don't miss your chance to grab these deals!"

2. Social Media Promotion

Social media platforms like **Instagram**, **Facebook**, **Twitter**, and **TikTok** are ideal for promoting your flash sale, engaging with your audience in real-time, and creating viral buzz.

Social Media Flash Sale Tactics:

- **Teaser Posts**: Use teaser posts in the days leading up to the sale to build excitement and curiosity. Share sneak peeks of the products that will be on sale, behind-the-scenes content, or a countdown to the sale's start.
    - Example: "Get ready... our biggest flash sale ever starts in 24 hours!"

- **Instagram and Facebook Stories**: Use Stories to share real-time updates about the sale. Include countdown stickers, product showcases, and links that take users directly to your sale page.
  - Example: "Only 3 hours left! Swipe up to get your 40% discount before it's gone!"
- **Live Video**: Host a live video on Instagram or Facebook at the start of your flash sale to announce the sale, showcase products, and answer questions. Live videos are highly engaging and can create a sense of urgency and excitement.
  - Example: "We're live! Join us now for exclusive offers during our flash sale."

3. Paid Advertising

Running **paid ads** on Facebook, Instagram, and Google can help you reach a wider audience and drive traffic to your flash sale. With paid ads, you can target specific demographics, retarget previous website visitors, and promote your limited-time offer to people who are more likely to convert.

Best Practices for Flash Sale Ads:

- **Target Your Ideal Audience**: Use advanced targeting features to reach your ideal customer base based on demographics, interests, and behaviors. You can also create **Lookalike Audiences** based on your existing customers to find new prospects.
- **Use Eye-Catching Visuals**: The visuals in your ad should highlight the product and emphasize the urgency of the offer. Use bold fonts, countdown timers, and bright colors to grab attention.
  - Example: "Flash Sale Today Only—Get 50% Off! Don't Miss Out!"
- **Retarget Visitors**: Use retargeting ads to reach people who have visited your website before or who have added items to their cart

but didn't complete their purchase. Remind them of the limited-time offer and encourage them to return and buy.

- Example: "You left something in your cart—get it now before the flash sale ends in 2 hours!"

Step 5: Maximizing Conversions During the Flash Sale

Once your flash sale is live, the focus shifts to **maximizing conversions** and ensuring a smooth buying experience. To make the most of your limited-time offer, you need to remove friction from the checkout process, offer excellent customer support, and capitalize on opportunities for upselling and cross-selling.

1. Simplify the Checkout Process

A complicated or slow checkout process can cause customers to abandon their carts, especially during a time-sensitive flash sale. Make sure your checkout is fast, easy, and mobile-friendly to accommodate the surge in traffic.

Checkout Optimization Tips:

- **Guest Checkout**: Allow customers to check out as a guest without creating an account, which speeds up the process and reduces friction.
- **Fast Payment Options**: Offer multiple payment options, including one-click payment solutions like PayPal, Apple Pay, or Google Pay.
- **Minimize Steps**: Reduce the number of steps in the checkout process by eliminating unnecessary fields or requirements.

2. Offer Real-Time Customer Support

During a flash sale, customers may have questions about the product, shipping, or the checkout process. Providing **real-time customer support**—whether through live chat, email, or social media—can help resolve issues quickly and prevent abandoned carts.

Best Practices for Flash Sale Support:

- **Live Chat**: Enable live chat on your website so customers can get instant answers to their questions while they're shopping.
- **Monitor Social Media**: Keep an eye on your social media channels for questions or concerns and respond promptly to engage customers and address any issues.
- **Automated Responses**: Set up automated email responses for common inquiries, such as shipping times or return policies, to handle frequently asked questions during the sale.

3. Upsell and Cross-Sell for Higher Average Order Value

A flash sale is the perfect opportunity to increase your average order value by offering **upsells** and **cross-sells** during the checkout process. By suggesting complementary products or encouraging customers to upgrade to a higher-priced option, you can maximize your revenue during the sale.

Upsell and Cross-Sell Strategies:

- **Offer Related Products**: Use product recommendation tools to suggest related or complementary products at checkout.
  - Example: "Complete your purchase with these matching accessories—add them to your cart now for 20% off!"
- **Free Shipping Threshold**: Encourage customers to spend more by offering free shipping on orders over a certain amount.
  - Example: "Spend $50 more to get free shipping—add these items to your cart to qualify!"
- **Limited-Time Add-Ons**: Offer exclusive add-ons or upgrades available only during the flash sale.
  - Example: "Upgrade to the premium version for just $20 more—today only!"

Conclusion

Flash sales and promotions are powerful tools for driving rapid sales, increasing customer acquisition, and creating excitement around your brand. By strategically using countdown timers, promoting your sale across multiple channels, and optimizing your checkout process for conversions, you can create a highly effective flash sale that generates significant revenue in a short period.

The key to a successful flash sale is to create a sense of urgency and scarcity that compels customers to act immediately. By offering irresistible deals, leveraging time-sensitive promotions, and engaging your audience through email, social media, and paid ads, you can maximize the impact of your flash sale and reach ambitious sales goals—like generating $100,000 in 24 hours.

With the strategies and techniques outlined in this chapter, you'll be well-equipped to run high-converting flash sales that not only drive immediate revenue but also build long-term customer loyalty and repeat business.

Chapter 24: Handling the Surge: Automating Customer Support

When you're running a campaign to generate $100,000 in 24 hours, or executing any high-volume sales event such as a flash sale or product launch, a significant surge in customer inquiries is inevitable. From pre-sale questions about product details to post-purchase support like tracking orders or resolving issues, effective customer service becomes critical to ensuring a smooth experience. If your customer support is overwhelmed during this surge, it can lead to delays, frustration, abandoned carts, and even lost customers. The solution lies in **automating customer support** to efficiently handle the influx of queries, provide real-time assistance, and maintain high levels of customer satisfaction without overwhelming your team.

In this chapter, we will explore the strategies and tools needed to **automate customer support**, ensuring that your team can handle high volumes of inquiries while providing timely and accurate responses. You'll learn how to set up chatbots, automate frequently asked questions, manage tickets efficiently, and integrate automation into your overall customer support system.

Step 1: Preparing for a Surge in Customer Inquiries

Before your high-volume sales event begins, it's essential to anticipate the potential surge in customer inquiries and ensure that your systems are prepared to handle the load. This includes creating an infrastructure that allows for quick and automated responses to common questions, as well as having contingency plans in place for more complex inquiries.

1. Anticipating Common Customer Questions

One of the first steps in preparing for a surge is understanding the types of questions your customers are most likely to ask. During high-volume sales events, customer inquiries often revolve around common themes, such as product availability, shipping details, payment issues, and returns.

Typical Questions During a Sales Surge:

- **Pre-Sale Inquiries**:
    - "Is this product still in stock?"
    - "What is the discount or offer?"
    - "How long will shipping take?"
- **Payment and Checkout Issues**:
    - "My payment isn't going through, what should I do?"
    - "Is there another way to pay?"
- **Post-Sale Questions**:
    - "How do I track my order?"
    - "When will my item be delivered?"
    - "What is your return policy?"

By identifying these common questions, you can automate responses to provide fast and accurate information, freeing your support team to focus on more complex issues.

2. Building a Comprehensive Knowledge Base

A **knowledge base** is a collection of help articles, FAQs, and guides that customers can access to find answers to their questions without contacting customer support. Having a well-organized knowledge base is a crucial first step in automating customer support, as it allows customers to help themselves before reaching out for additional assistance.

Key Components of an Effective Knowledge Base:

- **FAQs**: Create a section of frequently asked questions that covers common inquiries about products, shipping, pricing, and returns. Make sure these are easy to find on your website.
- **Product Guides**: Offer detailed product guides that explain how your products work, troubleshooting steps, and usage tips.

- **Order and Shipping Information**: Include a detailed section on order tracking, shipping times, and delivery estimates, as these are common questions during sales events.

Best Practices for a Knowledge Base:

- **Searchable Content**: Ensure that your knowledge base is easily searchable so customers can quickly find the information they need.
- **Clear and Concise Language**: Write help articles in simple, straightforward language that anyone can understand. Use bullet points or numbered lists to make content easy to scan.
- **Visual Aids**: Include screenshots, images, or videos where appropriate to help explain processes or guide customers through troubleshooting.

By having a comprehensive knowledge base in place, you can reduce the number of incoming inquiries and allow customers to find the answers they need quickly and independently.

Step 2: Leveraging Chatbots for Instant Customer Support

Chatbots are one of the most effective ways to automate customer support during a surge in inquiries. Powered by artificial intelligence (AI) or pre-programmed workflows, chatbots can provide instant responses to common questions, guide customers through the purchase process, and even escalate issues to a human agent if necessary.

1. Setting Up AI-Powered Chatbots

An **AI-powered chatbot** can handle customer interactions in real-time, mimicking human conversations to resolve queries quickly. These chatbots can be integrated into your website, social media channels, and even your email system to provide round-the-clock assistance without requiring human intervention.

Steps to Set Up an AI Chatbot:

- **Choose a Chatbot Platform**: Select a chatbot platform that integrates seamlessly with your website or eCommerce platform. Popular options include **Intercom**, **Zendesk Chat**, **Tidio**, **Drift**, and **LivePerson**.
- **Train the Bot**: Use AI to train the chatbot on common customer queries by inputting FAQs, product information, and troubleshooting guides. The more data the bot has, the more accurate and useful it will be in answering questions.
- **Configure Pre-Built Responses**: Program pre-built responses for specific inquiries. For example, you could configure the chatbot to handle questions like "What's your return policy?" or "Where can I track my order?"
- **Integrate Escalation Paths**: In cases where the chatbot can't resolve an issue, ensure that there's an escalation path that seamlessly connects the customer with a human agent. This ensures that more complex issues are handled efficiently.

Best Practices for AI Chatbots:

- **Personalization**: Make sure your chatbot can greet customers by name, remember past interactions, and provide personalized recommendations based on customer behavior.
- **Multichannel Integration**: Integrate your chatbot across multiple customer touchpoints, including your website, social media platforms (like Facebook Messenger), and email support, to provide a consistent experience.
- **Real-Time Order Tracking**: Integrate your chatbot with your order management system to provide real-time updates on order status. This reduces the number of inquiries related to shipping or delivery times.

2. Creating Rule-Based Chatbots

While AI chatbots are highly effective, **rule-based chatbots** can also be used to automate customer support for simpler, more predictable queries. These chatbots follow a decision-tree model, guiding customers through a series of options based on pre-programmed rules.

Example of a Rule-Based Chatbot Interaction:

1. **Customer Question**: "Where is my order?"
2. **Bot Response**: "Please enter your order number."
3. **Customer Input**: [Customer enters order number]
4. **Bot Response**: "Your order is currently in transit and expected to arrive on [Date]."

Rule-based chatbots are easy to set up and highly effective for handling repetitive queries like order tracking, shipping information, or simple product questions.

Step 3: Automating Email Support with Auto-Responders

Email is another critical channel for customer support, especially during high-traffic sales events. To prevent your team from being overwhelmed with emails, you can set up **auto-responders** to handle common queries and provide instant replies, giving customers the information they need without having to wait for a manual response.

1. Setting Up Auto-Responders for Common Inquiries

Auto-responders are pre-written email replies that are automatically triggered when a customer sends an email with specific keywords or selects a particular inquiry type in your contact form. These automated responses can address frequently asked questions or provide updates on order status.

Steps to Automate Email Support:

- **Identify Common Inquiries**: Start by identifying the most common reasons customers reach out via email during sales events. This could include questions about pricing, returns, shipping, or payment issues.
- **Create Pre-Written Responses**: Write clear, concise email templates that address these common inquiries. These should be personalized with the customer's name and provide all the necessary details to resolve their question.
  - Example: For a shipping inquiry, the auto-responder might say, "Thank you for your order, [Customer Name]! Your item is currently being processed and is expected to ship within 2-3 business days. You'll receive a tracking link once it's shipped."
- **Trigger Conditions**: Set up triggers for the auto-responders based on specific keywords (e.g., "shipping," "returns," "order status") or customer inquiry categories. The auto-responder will automatically send the appropriate reply when these conditions are met.

2. Using Automated Follow-Up Emails

In addition to initial auto-responders, you can also automate **follow-up emails** to keep customers informed throughout their purchase journey. This is especially helpful during sales surges, as it reduces the number of incoming inquiries related to order status.

Examples of Automated Follow-Up Emails:

- **Order Confirmation**: Send an immediate confirmation email after a purchase, including the order number, product details, and expected shipping time.

- ◦ Example: "Thank you for your purchase, [Customer Name]! Your order number is [Order Number]. We're processing your order and will notify you when it ships."
- **Shipping Notification**: Once an order has shipped, send an automated email with tracking information and an estimated delivery date.
  - ◦ Example: "Good news! Your order has shipped. Track your package here: [Tracking Link]. Estimated delivery: [Date]."
- **Delivery Confirmation**: After the order is delivered, send a follow-up email to confirm the delivery and request feedback or a review.
  - ◦ Example: "Your order has arrived! We hope you love it. Let us know what you think by leaving a review."

These follow-up emails provide customers with proactive updates, reducing the need for them to contact support for order-related inquiries.

Step 4: Efficiently Managing Support Tickets with Automation

When your customer support system is flooded with inquiries, managing and resolving tickets efficiently is critical. By using automation, you can streamline the ticket management process, prioritize urgent issues, and ensure that every customer receives timely assistance.

1. Automating Ticket Routing and Prioritization

During a high-volume sales event, certain customer inquiries will require urgent attention (e.g., payment issues or technical problems), while others may be less time-sensitive. To ensure that critical issues are resolved quickly, you can automate the **routing and prioritization** of support tickets.

How to Automate Ticket Routing:

- **Set Priority Levels**: Assign priority levels to different types of inquiries. For example, payment issues and cart abandonment may be high-priority, while general product questions may be lower-priority.
- **Automatic Routing**: Use automation to route tickets to the appropriate department or team based on the nature of the inquiry. For instance, technical issues can be routed to IT, while product inquiries go to customer service.
  - Example: "If a customer selects 'Payment Issue' in the support form, the ticket is automatically routed to the billing team for immediate resolution."
- **Escalation Rules**: Set up escalation rules that automatically escalate tickets to higher-level support agents if they haven't been resolved within a certain timeframe.

2. Using Ticket Automation for Status Updates

Customers who submit support tickets often want to know the status of their inquiry. You can automate status updates, keeping customers informed without requiring manual follow-up from your support team.

Examples of Automated Ticket Updates:

- **Ticket Acknowledgement**: As soon as a ticket is submitted, send an automated response acknowledging receipt of the ticket and providing an estimated resolution time.
  - Example: "We've received your support request, [Customer Name]. A member of our team is looking into it and will get back to you within 24 hours."
- **Status Updates**: Send automated status updates to customers when their ticket is being worked on or has been resolved.

- Example: "Good news! Your support request is being reviewed by our technical team. We'll follow up with a resolution shortly."

- **Resolution Confirmation**: Once the issue is resolved, send a final automated email confirming the resolution and asking if the customer is satisfied with the outcome.

  - Example: "Your issue has been resolved, [Customer Name]. If you're satisfied with the solution, no further action is needed. If you have any other questions, feel free to reach out."

Step 5: Integrating Automation with Human Support

While automation can handle a significant portion of customer inquiries, there will always be complex or sensitive issues that require human intervention. To ensure a smooth customer experience, it's important to have a system in place that seamlessly transitions customers from automated support to human agents when needed.

1. Creating Smooth Handoffs Between Bots and Agents

A common challenge with automated support is ensuring a smooth handoff when the chatbot or automation system reaches its limits. To avoid customer frustration, make it easy for customers to escalate their issues to a human agent.

Best Practices for Bot-to-Agent Handoffs:

- **Provide an Option for Human Support**: Always include an option in your chatbot or automated system that allows customers to request human assistance. This ensures that customers with more complex issues can speak to a real person.

  - Example: "Would you like to speak with a human agent? Type 'Agent' to be connected."

- **Transfer Customer Information**: When transferring a customer from a bot to a human agent, ensure that all relevant information (such as the customer's name, inquiry details, and previous interactions) is passed along to the agent. This avoids requiring the customer to repeat themselves.

- Example: The agent should receive a complete transcript of the customer's chatbot conversation before taking over the inquiry.

- **Prioritize Escalated Tickets**: Ensure that any tickets escalated from automated systems are flagged as high-priority and handled by your support team as quickly as possible.

2. Blending Automation with Personalized Human Support

Automation is highly effective for managing routine tasks and common inquiries, but personalized human support is essential for resolving complex issues or providing a premium customer experience. Your goal should be to blend automation with human support to create a seamless, efficient, and empathetic customer service experience.

When to Use Human Support:

- **Technical Problems**: Complex technical issues that require troubleshooting or specialized knowledge should be handled by human agents.
- **Payment or Billing Issues**: Payment disputes, refunds, or billing questions often require a personal touch to reassure customers and provide detailed explanations.
- **VIP Customers**: If you have high-value or VIP customers, consider routing their inquiries directly to human agents for personalized service. This can help build stronger relationships and ensure loyalty.

Conclusion

Handling a surge in customer inquiries during a high-volume sales event requires a combination of **automation** and **human support** to ensure a smooth and efficient customer experience. By leveraging chatbots, auto-responders, and ticket automation, you can provide instant assistance for common inquiries while freeing up your team to focus on more complex or urgent issues.

Automating customer support not only helps you manage large volumes of inquiries but also ensures that customers receive timely, accurate responses, which can prevent frustration and boost satisfaction. When done right, this approach can lead to higher conversion rates, lower cart abandonment, and more repeat customers—all while keeping your support team from becoming overwhelmed.

By following the strategies outlined in this chapter, you'll be well-equipped to handle the surge in customer inquiries that comes with a $100,000 launch or sales event, ensuring that your customers receive the support they need to complete their purchases and enjoy a seamless buying experience.

Chapter 25: Real-Time Sales Optimization

In a high-stakes, time-sensitive campaign like generating $100,000 in 24 hours, real-time optimization can make the difference between meeting your goal or falling short. While meticulous planning is critical, the ability to **analyze data and adjust your strategy on the fly** is equally important for maximizing sales. By tracking performance metrics, identifying bottlenecks, and making strategic tweaks during the sales window, you can increase conversions, reduce cart abandonment, and boost overall revenue.

In this chapter, we'll explore how to monitor key metrics, make data-driven decisions, and implement real-time adjustments to optimize sales during your 24-hour window. From changing pricing to adjusting ad targeting or tweaking messaging, real-time sales optimization requires quick thinking and strategic action to capitalize on every opportunity for growth.

Step 1: Tracking Key Performance Metrics in Real Time

The first step in optimizing your sales campaign in real time is having a system in place to **monitor key metrics** as they happen. You need to be able to track how your sales are performing, where customers are dropping off, and which strategies are driving the most conversions. By monitoring these metrics continuously, you'll be able to identify what's working, what needs adjustment, and where your biggest opportunities lie.

1. Essential Metrics to Track During the 24-Hour Window

To effectively optimize your campaign, it's critical to focus on the right metrics. These metrics will help you identify areas where you can make immediate improvements to boost sales.

Key Metrics to Monitor:

- **Conversion Rate**: The percentage of visitors who complete a purchase. A low conversion rate indicates friction in the buying process, such as a confusing checkout experience or unclear value proposition.

- **Cart Abandonment Rate**: The percentage of users who add items to their cart but fail to complete the purchase. A high cart abandonment rate could indicate issues with payment options, shipping costs, or a lack of urgency.
- **Traffic Sources**: Analyze where your traffic is coming from (organic search, social media, paid ads, email, etc.) and which sources are converting the best. Focus your resources on the highest-converting traffic channels.
- **Average Order Value (AOV)**: The average amount spent by customers per transaction. By monitoring AOV, you can identify opportunities for upselling or cross-selling to increase revenue.
- **Checkout Completion Rate**: The percentage of customers who complete the checkout process after starting it. If this rate is low, investigate potential obstacles in the checkout process that may be causing drop-offs.
- **Bounce Rate**: The percentage of visitors who leave your website without interacting. A high bounce rate could suggest that your landing page isn't aligned with customer expectations or that there's a lack of clarity in your offer.

2. Using Real-Time Analytics Tools

To effectively track these metrics during your 24-hour sales window, you'll need to use **real-time analytics tools** that provide up-to-the-minute data on customer behavior. These tools will allow you to quickly spot trends and make adjustments on the fly.

Popular Real-Time Analytics Tools:

- **Google Analytics**: Google Analytics provides real-time insights into traffic sources, user behavior, and conversion rates. Use this tool to monitor where your visitors are coming from and how they're interacting with your site.

- **Hotjar**: Hotjar offers heatmaps and session recordings that show how users are navigating your site. This helps you identify usability issues or obstacles in the customer journey.
- **Shopify Analytics** (or other eCommerce platforms): Shopify Analytics allows you to track sales, conversions, and customer behavior in real time. It also integrates with various marketing tools to give you a holistic view of your campaign.
- **Facebook Ads Manager and Google Ads**: If you're running paid ads, use these platforms' real-time analytics to track ad performance, click-through rates, and conversions. This will help you determine if you need to adjust your ad spend or targeting.

By using these tools, you can get a clear picture of how your campaign is performing and quickly identify areas for improvement.

Step 2: Identifying and Addressing Bottlenecks

Even with a solid plan in place, bottlenecks can occur during your sales campaign that slow down conversions or cause customers to abandon the buying process. These bottlenecks could be technical issues, poor user experience, or problems with your offer. The key is to quickly identify and address them to prevent lost sales.

1. Optimizing the Checkout Process

One of the most common bottlenecks during high-volume sales events is the **checkout process**. If customers encounter issues while trying to complete their purchase, they are likely to abandon their cart. Monitoring the checkout funnel closely will help you spot any friction points.

Common Checkout Issues to Watch For:

- **Complicated Checkout Forms**: Long, complex checkout forms that require too much information can frustrate customers and cause them to abandon their purchase. Simplify the form by only asking for essential information.

- **Lack of Payment Options**: If customers don't see their preferred payment method, they may abandon their cart. Ensure you offer a variety of payment options (e.g., credit card, PayPal, Apple Pay).
- **Unexpected Costs**: Surprise costs like shipping fees or taxes can cause customers to abandon their carts. Be transparent about costs upfront to avoid last-minute shocks.

Real-Time Fixes for Checkout Issues:

- **Enable Guest Checkout**: Allow customers to check out without creating an account to streamline the process.
- **Offer a Discount Code**: If you notice high cart abandonment, send an immediate email offering a discount code to encourage customers to complete their purchase.
- **Simplify Payment**: Add one-click payment options like PayPal Express Checkout or Google Pay to make the process faster and easier.

2. Adjusting Pricing and Offers in Real Time

During your 24-hour window, you may discover that your initial pricing or offer isn't converting as well as you anticipated. If you notice a lower-than-expected conversion rate, consider tweaking your pricing or adding additional incentives to drive urgency.

Real-Time Pricing Adjustments:

- **Introduce Time-Limited Discounts**: If sales are slower than expected, introduce a new time-limited discount or flash deal to reignite interest.
  - Example: "For the next 2 hours only, get an additional 10% off all orders!"

- **Bundle Offers**: If individual product sales are low, consider bundling complementary products together at a discounted price to increase perceived value and boost AOV.
  - Example: "Buy 2, get 1 free on all accessories!"
- **Free Shipping**: If you notice high cart abandonment due to shipping costs, offer free shipping for a limited time to encourage customers to complete their purchase.

3. Monitoring Website Performance

Technical issues can derail a high-stakes sales campaign. If your website is slow to load or crashes under heavy traffic, you risk losing potential customers. Use real-time monitoring to ensure that your site is functioning smoothly and fix any issues immediately.

Technical Bottlenecks to Watch For:

- **Slow Page Load Times**: If your pages take too long to load, customers may leave before even seeing your offer. Use tools like **Google PageSpeed Insights** to monitor load times and address performance issues.
- **Mobile Optimization**: Ensure that your site is fully optimized for mobile, as a large portion of traffic during sales events often comes from mobile devices. Test your site on multiple devices and browsers to ensure a seamless experience.
- **Server Downtime**: Use monitoring tools like **Pingdom** or **UptimeRobot** to ensure your website stays online throughout the sale. If you experience downtime, work with your hosting provider to resolve the issue as quickly as possible.

Step 3: Adjusting Marketing and Advertising Strategies

During your 24-hour campaign, you may need to make adjustments to your **marketing and advertising strategies** to optimize performance. If certain channels or ads are underperforming, or if you notice opportunities for improvement, making changes in real time can help you maximize your sales.

1. Tweaking Paid Ad Campaigns

If you're running paid ads through platforms like Facebook, Instagram, or Google Ads, use real-time data to adjust your campaigns for better results. Monitor your ad performance and be prepared to shift your ad spend or refine your targeting to boost conversions.

Real-Time Ad Optimization Tips:

- **Adjust Targeting**: If certain audience segments aren't converting as expected, refine your targeting to focus on more relevant or engaged demographics. Look at which age groups, locations, or behaviors are driving the most sales and adjust your ad sets accordingly.
  - Example: "We're seeing higher conversions from users aged 25-34. Let's allocate more budget to target this group."
- **Increase Ad Spend on High-Performing Campaigns**: If certain ads are driving a higher return on ad spend (ROAS), consider increasing your budget for those ads to capitalize on their success.
  - Example: "Our Instagram Story ad has a 3x ROAS—let's increase the budget by 20% to capture more traffic."
- **A/B Testing on the Fly**: Test different ad creatives, copy, or headlines in real time to see which variations perform best. If one version clearly outperforms the other, shift more of your budget to the winning ad.

2. Amplifying Organic Social Media Engagement

If you're seeing positive engagement on social media, capitalize on the momentum by ramping up your organic social media efforts. Real-time engagement on platforms like Instagram, Twitter, and Facebook can help amplify your message and drive additional traffic to your sales page.

Real-Time Social Media Strategies:

- **Host a Live Event**: Go live on Instagram, Facebook, or YouTube to answer questions, demonstrate your product, or announce exclusive time-limited offers. This can create excitement and drive immediate action.
  - Example: "Join us live at 2 PM for a behind-the-scenes look at our product and a special surprise for attendees!"
- **Engage with Comments and Mentions**: Actively monitor your social media mentions and comments throughout the day. Respond to customer questions, highlight positive feedback, and encourage users to share their purchases on social media.
  - Example: "Thanks for the shoutout, [Customer Name]! We can't wait for you to try our new product!"
- **Use Real-Time Story Updates**: Post Instagram Stories, Facebook Stories, and Twitter updates throughout the day to keep your audience informed about how much time is left, flash deals, and stock updates.

3. Sending Targeted Email Blasts

Email marketing is a powerful tool for driving immediate traffic during a sales campaign. Use email to notify your subscribers about limited-time offers, remind them of the time remaining in the sale, and encourage them to complete their purchases.

Real-Time Email Campaign Tactics:

- **Flash Sale Alerts**: Send a real-time email blast announcing any flash sales or special promotions during the 24-hour window. Highlight urgency with subject lines like "Hurry—Only 2 Hours Left to Save 30%!"

- **Cart Abandonment Emails**: If you notice high cart abandonment rates, trigger an automated cart abandonment email sequence to remind customers to complete their purchase. Include an incentive like free shipping or an additional discount to encourage them to buy.
    - Example: "You left something in your cart! Complete your purchase now and get free shipping."
- **Last-Chance Reminders**: As the end of the 24-hour window approaches, send a "last chance" email to create urgency and drive final conversions.
    - Example: "Only 3 hours left! Don't miss out on our biggest sale of the year."

Step 4: Upselling and Cross-Selling for Increased Revenue

To maximize your revenue during the 24-hour sales window, focus on **upselling and cross-selling** opportunities. By encouraging customers to purchase additional products or upgrade their order, you can increase your average order value (AOV) and drive more revenue.

1. Implementing Upsells at Checkout

One of the easiest ways to increase revenue is to offer upsells during the checkout process. This can include higher-priced versions of the product the customer is purchasing or complementary products that enhance the customer's experience.

Upsell Examples:

- **Product Upgrades**: Offer customers a premium version of the product they're buying for a slightly higher price.
    - Example: "Upgrade to the Pro Version for just $20 more and get exclusive features!"
- **Add-On Products**: Suggest related products that complement the customer's purchase. These could be accessories, warranties, or additional services.
    - Example: "Add a protective case to your order for just $15!"

2. Using Cross-Selling Techniques

Cross-selling involves recommending products from other categories that your customer might be interested in based on their purchase. This strategy not only boosts your AOV but also introduces customers to more of your product offerings.

Cross-Sell Examples:

- **Related Products**: Display related products on the checkout page that align with what the customer is buying.
    - Example: "Customers who bought this item also purchased [Related Product]. Add it to your cart now for 20% off!"
- **Post-Purchase Cross-Sells**: After a customer completes their purchase, use the confirmation page or follow-up email to recommend additional products.
    - Example: "Thanks for your purchase! Complete your collection with these must-have accessories."

Step 5: Monitoring Customer Feedback and Making Adjustments

During a high-volume sales campaign, customer feedback is invaluable for spotting issues you may not have anticipated. By monitoring feedback in real time and making quick adjustments, you can improve the customer experience and drive more sales.

1. Actively Monitoring Customer Support Channels

Keep a close eye on customer support channels, including live chat, social media, and email. If customers are experiencing common issues or expressing concerns, address them immediately to prevent further problems.

Examples of Real-Time Adjustments Based on Feedback:

- **Addressing Product Confusion**: If multiple customers are asking questions about product details, consider updating your sales page with clearer descriptions or adding a FAQ section.
    - Example: "We've received questions about sizing—here's a quick size guide to help you choose the right option."
- **Fixing Checkout Problems**: If customers report issues with the checkout process (e.g., payment failures or shipping options), work with your technical team to resolve these issues as quickly as possible.
    - Example: "We're aware of the payment issue and are working on it—please try again in a few minutes."

2. Collecting Post-Purchase Feedback

After the sale is completed, collecting post-purchase feedback can provide valuable insights for future campaigns. Use surveys or follow-up emails to ask customers about their experience and gather suggestions for improvement.

Post-Purchase Survey Questions:

- "How satisfied were you with your shopping experience?"
- "Did you encounter any issues during the checkout process?"
- "What could we improve next time?"

This feedback can help you identify pain points and make improvements for your next high-volume sales event.

Conclusion

Real-time sales optimization is an essential strategy for making the most of a high-volume sales campaign. By tracking key metrics, identifying and addressing bottlenecks, adjusting your marketing efforts, and optimizing the customer experience, you can significantly boost your sales and increase your chances of hitting ambitious revenue goals like $100,000 in 24 hours.

The ability to adapt quickly, make data-driven decisions, and implement real-time adjustments will set you apart in the fast-paced world of online sales. With the techniques outlined in this chapter, you'll be well-equipped to optimize your campaign on the fly, ensuring that every opportunity is captured and every potential customer is converted.

Chapter 26: Social Proof and Testimonials

One of the most powerful drivers of purchasing decisions is **social proof**—the idea that people are more likely to take action when they see others doing the same. During a high-stakes sales event, like aiming to generate $100,000 in 24 hours, showcasing social proof in the form of testimonials, reviews, and customer stories can significantly boost your conversions. When potential customers see that others have already purchased, benefited from, or recommend your product, they feel reassured that they're making a smart decision, reducing the perceived risk of buying.

In this chapter, we will explore how to **collect, display, and leverage testimonials and other forms of social proof** during your 24-hour campaign to maximize sales. We'll discuss various types of testimonials, how to collect them quickly, and the best ways to integrate them into your sales process for maximum impact.

Step 1: Understanding the Power of Social Proof

Social proof plays a crucial psychological role in influencing customer behavior, especially during time-sensitive sales events. It reassures potential buyers that others have already validated your product, which reduces uncertainty and builds trust. Social proof can come in various forms, such as customer testimonials, user-generated content, celebrity endorsements, and reviews.

1. Why Social Proof is Essential for High-Converting Sales

During a 24-hour sales event, potential customers have little time to make decisions, so building trust quickly is critical. **Testimonials and reviews** can do the heavy lifting by acting as third-party validation, confirming that your product delivers results and is worth the investment.

Key Benefits of Social Proof:

- **Builds Trust Quickly**: Seeing positive feedback from other customers reduces skepticism and builds trust in your product.

- **Increases Credibility**: When people see others endorsing or purchasing your product, it adds credibility to your brand, making new customers more confident in their purchase decision.
- **Reduces Perceived Risk**: Testimonials and reviews reassure customers that they're making a safe choice, especially if they're on the fence about purchasing.
- **Creates FOMO (Fear of Missing Out)**: Showcasing a large number of people buying or endorsing your product can create a sense of urgency and FOMO, encouraging potential customers to act quickly before the sale ends.

2. Types of Social Proof You Can Use

There are several forms of social proof that you can leverage during your sales event. Depending on your business, product, and customer base, you can mix and match these to create a compelling narrative around your offer.

Different Forms of Social Proof:

- **Customer Testimonials**: Positive feedback from real customers describing their experience with your product and the results they've achieved.
    - Example: "I've used [Product Name] for three months, and it has completely transformed my skin! Highly recommend it to anyone looking for real results."
- **User Reviews and Ratings**: Star ratings and reviews left by customers on your website or third-party platforms like Amazon, Google, or Yelp.
    - Example: "4.8 out of 5 stars based on 200+ reviews."
- **Case Studies**: In-depth customer stories that highlight how your product has helped solve a specific problem or achieve a significant goal.
    - Example: "Sarah used [Product Name] to double her sales in just 60 days. Here's how she did it."

- **Celebrity or Influencer Endorsements**: Social media influencers or celebrities recommending your product. This type of social proof can have a big impact if the influencer aligns with your target audience.
  - Example: "As seen in [Magazine Name] and endorsed by [Influencer Name] with over 1 million followers."
- **User-Generated Content**: Photos, videos, or posts created by your customers that showcase them using or enjoying your product. This content can be reposted on your social media channels or product pages.
  - Example: "Check out how our customers are styling their outfits with [Brand Name]! #CustomerStyle"
- **Sales Counters or Purchase Numbers**: Displaying the number of products sold during the sale or in the past can create urgency and provide validation that others are buying.
  - Example: "Over 1,000 units sold in the last 24 hours!"

Step 2: Collecting Testimonials and Reviews Quickly

To effectively showcase social proof during your 24-hour sales campaign, you'll need to **collect testimonials** and reviews quickly, especially if this is a product launch or if you're running a new promotion. Fortunately, there are several strategies you can use to gather feedback fast.

1. Reaching Out to Existing Customers

The fastest way to collect testimonials is by reaching out to your existing customers who have already used and benefited from your product. Send them a personalized email asking for feedback or a quick testimonial.

Steps to Request Testimonials:

- **Send a Personalized Email**: Reach out to satisfied customers via email and ask them to share their experience with your product.

Make it easy for them by including a few prompts or questions they can answer.

- Example: "Hi [Customer Name], we're thrilled that you've been using [Product Name]! Would you mind sharing a quick testimonial about your experience? Here are a few questions to guide you: What results have you seen since using our product? What would you say to someone considering it?"

- **Offer an Incentive**: To encourage quick responses, offer a small incentive, such as a discount on their next purchase or entry into a giveaway for those who submit testimonials.

  - Example: "Share your feedback, and we'll send you a 10% off coupon for your next order as a thank you!"

- **Use Automated Follow-Up Emails**: If you have an email automation system, send a follow-up email to recent purchasers asking them to leave a review. Automate these requests to go out 7-14 days after purchase, depending on the type of product.

2. Leveraging Social Media for Instant Feedback

Social media is a goldmine for collecting user-generated content and testimonials in real time. By encouraging your followers to share their experiences with your product, you can gather and display social proof quickly.

Strategies for Social Media Testimonials:

- **Run a Hashtag Campaign**: Create a unique hashtag and encourage your customers to share photos or videos of themselves using your product. Offer a prize or feature the best posts on your page.

  - Example: "Post a picture using [Product Name] with the hashtag #MyBrandExperience, and you could be featured on our page!"

- **Polls and Questions**: Use Instagram Stories or Twitter polls to ask your audience for quick feedback or testimonials. You can re-post the best responses as social proof.
    - Example: "What's your favorite thing about [Product Name]? Share your thoughts in the comments or via DM for a chance to be featured!"
- **Feature Customer Stories**: If you have dedicated customers who have shared their product experiences on social media, ask for permission to repost their stories or testimonials. Highlight their stories as part of your launch campaign.

3. Asking for Video Testimonials

Video testimonials are especially compelling because they add a personal, authentic touch to social proof. Customers talking about their positive experiences in their own words—and with emotion—are incredibly persuasive.

How to Collect Video Testimonials Quickly:

- **Reach Out to Happy Customers**: Contact your most satisfied customers and ask them to record a short video explaining how your product has helped them. Provide them with a simple script or outline if needed.
    - Example: "Would you be willing to record a short video telling us how [Product Name] has made a difference for you? Here's a quick guide to help: 1) Introduce yourself, 2) Tell us what problem you were facing before using our product, 3) Share the results you've seen."
- **Incentivize Video Submissions**: As with written testimonials, offering a small reward can encourage customers to submit video reviews faster.
    - Example: "Send us a video testimonial, and we'll give you 15% off your next order!"

- **Feature Videos on Your Sales Page**: Once you've collected the video testimonials, feature them prominently on your landing or product page to make a strong emotional connection with potential buyers.

Step 3: Showcasing Testimonials for Maximum Impact

Once you've collected testimonials, it's time to **showcase them in strategic places** to maximize their impact. The goal is to integrate social proof throughout your customer journey—on landing pages, product pages, emails, ads, and even during the checkout process—to continuously reinforce trust and credibility.

1. Displaying Testimonials on Your Sales Page

Your sales page is one of the most critical places to showcase social proof, as this is where potential customers are making the decision to buy. Adding testimonials, reviews, and case studies throughout the page will help build confidence and reduce friction.

Where to Place Testimonials on Your Sales Page:

- **Above the Fold**: Place one or two powerful testimonials at the top of your sales page, ideally above the fold, so they're immediately visible to visitors.
  - Example: "Here's what our customers are saying: '[Testimonial Quote]' — [Customer Name]."
- **Next to Call-to-Action Buttons**: Adding testimonials near your call-to-action buttons ("Buy Now," "Add to Cart," etc.) can reinforce the decision to purchase.
  - Example: "Thousands of customers are loving [Product Name]—'This product changed my life!' — [Customer Name]."
- **Throughout the Page**: Scatter different types of social proof throughout the sales page, including star ratings, customer stories, and case studies, so potential buyers encounter positive feedback as they scroll.

- Example: "Real customers, real results: '[Testimonial]' with photos or video clips."

2. Featuring Testimonials in Your Ads

Incorporating social proof into your paid advertising campaigns can boost the effectiveness of your ads, especially when you're targeting cold audiences who may be unfamiliar with your brand.

Ways to Use Testimonials in Ads:

- **Video Testimonials in Facebook and Instagram Ads**: Use short, authentic customer videos in your social media ads to show real people talking about their positive experiences. These types of ads perform particularly well because they come across as genuine and relatable.
  - Example: A Facebook video ad featuring a customer saying, "I've tried so many products, but nothing worked like [Product Name]. I saw results in just a week!"
- **Customer Quotes in Display Ads**: Use quotes from customer testimonials in display ads or Google Ads to build credibility and catch attention. Pair the quotes with images of the customer or product to create a cohesive message.
  - Example: "'[Product Name] changed my life!' — Sarah T. | Shop now to see for yourself."
- **Before-and-After Ads**: If your product delivers visible results (e.g., skincare, fitness, home improvement), use before-and-after testimonials in your ads to showcase the transformation your customers experience.

3. Including Social Proof in Checkout Pages and Email Campaigns

Adding testimonials to your checkout page and post-purchase email sequences can help reinforce trust and reduce buyer hesitation, especially during the critical moments when customers are deciding whether to complete their purchase.

Using Social Proof in Checkout Pages:

- **Testimonials on Checkout Page**: Place a short testimonial or star rating near the checkout button to give buyers extra reassurance before they complete their purchase.
  - Example: "Join thousands of satisfied customers! 'I couldn't be happier with my purchase.' — Emily W."
- **Urgency + Social Proof**: Combine social proof with urgency to encourage faster checkouts. Use statements like "Only 5 left in stock—100+ customers purchased today!" to create a sense of scarcity and social validation.

Leveraging Testimonials in Email Campaigns:

- **Pre-Launch Emails**: Include testimonials in your pre-launch emails to build anticipation and convince subscribers to take action when the sale goes live.
  - Example: "Don't just take our word for it—here's what [Customer Name] had to say: 'This product is worth every penny. I've never felt better!'"
- **Cart Abandonment Emails**: Use testimonials in cart abandonment emails to remind hesitant buyers of the positive experiences others have had with your product.
  - Example: "Still thinking about it? Here's what others are saying: '[Product Name] is a game-changer.' — Alex P."
- **Post-Purchase Follow-Up**: After a purchase, send follow-up emails featuring testimonials to encourage customers to leave their own review or recommend the product to friends.

Step 4: Leveraging User-Generated Content for Authentic Social Proof

While customer testimonials are highly effective, **user-generated content (UGC)**—such as photos, videos, and posts created by your customers—can provide an even more authentic form of social proof. When potential buyers see real people like them using and enjoying your product, it builds a deep sense of trust.

1. Encouraging Customers to Share UGC

To generate UGC, you'll need to actively encourage your customers to share their experiences with your product. You can do this through social media campaigns, email marketing, and even direct outreach.

Strategies to Encourage UGC:

- **Hashtag Campaigns**: Create a branded hashtag and encourage customers to use it when posting about your product on Instagram, Twitter, or TikTok. Repost the best content on your own channels to showcase real customer experiences.
  - Example: "Share your [Brand Name] look with #MyBrandStyle for a chance to be featured on our page!"
- **Photo Contests**: Run a photo contest where customers submit pictures of themselves using your product for a chance to win a prize. This not only generates UGC but also creates excitement around your product.
  - Example: "Snap a photo with your new [Product Name] and tag us for a chance to win a $100 gift card!"
- **Post-Purchase Email Request**: After a customer makes a purchase, send an email asking them to share their experience on social media with a specific hashtag or tag.
  - Example: "Love your new [Product Name]? Share a photo on Instagram and tag us @BrandName for a chance to be featured!"

2. Showcasing UGC on Your Website and Social Media

Once you've collected user-generated content, the next step is to showcase it prominently across your digital channels to provide social proof and inspire new customers.

Best Practices for Showcasing UGC:

- **Feature UGC on Product Pages**: Display customer photos or videos directly on your product pages to show potential buyers how others are using and enjoying the product.
    - Example: "Here's how our customers are using [Product Name]—scroll to see real customer photos!"
- **Create a UGC Gallery**: Dedicate a section of your website or landing page to a UGC gallery, where customers can browse photos and videos submitted by others. This creates a sense of community and shows real-world use cases for your product.
    - Example: "Check out our [Brand Name] community in action!"
- **Post UGC on Social Media**: Regularly repost user-generated content on your social media channels to build engagement and provide constant social proof. Be sure to credit the original poster and thank them for sharing their experience.
    - Example: "Loving this look from @CustomerName with our new [Product Name]—you look amazing!"

Conclusion

Social proof is one of the most effective tools for increasing conversions during a time-sensitive sales event. By collecting and showcasing **customer testimonials, reviews, and user-generated content**, you can build trust, reduce uncertainty, and provide the validation potential buyers need to make a purchase decision.

Whether through written testimonials, video reviews, or user-generated photos, integrating social proof into every step of your sales funnel can create a powerful sense of credibility and urgency, leading to higher sales and customer satisfaction. With the strategies outlined in this chapter, you'll be able to harness the full potential of social proof to drive more sales, boost customer confidence, and reach your goal of $100,000 in 24 hours.

Part 6: Post-Launch Optimization

Chapter 27: Turning Buyers Into Repeat Customers

One of the key elements of building a successful business is not only acquiring customers but turning them into **repeat buyers** who remain loyal to your brand over the long term. During a high-stakes sales event like generating $100,000 in 24 hours, the focus may be on driving immediate sales. However, the real value lies in your ability to **convert one-time buyers into lifelong clients**, creating a consistent revenue stream and building a loyal customer base that returns to purchase again and again.

In this chapter, we'll explore the strategies and tactics you can implement to nurture your relationship with customers after their first purchase, providing them with an exceptional experience that encourages repeat business. By understanding what motivates repeat purchases, using customer retention techniques, and implementing loyalty programs, you can transform first-time buyers into brand advocates who drive your business growth.

Step 1: Why Repeat Customers Are Essential to Long-Term Success

Before diving into tactics, it's important to understand why focusing on repeat customers is so crucial to long-term business success. While acquiring new customers is important, keeping those customers coming back can be even more valuable.

1. The Value of Repeat Customers

Repeat customers are **more valuable** than first-time buyers for several reasons:

- **Higher Lifetime Value (LTV)**: Repeat customers have a higher lifetime value because they make multiple purchases over time. The more a customer buys from you, the higher their overall contribution to your revenue.
  - Example: If a customer buys from you every 3 months, their value could be 5x or more compared to a one-time buyer.

- **Lower Customer Acquisition Costs (CAC)**: Acquiring new customers through ads, promotions, or marketing efforts can be expensive. With repeat customers, you've already made the initial investment, so every future purchase comes at a lower cost.
- **Word-of-Mouth Marketing**: Satisfied repeat customers are more likely to recommend your brand to friends and family, providing free word-of-mouth marketing that can lead to additional sales.
  - Example: A loyal customer may post about your product on social media, introducing their followers to your brand and driving new traffic.

2. The Psychology of Repeat Purchases

Customers are more likely to make repeat purchases when they feel connected to your brand, when they've had a positive experience, and when they trust that you'll continue to deliver value. Building customer loyalty requires **emotional connections**, **reliability**, and a sense of **belonging**.

Key Factors that Drive Repeat Purchases:

- **Trust and Satisfaction**: When customers are satisfied with their purchase and trust your brand, they're more likely to come back for more. Delivering on promises—whether it's quality, speed, or customer service—helps solidify that trust.
- **Convenience and Ease of Purchase**: Customers are more likely to repurchase when it's easy and convenient to do so. Streamlined checkout processes, fast shipping, and user-friendly websites contribute to a smooth customer experience that encourages repeat business.
- **Emotional Connection**: Customers who feel an emotional connection to your brand are more loyal. This connection could be built through shared values, exceptional customer service, or a brand identity that resonates with their lifestyle.

Step 2: Providing an Exceptional Post-Purchase Experience

The post-purchase experience is one of the most critical touchpoints in turning a one-time buyer into a repeat customer. By delivering value beyond the initial sale, you can create a lasting impression that encourages customers to return.

1. Personalized Post-Purchase Follow-Up

Once a customer has made a purchase, your next step is to continue the conversation. A well-crafted post-purchase email sequence can provide additional value, address potential concerns, and keep your brand top of mind.

Post-Purchase Email Sequence Ideas:

- **Thank You Email**: Send an immediate thank you email confirming the customer's order and expressing your appreciation for their business. This simple gesture helps build rapport and strengthens the relationship.
  - Example: "Thank you for your purchase, [Customer Name]! We're thrilled to have you as part of the [Brand Name] family. Your order is being processed, and we'll let you know once it ships."
- **Shipping Confirmation**: Follow up with a shipping confirmation email that includes tracking information, delivery expectations, and any additional information that might be helpful for the customer.
  - Example: "Good news! Your order is on its way. Track your shipment here: [Tracking Link]."
- **Product Usage Tips or Tutorials**: A few days after the product is delivered, send an email offering tips on how to get the most out of the product, a user guide, or a tutorial video. This not only adds value but also ensures customer satisfaction.
  - Example: "Now that you've received your [Product Name], here are some tips to help you get started!"

- **Customer Satisfaction Survey**: A week or two after the purchase, send a survey asking for feedback on the product and their experience. This shows that you value their opinion and are committed to continuous improvement.
  - Example: "How are you enjoying your [Product Name]? We'd love to hear your feedback."

2. Providing Outstanding Customer Support

Exceptional customer support is one of the key differentiators in building long-term customer loyalty. If a customer has an issue with their purchase, how you handle it can determine whether they become a repeat buyer or leave for a competitor.

Strategies for Outstanding Post-Purchase Support:

- **Easy Returns and Exchanges**: Make the process of returning or exchanging products simple and hassle-free. Customers are more likely to buy again if they know they can easily return items if needed.
  - Example: "Not 100% satisfied with your purchase? No problem! Start your return or exchange here: [Link]."
- **24/7 Customer Support**: Offer accessible customer support channels, such as live chat, email, or phone support, to assist customers with any post-purchase issues or questions.
  - Example: "Need help? Our support team is available 24/7 to answer any questions you may have."
- **Proactive Problem Solving**: If there's an issue with the product or delivery, proactively reach out to the customer to offer a solution, such as a refund, replacement, or discount on their next purchase.
  - Example: "We noticed there was a delay with your order, and we apologize for the inconvenience. To make it right, we're offering you 10% off your next purchase."

3. Personalizing the Customer Journey

Personalization plays a major role in customer retention. When customers feel like a brand understands their preferences, habits, and needs, they're more likely to return. Use customer data to tailor the post-purchase experience and make customers feel valued.

Ways to Personalize the Post-Purchase Experience:

- **Personalized Product Recommendations**: Use data from the customer's past purchases to recommend complementary products they might like in future emails or on the website.
  - Example: "Based on your recent purchase, you might love these items too: [Product Recommendations]."
- **Segmented Email Campaigns**: Create email campaigns tailored to specific customer segments based on their purchase history, interests, or behavior.
  - Example: Send an email to customers who have purchased skincare products recommending new arrivals in the same category.
- **Birthday or Anniversary Offers**: Send personalized offers to celebrate milestones, such as the anniversary of their first purchase or their birthday.
  - Example: "Happy Birthday, [Customer Name]! Enjoy 15% off your next order as our gift to you."

Step 3: Encouraging Repeat Purchases with Incentives

To encourage repeat purchases, consider offering incentives that motivate customers to return to your store. These incentives can range from special discounts to exclusive offers that make your brand stand out from competitors.

1. Offering Discounts and Special Promotions

One of the most effective ways to encourage repeat purchases is by offering exclusive discounts or promotions to your existing customers.

These offers make customers feel valued and appreciated while also providing a tangible reason to return.

Types of Promotions for Repeat Customers:

- **Exclusive Discounts**: Offer a special discount to customers who have made a previous purchase. This could be presented as a "thank you" for their loyalty.
    - Example: "Thank you for being a loyal customer! Enjoy 20% off your next order with code LOYALTY20."
- **Loyalty Discounts**: Offer increasing discounts based on the number of purchases a customer has made. For example, after their third purchase, they receive a higher discount than after their first purchase.
    - Example: "You've made 3 purchases with us—here's 25% off your next order as a thank you for your loyalty!"
- **Bundle Offers**: Encourage customers to purchase more by offering discounted bundles of complementary products.
    - Example: "Buy any 2 skincare products and get the 3rd one free!"

2. Launching a Loyalty Program

Loyalty programs reward customers for repeat purchases, creating a cycle where the more they buy, the more benefits they receive. These programs not only encourage customers to return but also foster long-term loyalty by making them feel part of an exclusive group.

How to Set Up an Effective Loyalty Program:

- **Points-Based System**: Set up a system where customers earn points for every purchase they make. These points can then be redeemed for discounts, free products, or special rewards.
    - Example: "Earn 10 points for every $1 spent! Redeem points for discounts on your next order."

- **Tiered Loyalty Program**: Offer different levels of rewards based on customer spending or engagement. The higher the tier, the more exclusive the rewards, creating an incentive for customers to increase their purchases.
  - Example: "Join our Silver, Gold, or Platinum tier loyalty program and unlock exclusive perks like early access to sales, free shipping, and more."
- **Referral Rewards**: Encourage repeat customers to refer friends and family in exchange for rewards. Not only does this generate new customers, but it also gives the original customer a reason to return.
  - Example: "Refer a friend and earn $10 off your next purchase when they place their first order."

3. Creating VIP and Exclusive Offers

Another powerful incentive to drive repeat purchases is offering VIP or **exclusive deals** that are only available to returning customers. This creates a sense of exclusivity and makes customers feel like they're part of a special group.

Exclusive Offer Strategies:

- **Early Access to New Products**: Give your repeat customers early access to new product launches before they're available to the general public.
  - Example: "As a valued customer, you're invited to shop our new collection before anyone else! Use code VIPEARLY for exclusive access."
- **Special VIP Events or Sales**: Host private sales or events for your best customers, offering them exclusive discounts or products that aren't available to others.
  - Example: "Join our VIP members-only sale and enjoy 30% off sitewide—this weekend only!"

- **Free Gifts with Purchase**: Offer returning customers a free gift with their next purchase as a reward for their loyalty.
  - Example: "As a thank you for being a loyal customer, enjoy a free travel-sized product with your next order!"

Step 4: Building Long-Term Customer Relationships

Building **long-term relationships** with your customers requires consistent effort, communication, and a focus on delivering value at every touchpoint. When customers feel connected to your brand and confident that you'll continue to meet their needs, they're far more likely to remain loyal over time.

1. Maintaining Consistent Communication

Stay top-of-mind with your customers by maintaining consistent, meaningful communication. This doesn't mean bombarding them with promotional emails—it means providing valuable content, up-dates, and offers that align with their interests and needs.

Best Practices for Consistent Customer Communication:

- **Regular Newsletters**: Send regular email newsletters that feature product updates, helpful content (such as tips or guides), and exclusive offers for subscribers.
  - Example: "Here's what's new this month at [Brand Name]—plus, enjoy 10% off your next order!"
- **Personalized Messages**: Use data to personalize your communication, such as sending product recommendations based on their purchase history or offering birthday discounts.
- **Engagement on Social Media**: Stay engaged with your customers on social media by responding to comments, sharing customer posts, and showcasing your brand's personality.

2. Continuously Adding Value

One of the best ways to build customer loyalty is by continuously adding value, even after the purchase. This could mean offering educational content, creating a sense of community, or providing unexpected bonuses that make customers feel appreciated.

Ways to Add Value for Repeat Customers:

- **Educational Content**: Provide ongoing value through educational content, such as how-to guides, tutorials, or webinars, that help customers get the most out of your products.
    - Example: "Check out our latest blog post: '5 Ways to Maximize Your Results with [Product Name].'"
- **Surprise and Delight**: Occasionally surprise customers with unexpected perks, such as free samples, handwritten notes, or bonus products in their orders.
    - Example: "We've included a little something extra in your order—enjoy this free sample of our new product!"
- **Exclusive Content and Community**: Create a sense of belonging by offering exclusive content, such as behind-the-scenes looks, early access to events, or a dedicated community space where customers can engage with each other and your brand.

3. Turning Customers Into Brand Advocates

Loyal repeat customers can become your brand's most powerful advocates. When customers love your products and have had consistently positive experiences, they're more likely to recommend you to their network, write positive reviews, and share their experience on social media.

Encouraging Customer Advocacy:

- **Referral Programs**: Offer incentives for customers to refer friends and family to your brand, rewarding both the referrer and the new customer.
    - Example: "Invite a friend to shop with us and you'll both get $15 off your next order!"

- **Social Media Sharing**: Encourage customers to share their experience with your brand on social media by offering prizes, reposting user-generated content, or simply asking for their feedback.
  - Example: "Love your new [Product Name]? Tag us in your post for a chance to be featured on our page!"
- **Positive Reviews**: Request reviews from satisfied customers, offering them a small incentive (such as a discount or free sample) for leaving feedback on your website or third-party platforms.
  - Example: "We'd love to hear your thoughts! Leave a review and get 10% off your next order as a thank you."

Conclusion

Turning one-time buyers into repeat customers is not only crucial for long-term success but also provides a sustainable foundation for consistent growth. By focusing on delivering exceptional post-purchase experiences, providing personalized incentives, and building strong relationships, you can create a loyal customer base that continues to return to your brand, purchase again, and spread the word.

With the strategies outlined in this chapter, you'll be well-equipped to nurture repeat business, turn customers into lifelong clients, and create a customer experience that encourages loyalty and advocacy. By investing in your existing customers, you'll increase your lifetime customer value and drive the sustained growth of your brand well beyond your initial 24-hour sales campaign.

Chapter 28: Scaling Beyond the First 24 Hours

After achieving the impressive milestone of generating $100,000 in 24 hours, the challenge becomes how to **capitalize on that momentum** and continue generating revenue consistently. While the initial campaign's success sets a solid foundation, long-term growth requires a strategic plan to **scale beyond the launch**, ensuring ongoing sales, customer retention, and a sustainable business model.

This chapter will delve into strategies to keep the momentum going, including expanding your reach, improving your processes, and optimizing your marketing. We'll explore how to take the success of the initial 24-hour campaign and convert it into long-term profitability through customer retention, scaling operations, and diversifying your income streams.

Step 1: Analyzing the 24-Hour Campaign Results

Before you can effectively scale, it's important to understand **what worked** in the first 24 hours. By analyzing the performance of your initial campaign, you can identify key drivers of success and areas for improvement. This insight will guide your next steps and ensure that your scaling efforts are targeted and efficient.

1. Measure Key Metrics

Start by examining the key performance indicators (KPIs) of your campaign. These metrics will help you determine which areas to expand on and which aspects to tweak or optimize.

Metrics to Analyze:

- **Conversion Rate**: What percentage of visitors converted into paying customers? How did this vary by traffic source, product type, or campaign? Understanding where conversions were strongest helps you target your most valuable channels for future growth.
    - Example: If Facebook ads had a 10% conversion rate compared to email marketing's 3%, focusing more on paid social media might yield better results.

- **Traffic Sources**: Identify the best-performing traffic sources during your campaign. Did paid ads, organic traffic, email campaigns, or social media generate the most sales? This analysis helps you invest in the highest-return channels moving forward.
  - Example: Instagram might have driven 60% of traffic but only resulted in 20% of sales, suggesting the need to optimize content for conversions.
- **Average Order Value (AOV)**: Calculate the AOV during your 24-hour sale. Were there opportunities for upselling or bundling that could have increased the AOV? Understanding this metric helps you explore ways to boost revenue without necessarily increasing customer numbers.
- **Customer Acquisition Cost (CAC)**: How much did you spend on marketing to acquire each customer? If CAC is too high, refining your marketing strategy could help reduce costs in future campaigns.

By measuring these KPIs, you'll have a clearer picture of what worked well and where adjustments are needed.

2. Gather Customer Feedback

Post-campaign, it's essential to gather **customer feedback** to understand their experience. This can provide valuable insights into how to improve your product, sales process, or customer service, all of which impact future sales.

Ways to Collect Feedback:

- **Post-Purchase Surveys**: Send out a short survey asking customers about their experience with the purchase process, product quality, and any suggestions for improvement.
  - Example: "How satisfied are you with your purchase? What could we improve?"

- **Email Follow-Ups**: Encourage customers to reply to a follow-up email with their thoughts on the buying experience and the product itself.
- **Social Media Engagement**: Monitor social media for customer comments, reviews, or posts about your product, as these can provide candid feedback.

Customer feedback not only helps refine your product and sales process but also builds trust by showing that you care about their opinions.

Step 2: Building on Success With Immediate Post-Campaign Actions

The hours and days immediately after your 24-hour campaign are crucial for keeping the energy alive. Instead of letting the momentum fizzle out, you need to take proactive steps to maintain customer engagement and drive additional sales.

1. Offer Follow-Up Promotions

A follow-up promotion or **flash sale** aimed at the same audience can extend the excitement generated by the initial campaign. By offering time-sensitive discounts, you can capitalize on customers who may have missed the original sale or want to buy more.

Examples of Follow-Up Promotions:

- **Exclusive Discount for New Buyers**: Offer a small discount (e.g., 10-15%) to customers who bought during the 24-hour campaign, encouraging them to make a second purchase.
  - Example: "Loved your recent purchase? Get 15% off your next order—valid for the next 48 hours only!"
- **Second-Chance Offer**: For customers who didn't convert during the 24-hour sale, send a "last chance" email with a limited-time offer.

    ◦ Example: "Missed out? Our sale was so popular that we're extending it for another 24 hours—don't miss your final chance to save!"

2. Implement Upselling and Cross-Selling Strategies

Now that you've acquired a wave of new customers, it's essential to increase **customer lifetime value** (CLV) by encouraging them to purchase more or higher-value products. Upselling and cross-selling are effective strategies to maximize revenue without acquiring new customers.

Tactics for Upselling and Cross-Selling:

- **Product Recommendations**: Use email campaigns or website pop-ups to suggest complementary products based on the customer's initial purchase.
    - ◦ Example: "You purchased [Product A]—complete the set with [Product B] at a special price."
- **Loyalty Discounts**: Offer returning customers an exclusive discount for upgrading to a premium version of the product or purchasing additional items.
    - ◦ Example: "Upgrade to the premium edition of [Product Name] and save 20%—offer valid for returning customers only."

3. Optimize Post-Purchase Email Sequences

A strong **post-purchase email sequence** can nurture new customers into loyal, repeat buyers. Use this opportunity to build a deeper connection with your audience and introduce them to more of your product line.

Effective Post-Purchase Emails:

- **Thank-You Email**: Immediately after purchase, send a thank-you email that reinforces the customer's positive decision and sets the stage for future communication.
    - Example: "Thank you for your purchase! We're thrilled to have you as part of the [Brand Name] community."
- **Product Use Tips and Guides**: A few days later, send an email offering helpful tips on how to get the most out of the product. This not only adds value but also enhances customer satisfaction.
    - Example: "Here are 5 ways to make the most of your new [Product Name]."
- **Referral Program Invitation**: Introduce your referral program (if applicable) to incentivize customers to refer friends or family, further extending your reach.
    - Example: "Love your purchase? Share it with a friend and earn $10 off your next order!"

Step 3: Expanding Your Reach With New Marketing Strategies

Scaling beyond the first 24 hours requires **expanding your reach** to new audiences and optimizing your marketing strategies to attract more potential buyers. This can be done by broadening your advertising efforts, creating ongoing content, and leveraging partnerships.

1. Invest in Paid Advertising

If paid ads were a major driver of success during the 24-hour campaign, now is the time to **scale those efforts**. Reinvest some of the revenue generated from the initial campaign into expanding your ad reach, experimenting with new platforms, and targeting different customer segments.

Paid Advertising Tactics for Scaling:

- **Lookalike Audiences**: Use Facebook, Instagram, or Google's algorithms to create lookalike audiences based on your existing customers. This allows you to target people who are likely to have similar interests and behaviors as those who purchased during your 24-hour sale.
    - Example: "We generated $100,000 in 24 hours using Facebook Ads. Now, let's create a lookalike audience to scale those results."
- **Retargeting Campaigns**: Retarget visitors who showed interest during the campaign but didn't convert. Use ads to bring them back to your site and offer a new incentive.
    - Example: "You browsed [Product Name]—come back and get 10% off your first order!"
- **Expanding to New Ad Platforms**: Test new advertising platforms such as TikTok, Pinterest, or YouTube to reach untapped audiences.
    - Example: "Our Facebook ads worked well—let's replicate that success on TikTok with a product demo video."

2. Leverage Content Marketing for Ongoing Engagement

Content marketing can help maintain momentum by keeping your brand top-of-mind and continuously engaging your audience. Creating **valuable content** that speaks to your customers' needs, interests, and pain points can drive organic traffic, build your brand authority, and increase sales over time.

Content Marketing Strategies:

- **Create Blog Posts**: Write blog posts that provide solutions to your customers' problems, using your products as the ideal solution. SEO-optimized content can help drive organic traffic to your site.
  - Example: "5 Ways to Improve Your Home Office Using [Product Name]" (with links to your products throughout the article).
- **Build a YouTube Channel**: Video content is highly engaging and can showcase your product in action. Create how-to videos, product demonstrations, and customer testimonials to attract new audiences.
  - Example: "Watch how [Product Name] can streamline your morning routine."
- **Email Newsletters**: Keep your customers engaged by sending regular newsletters that feature product updates, tips, customer success stories, and special offers.
  - Example: "Stay in the loop! Here's what's new at [Brand Name] this month."

3. Establish Strategic Partnerships

Partnering with **influencers, affiliates, or complementary brands** can help you expand your reach to new audiences. These collaborations allow you to tap into established customer bases and gain credibility through trusted recommendations.

Examples of Strategic Partnerships:

- **Influencer Collaborations**: Partner with influencers who align with your brand to promote your products through sponsored posts, reviews, or giveaways.

- Example: "Collaborate with influencers in the health and wellness space to promote your products to their engaged followers."
- **Affiliate Marketing**: Set up an affiliate program where content creators or bloggers earn a commission for promoting your products and driving sales.
  - Example: "Invite bloggers in your niche to join your affiliate program and earn 10% commission on every sale they generate."
- **Brand Collaborations**: Team up with complementary brands to offer exclusive bundles or co-branded products, creating opportunities to cross-promote to each other's audiences.
  - Example: "Partner with a skincare brand to offer a wellness bundle that includes both companies' best-sellers."

Step 4: Scaling Operations for Long-Term Growth

As you expand your reach and drive more sales, you'll need to ensure that your **operations** can handle the increased demand. Efficient fulfillment, strong customer service, and effective inventory management are crucial to sustaining long-term growth.

1. Streamline Fulfillment and Shipping

Scaling your sales means you'll need to **streamline your fulfillment process** to keep up with demand while ensuring fast, reliable delivery. Delays or mistakes can harm your reputation, so it's important to optimize logistics early on.

Fulfillment Strategies:

- **Partner with a Fulfillment Center**: If you anticipate ongoing high-volume sales, consider outsourcing to a fulfillment center that can handle storage, packing, and shipping.
  - Example: "Outsource order fulfillment to a third-party logistics provider (3PL) to focus on scaling the business without being overwhelmed by logistics."

- **Automate Inventory Management**: Use inventory management software to track stock levels, set reorder alerts, and prevent stockouts or over-ordering.
  - Example: "Automate inventory tracking to ensure we're always well-stocked for our best-selling products."
- **Negotiate Shipping Rates**: As you scale, negotiate better shipping rates with carriers to reduce costs and offer competitive shipping options to your customers.
  - Example: "Leverage higher order volumes to negotiate discounts with shipping providers."

2. Enhance Customer Support

As your customer base grows, maintaining excellent **customer support** becomes even more important. Investing in customer service tools and automation ensures that you can scale your support operations without compromising the quality of service.

Customer Support Scaling Tactics:

- **Live Chat and Chatbots**: Implement live chat or AI-driven chatbots on your website to handle common customer queries and provide instant support, reducing the burden on your team.
  - Example: "Set up a chatbot to answer common questions like 'Where's my order?' or 'What are your return policies?'"
- **Outsource Customer Service**: If your customer service team is overwhelmed, consider outsourcing to a reputable service provider that can handle customer inquiries and issues professionally.
  - Example: "Hire a customer support agency to manage phone, email, and chat inquiries as we scale."
- **Proactive Communication**: Keep customers informed with proactive communication, such as order updates, shipment track-

ing, and issue resolution emails, to build trust and reduce support requests.

Step 5: Diversifying Income Streams for Long-Term Stability

To scale beyond the 24-hour campaign, it's essential to **diversify your income streams**. Relying solely on one product or sales channel can limit growth and expose your business to risk. By introducing new products, exploring different sales models, and expanding your revenue streams, you can build a more resilient and scalable business.

1. Introduce New Products or Services

One of the easiest ways to scale is by expanding your product line or introducing complementary services. New products can attract both returning customers and new buyers, increasing your overall revenue potential.

Ideas for New Products/Services:

- **Upsell Premium Versions**: Offer upgraded or premium versions of your original product with enhanced features or higher value.
    - Example: "Launch a premium edition of [Product Name] with additional features at a higher price point."
- **Offer Subscription Services**: If applicable, consider introducing a subscription model where customers receive your product on a recurring basis.
    - Example: "Launch a subscription box for monthly deliveries of your product, providing customers with a hassle-free experience."
- **Expand to New Categories**: Introduce related product categories to serve a wider range of customer needs.
    - Example: "Expand your skincare line to include haircare or wellness products, appealing to a broader customer base."

2. Explore New Sales Channels

Scaling your business often requires expanding beyond your current sales channels. Diversifying where and how you sell can help you reach new audiences and reduce reliance on a single platform.

Sales Channel Expansion Strategies:

- **Sell on Marketplaces**: Expand to popular online marketplaces like Amazon, eBay, or Etsy to reach new customers who may not be familiar with your brand.
    - Example: "Launch your best-selling products on Amazon to tap into a global customer base."
- **Retail Partnerships**: If applicable, partner with physical retailers or boutiques to stock your products, creating an additional revenue stream.
    - Example: "Partner with local boutique stores to feature your products on their shelves."
- **Wholesale or B2B**: Explore the option of selling your products wholesale to other businesses or retailers, creating a steady revenue stream through bulk sales.
    - Example: "Offer wholesale pricing for bulk orders to retailers or businesses looking to stock your products."

3. Launch Membership Programs

Another way to create long-term stability is by launching a **membership program** that offers exclusive benefits to your most loyal customers. Memberships provide consistent revenue and incentivize customers to stay engaged with your brand.

Examples of Membership Models:

- **Paid Membership**: Offer a paid membership that provides members with exclusive discounts, early access to new products, or free shipping.
    - Example: "Join our VIP membership for $99/year and enjoy 20% off all purchases, free shipping, and early access to sales."
- **Rewards-Based Membership**: Launch a loyalty program where customers earn points for each purchase, which can be redeemed for discounts or free products.
    - Example: "Earn 1 point for every $1 spent—redeem points for exclusive rewards and discounts!"

Conclusion

Scaling beyond your first 24-hour campaign requires a combination of **strategic marketing**, **optimized operations**, and **diversified revenue streams**. By analyzing the success of your initial campaign, maintaining customer engagement through upselling and follow-up promotions, and expanding your reach through new marketing efforts, you can build on your momentum and ensure long-term, sustainable growth.

With the right tactics in place, you'll be able to turn the short-term excitement of a 24-hour sales campaign into a powerful, scalable business model that continues to generate revenue and grow your brand for years to come. By constantly iterating, improving, and diversifying, you can transform your $100,000 launch into ongoing success and create a thriving business that reaches new heights.

Chapter 29: Debrief and Data Analysis

After a successful 24-hour campaign that generated $100,000 in sales, the next critical step is conducting a **debrief** and performing a detailed **data analysis**. Understanding the metrics and insights gained from this intensive campaign will allow you to optimize future launches, improve marketing strategies, and fine-tune your sales funnel for even greater success.

In this chapter, we'll break down the process of reviewing your campaign performance, analyzing the data, and drawing actionable insights. This comprehensive analysis will help you replicate your successes, fix any shortcomings, and implement data-driven decisions for future campaigns.

Step 1: The Importance of a Post-Campaign Debrief

A debrief allows you to evaluate what worked, what didn't, and how your team and processes performed during the 24-hour sales event. Without this reflection, you miss valuable opportunities for learning and growth, which are essential for scaling and optimizing future campaigns.

1. The Purpose of the Debrief

The purpose of a debrief is to gather all the information about your campaign performance, customer interactions, sales metrics, and team execution to improve upon in future campaigns.

Objectives of a Debrief:

- **Identify Strengths**: What went well during the campaign? Which aspects exceeded expectations? Highlighting your campaign's strengths helps you double down on the most effective strategies.

- **Pinpoint Weaknesses**: Where were the bottlenecks or challenges? Identifying issues helps you troubleshoot and correct them before your next launch.
- **Generate Insights for Growth**: What data or trends emerged that could guide future campaigns? Identifying key trends will allow you to scale more effectively.
- **Evaluate Team and Process Efficiency**: How well did your team execute the campaign plan? Were there any operational inefficiencies that could be streamlined for better performance next time?

Conducting a thorough debrief ensures you approach the next campaign with a deeper understanding and a more optimized process.

2. How to Conduct a Debrief

To ensure your debrief is thorough and effective, consider gathering input from all team members involved in the campaign. This could include marketing, sales, customer support, fulfillment, and technical teams.

Debrief Steps:

- **Hold a Team Meeting**: Schedule a post-campaign meeting where each team member can share their insights, observations, and feedback.
- **Review Campaign Metrics**: Bring in relevant data on sales performance, traffic, conversions, and customer behavior to the meeting.
- **Document Key Findings**: Keep a record of key takeaways, focusing on both qualitative feedback (team experience) and quantitative insights (data analysis).
- **Highlight Action Items**: Identify clear next steps and assign responsibilities for addressing issues or capitalizing on successes.

By gathering insights from all angles, you'll have a complete view of what happened during the campaign and how to improve.

Step 2: Analyzing Sales and Marketing Data

Once the debrief is complete, it's time to dig deeper into the **data** to extract actionable insights. By examining your campaign metrics, you can understand where your revenue came from, how effective each element of the campaign was, and how to refine future strategies.

1. Sales Performance Metrics

The most critical aspect of your data analysis will involve evaluating how your sales performed during the 24-hour window. This includes looking at your overall sales numbers, the performance of specific products, and the behavior of your customers throughout the funnel.

Key Sales Metrics to Analyze:

- **Total Revenue**: Calculate your total revenue during the 24-hour campaign. How does this compare to your $100,000 goal? Did certain product categories or offers contribute more to the total than others?
    - Example: "We generated $120,000 in revenue, with 60% coming from our premium product bundle."
- **Sales by Product**: Break down sales by individual products to see which ones performed the best. Were there any surprises in terms of top sellers or underperforming products?
    - Example: "Product A accounted for 40% of sales, while Product B underperformed with only 10%."
- **Average Order Value (AOV)**: Calculate the average order value during the campaign. Did customers purchase more when presented with upsells or cross-sells?
    - Example: "Our AOV was $150, driven by successful upsell offers."
- **Conversion Rate**: Review the overall conversion rate, as well as the conversion rates for different customer segments or traffic sources. This will help you understand where your highest-value

customers came from and where you might have lost potential buyers.

- ◦ Example: "Our website had a conversion rate of 8%, but traffic from Instagram ads only converted at 3%, indicating the need for further optimization."

By breaking down sales metrics, you'll gain a clearer picture of how to allocate resources, optimize product offerings, and improve conversion strategies in future campaigns.

2. Marketing Performance Metrics

Next, analyze the performance of your **marketing channels** to see which strategies drove the most traffic, conversions, and revenue. Understanding how each marketing channel performed will allow you to allocate budgets more effectively for future campaigns.

Marketing Metrics to Review:

- **Traffic by Source**: Break down traffic by source (organic, paid ads, social media, email marketing, etc.) to see which channels brought in the most visitors and which converted the best.
  - ◦ Example: "Paid traffic accounted for 70% of sales, with Facebook Ads driving the highest volume."
- **Cost Per Acquisition (CPA)**: For each marketing channel, calculate the cost per acquisition. How much did it cost to acquire a customer from each platform, and how does that compare to the revenue they generated?
  - ◦ Example: "Our CPA on Google Ads was $25, while Facebook Ads had a CPA of $18, making Facebook more cost-effective."
- **Email Campaign Performance**: Review the open rates, click-through rates, and conversion rates of your email marketing efforts. Did certain emails outperform others in terms of driving sales?

- ◦ Example: "The final 'last chance' email had a 40% open rate and drove 15% of total sales."
- **Ad Performance**: If you ran paid ads, look at which ad creatives, targeting strategies, and platforms delivered the best return on ad spend (ROAS).
  - ◦ Example: "Our Instagram Stories ads generated a 4x ROAS, while Google Display ads only achieved a 1.5x ROAS."

This data will help you refine your marketing strategy and determine which channels to prioritize for future campaigns.

3. Customer Behavior and Segmentation

Understanding how different segments of your audience behaved during the campaign can reveal valuable insights for improving personalization and targeting in future campaigns. Segment your customer base to see who spent the most, who engaged the most, and which offers resonated with different demographics.

Customer Segmentation Metrics:

- **New vs. Returning Customers**: Break down your sales into new customers vs. returning customers. Were your existing customers more likely to buy, or did you bring in a significant number of new buyers?
  - ◦ Example: "60% of sales came from new customers, indicating a successful campaign in terms of customer acquisition."
- **Customer Lifetime Value (CLV)**: For returning customers, calculate their CLV and see how that compares to new customers. This can help you determine the potential long-term value of newly acquired buyers.
  - ◦ Example: "Returning customers had a higher CLV of $300 compared to $150 for new customers."

- **Geographic Segmentation**: Analyze where your customers came from. Did certain regions or countries convert better than others? Understanding geographical data can help you refine your targeting for future campaigns.
  - ∘ Example: "We saw the highest conversion rates from the U.S. and U.K., but lower conversion rates in Canada and Australia."
- **Behavioral Segmentation**: Examine how customers interacted with your site. Did certain types of users spend more time on specific product pages or respond better to certain offers?
  - ∘ Example: "Customers who engaged with the product demo video had a 20% higher conversion rate than those who didn't."

By segmenting your audience and analyzing their behavior, you can tailor your messaging and offers to specific customer groups, increasing your chances of driving conversions.

Step 3: Analyzing Customer Experience and Feedback

Your customers' experience during the campaign plays a significant role in your long-term success. By analyzing customer feedback and experience-related metrics, you can improve future campaigns and reduce friction in the buyer journey.

1. Customer Satisfaction Metrics

Measuring customer satisfaction post-purchase is essential for retaining customers and turning them into repeat buyers. Use surveys, feedback forms, and reviews to gauge how satisfied your customers were with their experience.

Metrics to Measure Customer Satisfaction:

- **Net Promoter Score (NPS)**: This is a popular customer loyalty metric that measures how likely customers are to recommend your product to others. Send out a post-purchase survey asking customers how likely they are to refer your product on a scale of 1-10.

- Example: "Our NPS score was 85, indicating high satisfaction and a likelihood of referrals."

- **Customer Reviews and Testimonials**: Encourage customers to leave reviews and testimonials about their experience. Analyze both positive and negative reviews to identify patterns.
  - Example: "Customers praised our fast shipping but mentioned that the product packaging could be improved."

- **Customer Support Interactions**: Review how many customers contacted support during the campaign and what the nature of their inquiries was. Were there common issues, such as problems with the checkout process, product confusion, or shipping delays?
  - Example: "30% of support inquiries were related to shipping questions, indicating a need for clearer communication during checkout."

Understanding customer satisfaction will help you address any issues that could negatively impact future campaigns and boost loyalty among new customers.

2. Analyze Checkout and Fulfillment Processes

Any friction in the checkout or fulfillment process can lead to cart abandonment, negative customer experiences, and lost sales. Use data from your checkout funnel and fulfillment system to identify areas for improvement.

Checkout and Fulfillment Metrics to Review:

- **Cart Abandonment Rate**: How many customers added products to their cart but didn't complete the purchase? A high cart abandonment rate could indicate issues with pricing transparency, payment options, or trust.

- ◦ Example: "Our cart abandonment rate was 40%, with many drop-offs happening at the shipping cost stage."
- **Checkout Completion Rate**: Measure how many customers who initiated the checkout process completed their purchase. A low completion rate might suggest the need to simplify your checkout process.
  - ◦ Example: "Our checkout completion rate was 85%, with a slight drop at the payment stage."
- **Fulfillment Speed**: How quickly were orders fulfilled after purchase? Delays in shipping or fulfillment can negatively affect customer satisfaction and lead to negative reviews or refund requests.
  - ◦ Example: "Fulfillment times averaged 48 hours, but we had some delays due to a high volume of orders. We may need to partner with a third-party fulfillment provider next time."

Optimizing your checkout and fulfillment processes can reduce friction and increase customer satisfaction, leading to higher conversion rates and repeat business in future campaigns.

Step 4: Drawing Actionable Insights for Future Campaigns

Once you've gathered and analyzed all relevant data, the next step is to draw **actionable insights** that will inform your future campaigns. By understanding the key takeaways from your analysis, you can refine your approach and ensure even greater success the next time around.

1. Identify High-Impact Strategies

Look for the strategies that had the biggest positive impact on your campaign and focus on expanding or replicating them in future launches.

Examples of High-Impact Insights:

- **Best-Performing Traffic Sources**: If a particular traffic source, such as Facebook Ads or your email list, delivered exceptional results, allocate more resources to those channels in future campaigns.

  ◦ Example: "Facebook Ads generated 50% of our sales at a low CPA—let's increase our ad spend there for the next campaign."

- **Successful Product Bundling**: If certain product bundles or offers performed better than expected, create similar bundles in future campaigns to maximize AOV.

  ◦ Example: "Our premium product bundle sold out quickly, so we'll introduce more bundle options next time."

2. Address Underperforming Areas

It's equally important to identify any **underperforming areas** of the campaign so that you can address them and improve for the future. These might include marketing channels with a low ROI, underwhelming product offers, or issues with customer support.

Examples of Actionable Improvements:

- **Optimize Underperforming Ads**: If certain ads didn't convert well, analyze the messaging, targeting, or design to see where improvements can be made. Consider A/B testing different creatives or audiences in the next campaign.

  ◦ Example: "Our Google Ads didn't perform as well as expected—let's test different headlines and retargeting strategies next time."

- **Improve Checkout Flow**: If you had a high cart abandonment rate, optimize the checkout process by reducing steps, offering guest checkout, or making shipping costs more transparent upfront.

  ◦ Example: "We'll simplify the checkout process by removing unnecessary form fields and offering free shipping for orders over $100."

3. Set Clear Goals for Future Campaigns

Based on your data analysis, set **clear goals** for your next campaign. These goals should be specific, measurable, and aligned with the insights you gained from the debrief and data review.

Examples of Future Campaign Goals:

- **Increase Conversion Rate**: Set a goal to increase the conversion rate by a specific percentage, based on improvements to your sales funnel or marketing strategy.
  - Example: "Our goal is to increase the conversion rate by 5% in the next campaign through optimized landing pages and targeted email sequences."
- **Lower CPA**: If your customer acquisition cost was high, set a goal to reduce it by refining your ad targeting or investing in more cost-effective channels.
  - Example: "We aim to lower CPA by 15% by shifting more of our budget to high-ROI platforms like Instagram Stories."

Conclusion

A thorough debrief and data analysis are essential for understanding the full impact of your 24-hour campaign and identifying the key drivers of success and areas for improvement. By analyzing sales performance, marketing effectiveness, customer behavior, and feedback, you can refine your strategy and optimize future campaigns for even greater results.

This chapter equips you with the tools and frameworks needed to draw actionable insights from your campaign data, ensuring that each subsequent launch builds on the success of the last. By continuously improving based on data-driven decisions, you can replicate and scale your $100,000 campaign to achieve even more ambitious goals in the future.

Chapter 30: Leveraging Success for Future Launches

Achieving $100,000 in sales within 24 hours is a remarkable feat, but the true power lies in turning that success into a **repeatable business model**. The goal is to use the momentum, insights, and strategies that led to your initial success to consistently generate high revenue with each future launch. By refining your processes, improving your products or offers, and replicating the elements that worked, you can build a scalable and sustainable system that drives significant sales with every campaign.

In this chapter, we'll explore how to transform your $100,000 success into a formula you can apply to future launches. This involves optimizing your launch strategy, enhancing customer relationships, and creating a framework that ensures your business remains profitable over the long term.

Step 1: Establishing a Repeatable Launch Framework

The foundation of turning a one-time success into a repeatable business model is creating a **launch framework** that you can use for future campaigns. By systematizing your process, you'll be able to execute each launch efficiently, ensuring you can replicate your results and even improve upon them.

1. Documenting Your Launch Process

Start by documenting every step of your $100,000 launch, from initial planning through execution. This helps ensure that you and your team can replicate the exact same steps (or refine them) for the next launch.

Elements to Document:

- **Campaign Timeline**: Create a detailed timeline that includes key milestones such as product creation, marketing prep, content creation, ad launch, email sequences, and customer outreach.

- Example: "Week 1: Finalize product. Week 2: Create landing page and email copy. Week 3: Launch ads. Week 4: Open cart for 24-hour sale."
- **Marketing Strategy**: Record which marketing strategies and platforms were most effective in driving traffic and conversions.
  - Example: "Facebook Ads generated 60% of traffic, email marketing converted at 8%, and Instagram Stories drove significant engagement."
- **Sales Funnel**: Document how your sales funnel performed, from landing pages to checkout. Were there any key touchpoints that contributed most to conversions?
  - Example: "Landing page conversion rate: 10%. Cart abandonment rate: 15%. Upsells contributed 25% of total revenue."
- **Team Responsibilities**: Outline the roles and responsibilities of each team member, from copywriting and design to customer support and fulfillment.

By documenting the entire process, you create a **launch blueprint** that can be used as a guide for future campaigns.

2. Creating a Launch Checklist

Turn your documented process into a **launch checklist** that you can follow for every future launch. This checklist should include all the tasks, deadlines, and deliverables necessary for executing a successful campaign.

Sample Launch Checklist:

- **Product Development**:
  - Finalize product or offer
  - Ensure product inventory is ready (if physical product)
  - Set up product in eCommerce platform
- **Marketing Prep**:
  - Write sales page copy and design

- Create email sequences (pre-launch, launch day, cart abandonment, follow-ups)
  - Design ad creatives and copy
  - Set up retargeting ads
- **Technical Setup**:
  - Set up sales funnel (landing page, checkout page, thank-you page)
  - Test payment processing and checkout flow
  - Ensure email list is segmented and ready
- **Launch Day Tasks**:
  - Send out launch emails
  - Monitor traffic and conversion metrics
  - Respond to customer inquiries and comments
  - Optimize ads and retargeting in real time
  - Track revenue in real time and adjust strategies as needed

With this checklist, you'll have a clear roadmap to follow for each launch, making it easier to maintain consistency and efficiency.

Step 2: Scaling Your Offer and Expanding Your Reach

To consistently replicate and grow your success, it's essential to **scale your offer** and expand your reach. This involves increasing the visibility of your launches, attracting new customers, and offering products or services that provide even greater value.

1. Expanding to New Audiences

One of the most effective ways to scale your future launches is by **reaching new audiences**. By leveraging new marketing channels, audiences, and partnerships, you can increase the potential pool of customers for each launch.

Strategies to Reach New Audiences:

- **Leverage Lookalike Audiences**: Use data from your existing customer base to create lookalike audiences on platforms like Facebook or Google Ads. These are people who share similar characteristics and behaviors to your best customers, making them more likely to convert.

- ○ Example: "Create a lookalike audience based on high-spending customers from the initial $100,000 launch."

- **Influencer and Affiliate Marketing**: Partner with influencers or affiliates who can introduce your product to their followers. This can significantly boost your reach, especially if the influencer's audience is aligned with your target market.
  - ○ Example: "Collaborate with industry influencers to promote your next launch through sponsored posts or affiliate partnerships."

- **Expand to New Marketing Channels**: Test new platforms, such as YouTube, Pinterest, or TikTok, to see if they offer access to untapped audiences that can further scale your reach.
  - ○ Example: "Create video content for TikTok that showcases product benefits and targets younger demographics."

Expanding your reach ensures that each new launch builds on your previous successes and taps into new customer segments.

2. Offering Tiered Pricing or Premium Versions

Another effective way to scale your offer is by introducing **tiered pricing** or premium versions of your product. This allows you to cater to different customer segments—those who are willing to pay more for additional value and those who may want a more affordable entry-level option.

Examples of Tiered Pricing Models:

- **Basic, Standard, and Premium Tiers**: Offer different versions of the product at varying price points. The higher tiers include additional features, services, or bonuses that justify a premium price.

- Example: "Offer a basic version for $100, a standard version with added bonuses for $250, and a premium version with exclusive content for $500."
- **Upsells and Add-Ons**: Provide customers with opportunities to purchase add-ons or upgrades during the checkout process. This can increase your average order value (AOV) without requiring new customer acquisition.
  - Example: "Offer an upsell for a VIP package that includes one-on-one coaching or an extended warranty."

By offering multiple tiers or premium options, you can maximize revenue from each customer, catering to those who are willing to invest more in your product or service.

3. Creating Evergreen and Automated Launches

While your initial $100,000 success may have come from a time-sensitive 24-hour campaign, you can expand your revenue potential by creating **evergreen** versions of your launch that continue generating sales automatically.

How to Build an Evergreen Launch:

- **Automate the Sales Funnel**: Set up an automated sales funnel that runs continuously. This could involve using paid traffic or content marketing to drive people to your landing page, where they can purchase the product at any time.
  - Example: "Turn your 24-hour campaign into an evergreen funnel that uses retargeting ads and email sequences to drive ongoing sales."
- **Evergreen Email Campaigns**: Create an automated email sequence that nurtures new subscribers and directs them to your product over time. These emails can educate potential customers, address objections, and eventually drive them to purchase.
  - Example: "Set up a 7-email sequence that nurtures new subscribers before pitching them the product."

- **Optimize for Consistent Conversions**: Continuously optimize your funnel based on the data from your previous launches. Track conversion rates, split-test landing pages, and refine your messaging to keep the funnel performing well over time.
  - Example: "Test different headline variations on your sales page to see which one drives higher conversions for the evergreen launch."

An evergreen launch system allows you to generate revenue on autopilot, reducing the need to constantly create time-limited campaigns.

Step 3: Building a Customer-Centric Business Model

To ensure long-term success, it's essential to build a **customer-centric business model** that focuses on nurturing relationships, retaining customers, and encouraging repeat purchases. Loyal customers are the foundation of any successful business, as they tend to spend more over time and advocate for your brand.

1. Nurturing Customer Relationships

Strong customer relationships lead to repeat purchases, higher customer lifetime value (CLV), and valuable word-of-mouth marketing. To build these relationships, focus on **delivering value** beyond the initial sale.

Tactics for Nurturing Relationships:

- **Consistent Communication**: Stay in touch with customers through regular email newsletters, offering them exclusive content, product tips, and updates on upcoming launches.
  - Example: "Send a monthly email newsletter that provides helpful content and early access to future products."
- **Loyalty Programs**: Implement a loyalty program that rewards customers for repeat purchases or referrals, incentivizing them to continue buying from you.

- Example: "Create a points-based loyalty program where customers earn points for every purchase, redeemable for discounts or free products."
- **Personalized Offers**: Use customer data to personalize marketing messages and offers based on their previous purchases or behavior.
  - Example: "Send personalized product recommendations based on a customer's buying history."

By nurturing your customer base, you can build long-term relationships that lead to consistent, recurring revenue.

2. Turning Customers Into Brand Advocates

Satisfied customers can become your best brand advocates, spreading the word about your product and driving new customers to your business through **word-of-mouth marketing**.

Strategies for Turning Customers Into Advocates:

- **Referral Programs**: Encourage satisfied customers to refer their friends and family in exchange for rewards or discounts.
  - Example: "Offer customers a $10 credit for every successful referral, with no limit on how many people they can refer."
- **Social Proof**: Encourage customers to leave reviews, testimonials, and social media posts about your product. Highlight these reviews on your website and marketing materials to build trust with potential buyers.
  - Example: "Feature user-generated content and customer testimonials prominently on your sales page."
- **Create a Community**: Build a sense of community around your brand by offering exclusive Facebook groups, webinars, or live events where customers can engage with each other and with you.
  - Example: "Create a private Facebook group where customers can share tips, ask questions, and connect with others who've purchased your product."

When customers feel connected to your brand, they're more likely to promote your product and bring in new customers organically.

Step 4: Refining and Scaling Over Time

The key to maintaining a successful, repeatable business model is **continuous improvement**. Even after reaching $100,000 in 24 hours, you should always look for ways to optimize and scale further.

1. Refining Your Offers and Products

As your business grows, you'll need to refine your offers to meet evolving customer needs, introduce new features, and stay competitive in the market.

Ways to Refine Your Offer:

- **Product Upgrades**: Continuously improve your products or services based on customer feedback. Introducing new features or addressing pain points can increase customer satisfaction and drive repeat purchases.
  - Example: "Release an updated version of your product with new features based on customer feedback."
- **Seasonal Offers**: Introduce seasonal or limited-time offers to create urgency and increase sales during specific times of the year.
  - Example: "Run a special holiday promotion with a limited-edition version of your product."

2. Scaling Your Marketing and Sales Systems

To scale your business further, you'll need to invest in more **robust marketing and sales systems** that allow you to handle higher volumes of traffic, orders, and customers.

Tactics for Scaling:

- **Advanced Analytics and Tracking**: Use advanced analytics tools to track customer behavior, monitor key performance indicators (KPIs), and optimize your sales funnel in real-time.

- ○ Example: "Use Google Analytics and heat mapping tools to track user behavior on your sales page and identify areas for improvement."
- **Sales Automation Tools**: Implement automation tools that streamline your marketing, sales, and customer support processes, freeing up time to focus on scaling.
  - ○ Example: "Use a customer relationship management (CRM) tool to automate follow-up emails and track customer interactions."
- **Expand Team and Resources**: As your business grows, you may need to hire additional team members or outsource certain tasks to keep up with demand.
  - ○ Example: "Hire a marketing agency to manage paid ads while you focus on product development."

Scaling your systems will enable you to handle larger volumes of customers and continue growing your business without compromising on quality or customer experience.

Conclusion

Turning your $100,000 success into a repeatable business model requires **systematizing your launch process**, scaling your reach, nurturing customer relationships, and continuously refining your offers. By creating a blueprint for future launches, expanding to new audiences, and leveraging customer loyalty, you can replicate your initial success and build a scalable, sustainable business.

As you refine and optimize your systems over time, you'll be able to achieve even greater results with each campaign, ensuring long-term growth and profitability. With the right strategy in place, you can transform a one-time success into a thriving, repeatable model that continues to generate significant revenue and business growth.

Part 7: Advanced Strategies for Bigger Earnings

Chapter 31: High-Ticket Webinars and Live Sales Events

Webinars and live sales events are incredibly effective tools for closing **high-ticket offers** quickly. These virtual events create a direct connection between you and your audience, allowing you to demonstrate the value of your product or service, address customer objections in real time, and build a sense of urgency for purchasing. When executed properly, high-ticket webinars can generate substantial revenue in a single session by converting interested prospects into paying customers.

In this chapter, we'll explore how to create and deliver **high-converting webinars and live sales events** that maximize your chances of closing big-ticket deals. From crafting the right offer to engaging your audience and handling objections, we'll break down every step to ensure your webinar drives significant results.

Step 1: Why Webinars Are Effective for High-Ticket Offers

Webinars provide a powerful platform for selling high-ticket offers because they combine **education, engagement, and sales** in a single format. Unlike traditional sales pages, webinars give you the opportunity to build trust and rapport with your audience, demonstrate the value of your offer, and answer questions on the spot—all of which are crucial for closing high-ticket deals.

1. The Psychology Behind Webinars

When selling high-ticket offers, your audience needs to feel confident in their decision to invest. Webinars allow you to address these psychological needs by providing **personalized, real-time interaction** and delivering an experience that goes beyond a simple product pitch.

Key Psychological Factors:

- **Trust Building**: The live nature of webinars builds trust with potential buyers. They can see you, hear your voice, and interact with you in real time, which helps establish a personal connection and credibility.

- Example: By sharing your personal story or client success stories during the webinar, you humanize your brand and create trust with the audience.
- **Demonstrating Expertise**: Webinars provide an opportunity to showcase your expertise in a way that's more immersive than text or video content. You can present valuable insights, case studies, and real-life examples to demonstrate why you're the authority in your niche.
  - Example: Use detailed case studies of clients who have achieved significant results using your service, showing exactly how you helped them reach their goals.
- **Creating Urgency**: Webinars allow you to use **scarcity** and **urgency** to drive immediate action. By offering limited-time bonuses or discounts for attendees who purchase during the live event, you incentivize quick decision-making.
  - Example: "If you purchase today before the webinar ends, you'll receive an exclusive 1-on-1 strategy session valued at $1,000—completely free!"

Webinars are highly engaging and interactive, which makes them ideal for persuading potential customers to make a significant investment.

2. Ideal Products and Services for High-Ticket Webinars

Not every product is suited for a high-ticket webinar. Webinars work best for **premium products and services** that require a higher level of explanation, trust-building, and customer commitment. These might include coaching programs, consulting services, software, mastermind groups, or luxury physical products.

Criteria for High-Ticket Webinar Offers:

- **Complexity or Customization**: Products or services that require in-depth explanations or personalization are ideal for webinars. The webinar format gives you the time to explain the benefits in detail.

- Example: A $10,000 business coaching program or a custom-built software solution.

- **High Perceived Value**: The offer must provide significant value that justifies the high price tag. Customers need to understand the transformation they will experience by purchasing your product or service.

  - Example: A health coaching program that promises a complete lifestyle transformation, with step-by-step guidance and accountability.

- **Immediate Results or Benefits**: Offers that provide clear, tangible results in a relatively short time frame often perform well in high-ticket webinars. The more concrete the outcome, the easier it is to sell.

  - Example: A six-week marketing consulting package that helps businesses increase their revenue by 20%.

Understanding the psychology behind webinars and knowing which products or services are best suited for this sales strategy is the first step toward creating a high-converting webinar.

Step 2: Crafting Your High-Ticket Offer for a Webinar

The success of your high-ticket webinar depends largely on the strength of your **offer**. For a high-ticket product to sell during a live event, it needs to be clear, compelling, and **value-packed**. Your offer must convince attendees that the transformation or result they'll achieve is worth the investment.

1. Structuring a High-Value Offer

When crafting your offer, it's important to clearly communicate **what you're offering, how it benefits the customer**, and **why it's worth the price**. High-ticket offers often include multiple elements or bonuses that add value, making the overall package more appealing.

Components of a High-Ticket Offer:

- **Core Offer**: This is the primary product or service you're selling, whether it's a coaching program, consulting package, or premium product. Be clear about what's included and how it solves the customer's problem.
  - Example: A 12-week business coaching program that includes weekly group coaching calls, personalized action plans, and access to a private community.
- **Exclusive Bonuses**: To add perceived value and incentivize quick purchases, offer **exclusive bonuses** that are only available during the webinar. These could be additional services, digital resources, or 1-on-1 sessions.
  - Example: "Sign up today and get a free 1-on-1 strategy session, a bonus workbook, and lifetime access to my online course."
- **Scarcity or Limited Access**: Create a sense of urgency by offering limited access, such as only accepting a small number of clients or capping enrollment at a certain number.
  - Example: "This offer is only available for the first 10 people who sign up today. Once these spots are filled, we'll close the doors."

The goal is to make the offer so attractive that your audience feels compelled to take action during the webinar.

2. Communicating the Transformation

High-ticket buyers are less interested in the specifics of your product and more interested in the **transformation** they'll experience. Focus on the **outcomes** and **results** your offer delivers, and explain how their lives or businesses will change by investing in your solution.

Steps to Communicate the Transformation:

- **Identify Pain Points**: Speak to the specific pain points or challenges your audience is facing. Show that you understand their problems and have the perfect solution.
  - Example: "Are you struggling to scale your business and hit consistent revenue targets? This program is designed to give you a proven roadmap to grow and sustain your business."
- **Describe the Desired Outcome**: Paint a vivid picture of the result they'll achieve by purchasing your offer. Help them visualize the end result and how much better their life or business will be after working with you.
  - Example: "Imagine in just 12 weeks, you'll have a fully scalable business model, automated systems in place, and the confidence to consistently generate $10,000 a month."
- **Use Social Proof**: Share testimonials, case studies, and success stories from clients who have already experienced the transformation you're offering. This builds trust and credibility.
  - Example: "John joined our program six months ago, and today, he's running a six-figure business with clients from all over the world."

By focusing on the transformation and leveraging social proof, you make your high-ticket offer irresistible to potential buyers.

Step 3: Creating a High-Converting Webinar Presentation

The content of your webinar must be structured to **educate**, **engage**, and **sell**. A well-designed webinar presentation builds rapport, provides value, and seamlessly leads into your sales pitch. The key is to strike a balance between giving valuable insights and creating a strong case for your high-ticket offer.

1. **Structuring the Webinar Content**

Your webinar should follow a proven structure that leads attendees from **problem awareness** to **solution**, and finally to the **offer**. Each section of your webinar plays a role in guiding prospects toward making a purchase decision.

Webinar Structure:

- **Introduction (5-10 minutes)**: Introduce yourself, establish your credibility, and set the tone for the webinar. Share your personal story or your journey to build a connection with the audience.
    - Example: "Hi, I'm Sarah, and over the last 10 years, I've helped hundreds of entrepreneurs build six-figure businesses. Today, I'm going to share the exact strategies I used to achieve that."
- **The Problem (10-15 minutes)**: Identify the specific problem your audience is facing and validate their struggles. Show empathy and understanding.
    - Example: "If you're here today, you've probably struggled to scale your business past $5,000 a month. Maybe you're stuck in client acquisition or overwhelmed with too many manual processes."
- **The Solution (20-30 minutes)**: Teach key strategies or insights that help solve the problem. This should be high-value content that establishes you as an expert and gives them a taste of what's possible.
    - Example: "I'm going to walk you through the three-step framework I use to help businesses automate their processes and scale to six figures."
- **Case Studies and Social Proof (10 minutes)**: Share real-life examples of how your product or service has transformed other

clients' businesses or lives. Use testimonials, case studies, and metrics to demonstrate results.

- Example: "John applied this framework, and within three months, he had doubled his revenue and was working fewer hours."

- **The Offer (15-20 minutes)**: Transition into your pitch. Present your high-ticket offer and clearly explain what's included, the price, and any bonuses. Emphasize the value of the offer and why attendees should act now.

  - Example: "Now, I want to invite you to join my 12-week business growth program, where I'll personally guide you through this process. You'll get access to exclusive training, weekly coaching calls, and lifetime access to my course."

2. Engaging Your Audience

To keep your audience engaged throughout the webinar, you need to encourage interaction and maintain a dynamic flow of content. Engagement keeps attendees focused and builds excitement around your offer.

Engagement Techniques:

- **Ask Questions**: Periodically ask your audience questions to get them thinking and participating. This can be as simple as asking them to drop their answers in the chat box.
  - Example: "What's your biggest challenge with scaling your business? Let me know in the chat!"
- **Use Polls or Surveys**: Incorporate live polls or surveys during the webinar to gauge interest and keep attendees engaged.
  - Example: "I'm going to launch a quick poll—how many of you have tried online advertising before? Yes or no?"
- **Offer a Q&A Session**: Host a Q&A session at the end of the webinar to address any questions or objections attendees may have. This gives you the opportunity to handle concerns in real time.

- Example: "I'll be taking your questions now—type them in the chat, and I'll answer them live."

By maintaining high engagement, you increase the likelihood that attendees will stay until the end and be more receptive to your offer.

Step 4: Closing the Sale During the Webinar

The final and most important part of the webinar is closing the sale. This is where you present your **high-ticket offer** in a way that emphasizes urgency and value, making it easy for attendees to say "yes."

1. Creating Urgency and Scarcity

To drive immediate action, it's essential to create a sense of **urgency** and **scarcity**. This can be done by offering limited-time bonuses, exclusive discounts, or capping the number of spots available.

Ways to Create Urgency:

- **Time-Sensitive Bonuses**: Offer exclusive bonuses that are only available to those who purchase during or immediately after the webinar. This incentivizes attendees to act quickly.
  - Example: "If you sign up within the next 24 hours, you'll get a free 1-on-1 coaching session with me—this is only available to webinar attendees."
- **Limited Spots**: For services or programs with limited availability (like coaching or consulting), emphasize that there are only a certain number of spots available.
  - Example: "I'm only accepting 10 people into this program to ensure everyone gets the attention they deserve. Once those spots are filled, the doors will close."
- **Fast-Action Discounts**: Offer a discount for attendees who take action before the webinar ends or within a set timeframe after the webinar.
  - Example: "If you enroll before the end of today, you'll get $500 off the full price."

Urgency and scarcity are powerful psychological drivers that encourage attendees to make a decision during the webinar rather than delaying.

2. Handling Objections

During the sales pitch, you'll likely encounter common **objections** such as concerns about price, time, or confidence in the program. It's essential to anticipate these objections and address them head-on.

Strategies for Handling Objections:

- **Price Objections**: Emphasize the value of your offer by comparing it to the potential ROI or the cost of not solving the problem. Offer payment plans if necessary to make the investment more accessible.
  - Example: "Yes, the investment is $5,000, but think about how much revenue you could generate once you implement this system—it's a fraction of what you'll earn back."
- **Time Objections**: Address concerns about time commitment by breaking down how the program or product can be integrated into their current schedule and how it will save them time in the long run.
  - Example: "You'll only need to dedicate 2 hours per week to this program, and the systems we'll build will save you hours every day."
- **Confidence Objections**: For those who doubt their ability to succeed, offer testimonials from clients who were once in their shoes and reassure them of your support.
  - Example: "Many of my clients started where you are now, unsure if they could make it work. With the right guidance, they achieved amazing results, and I'll be there to support you every step of the way."

By preemptively addressing objections, you remove barriers to purchase and increase conversion rates.

Step 5: Following Up After the Webinar

Even after the webinar ends, the selling process continues. **Follow-up** is crucial for converting attendees who may need more time to make a decision. An effective post-webinar follow-up strategy can significantly boost your overall sales.

1. Email Follow-Up Sequences

Set up a **post-webinar email sequence** that nurtures attendees and reminds them of the offer. Include additional value, such as bonus resources, case studies, or answers to common questions.

Email Sequence Example:

- **Day 1: Replay and Offer Reminder**: Send a replay of the webinar along with a reminder of the offer and bonuses.
  - Example: "In case you missed it, here's the replay of yesterday's webinar. Don't forget, you can still get the exclusive bonuses if you enroll today!"
- **Day 2: Social Proof and Case Studies**: Share more success stories or case studies that reinforce the value of your offer.
  - Example: "Here's how one of my clients went from struggling to earning six figures within 6 months using this program."
- **Day 3: Last Chance Reminder**: Send a final email reminding attendees that the offer and bonuses are expiring soon.
  - Example: "This is your last chance to take advantage of the exclusive bonuses—enroll by midnight tonight to secure your spot."

2. Personal Outreach

For high-ticket offers, consider **personal outreach** to attendees who showed interest but haven't yet purchased. This could be a phone call, personalized email, or even a follow-up consultation offer.

Personal Outreach Example:

- "Hi [Attendee Name], I noticed you attended the webinar and seemed interested in the program. I'd love to hop on a quick call to answer any questions and see how we can make this work for you."

This personal touch can be especially effective for high-ticket sales, as it shows your commitment to helping them succeed.

Conclusion

High-ticket webinars and live sales events are powerful tools for closing large deals quickly. By crafting a compelling offer, delivering valuable content, engaging with your audience, and creating urgency, you can convert prospects into paying customers with ease.

With the strategies outlined in this chapter, you'll be able to design and host webinars that not only educate but also sell, driving significant revenue from high-ticket offers in a short period of time. As you refine your process and optimize each element, webinars can become a repeatable, scalable model for generating substantial sales and growing your business.

Chapter 32: Mastering Retargeting

Not every visitor will purchase the first time they visit your sales page or webinar. In fact, studies show that up to **98% of visitors** leave a website without converting. This is where **retargeting** comes into play. Retargeting ads allow you to re-engage with those potential customers who have shown interest in your product but left before making a purchase. By strategically reminding them of your offer, you can recover lost sales and significantly increase your overall conversion rates.

This chapter will provide a comprehensive guide on how to **master retargeting** to recover lost sales. We'll cover how to set up effective retargeting campaigns, segment your audience, craft compelling ads, and optimize your strategy for maximum ROI.

Step 1: Understanding Retargeting and Its Benefits

Retargeting is a form of online advertising that allows you to display ads to users who have previously visited your website or engaged with your content but didn't complete a desired action, such as making a purchase. These ads are served across various platforms, including social media (Facebook, Instagram), search engines (Google Ads), and even other websites they visit.

1. How Retargeting Works

When a user visits your website, a small piece of code known as a **pixel** (e.g., Facebook Pixel, Google Ads Pixel) tracks their behavior and tags them for retargeting. This allows you to display specific ads to these users as they browse the web, keeping your product or offer top-of-mind.

Example of Retargeting Flow:

- A potential customer visits your website and browses a product page but leaves without making a purchase.
- Your pixel tags this visitor as part of your retargeting audience.
- The next time they browse Facebook, Instagram, or another website with ad placements, they see an ad for the product they

viewed, encouraging them to return to your site and complete the purchase.

2. Why Retargeting Is Effective for Recovering Lost Sales

Retargeting is an essential component of any sales strategy, particularly for high-ticket offers or complex products that require multiple touchpoints before a customer is ready to buy.

Key Benefits of Retargeting:

- **Reminds and Reinforces**: Retargeting ads serve as reminders, bringing your offer back into the prospect's awareness. This reinforcement is crucial for potential buyers who need time to consider the purchase.

- **Addresses Objections**: Retargeting provides an opportunity to address common objections or concerns directly through your ads. For instance, you can showcase customer testimonials, product features, or special promotions to nudge them toward conversion.

- **Increases Conversion Rates**: Retargeting visitors who have already shown interest in your offer tends to yield higher conversion rates compared to cold audiences. These visitors are already familiar with your brand, making them more likely to respond positively to follow-up ads.

- **Improves Return on Ad Spend (ROAS)**: Because retargeting ads target users who are already familiar with your brand, they are generally more cost-effective and deliver a higher return on investment than traditional ads aimed at cold audiences.

With a strong retargeting strategy, you can turn hesitant prospects into paying customers, ultimately boosting your bottom line.

Step 2: Setting Up Effective Retargeting Campaigns

The success of retargeting depends on properly setting up your campaigns. This involves installing tracking pixels, defining your retargeting audience segments, and creating ad creatives tailored to each stage of the customer journey.

1. Installing Tracking Pixels

The first step to retargeting is to install tracking pixels on your website. A **tracking pixel** is a snippet of code provided by ad platforms like Facebook, Instagram, and Google. This pixel tracks user behavior on your site, such as page views, product interactions, and abandoned carts.

How to Install Tracking Pixels:

- **Facebook Pixel**: Create a Facebook Pixel in your Facebook Ads Manager and install the pixel code on your website. The pixel will track visitors' actions, allowing you to retarget them with Facebook and Instagram ads.
  - Example: "Place the pixel code in the header section of your website to track all page views, and set up custom events like 'Add to Cart' and 'Initiate Checkout' for more targeted retargeting."
- **Google Ads Pixel**: Use the Google Ads pixel (also known as a remarketing tag) to track visitors and their interactions on your website. This enables you to retarget users across Google's display network, including YouTube.
  - Example: "Add the Google Ads pixel to your website and configure custom remarketing lists, such as users who visited the pricing page but didn't convert."

Installing these pixels is essential for tracking user behavior, segmenting your audience, and delivering highly targeted ads to those who are most likely to convert.

2. Segmenting Your Retargeting Audience

One of the most powerful aspects of retargeting is the ability to **segment your audience** based on their behavior. Different segments require different messaging, so it's crucial to customize your ads for each group.

Common Retargeting Segments:

- **Website Visitors**: People who visited your website but did not take a specific action, such as making a purchase or signing up for a webinar.
  - Example: "Target users who visited your homepage but didn't click through to the product page, indicating potential interest but hesitation."
- **Product Page Viewers**: Visitors who viewed a particular product page but left without adding the product to their cart.
  - Example: "Serve ads highlighting the key benefits of the product to those who visited the product page."
- **Cart Abandoners**: Users who added items to their cart but left before completing the checkout process. These individuals are often closer to purchasing and need a final push.
  - Example: "Target cart abandoners with ads offering a limited-time discount or free shipping to encourage them to complete their purchase."
- **Video Viewers and Webinar Attendees**: For those who watched a product demo video or attended a webinar, retargeting ads can reinforce the value of your offer and address any lingering objections.
  - Example: "Retarget webinar attendees with ads promoting an exclusive bonus for signing up within 48 hours."

Segmenting your audience allows you to tailor your messaging for each group, increasing the relevance and effectiveness of your retargeting ads.

Step 3: Crafting Compelling Retargeting Ads

The content and messaging of your retargeting ads are key to recovering lost sales. Your ads should be tailored to the audience segment you're targeting, addressing their specific concerns, highlighting benefits, and offering incentives to return.

1. Addressing Common Objections

Retargeting ads give you the opportunity to address potential objections that may have prevented users from purchasing the first time. By preemptively tackling these objections, you increase the likelihood of conversion.

Examples of Objection-Handling Ads:

- **Price Concerns**: If cost is a common objection, showcase the product's value and offer a discount or payment plan.
  - Example: "Still thinking it over? Get an exclusive 10% discount on your purchase—valid for the next 24 hours!"
- **Lack of Trust**: Use customer testimonials, case studies, or guarantees to build trust and credibility.
  - Example: "Don't just take our word for it—hear from our customers! 'This product changed my life—worth every penny!'"
- **Uncertainty About Benefits**: Highlight key benefits and features, focusing on how the product can solve their problem or improve their life.
  - Example: "Our coaching program has helped over 500 entrepreneurs scale their businesses. You could be next!"

2. Offering Incentives to Encourage Action

Incentives such as discounts, free shipping, bonuses, or limited-time offers can provide the extra nudge that prospects need to complete their purchase.

Incentive-Based Ad Examples:

- **Discount Codes**: Offer a discount to cart abandoners to motivate them to return and finish their purchase.

- ◦ Example: "Complete your order now and enjoy 15% off with code SAVE15—offer expires in 24 hours!"
- **Free Shipping**: For eCommerce products, offering free shipping can remove a common barrier to purchase.
  - ◦ Example: "Still want that [Product]? Get free shipping if you order within the next 48 hours!"
- **Exclusive Bonuses**: For high-ticket offers, include an exclusive bonus for returning customers.
  - ◦ Example: "Enroll today and receive a free 30-minute strategy session as a thank you for joining our community."

3. Using Visuals and Dynamic Content

Visual content plays a crucial role in grabbing attention and conveying your message quickly. For eCommerce products, use **dynamic ads** that automatically show users the specific products they viewed or added to their cart.

Visual Ad Examples:

- **Carousel Ads**: Use carousel ads to display multiple product images, features, or testimonials in a single ad unit, allowing users to swipe through the content.
  - ◦ Example: "Check out these best-sellers you viewed! Swipe through to see more and grab yours now."
- **Dynamic Product Ads**: Create dynamic ads that display the exact product a user viewed on your website, including an image, price, and call-to-action button.
  - ◦ Example: "Don't miss out! The [Product Name] you were interested in is still available. Buy now before it's gone!"

By using engaging visuals and personalized content, you can capture attention and remind prospects of the items they were interested in.

Step 4: Optimizing and Scaling Your Retargeting Campaigns

Once your retargeting campaigns are live, it's important to **monitor performance** and **optimize** your ads for better results. Testing different elements, adjusting targeting, and scaling successful campaigns can help you maximize your return on ad spend (ROAS).

1. A/B Testing Your Ads

To determine what resonates best with your audience, conduct **A/B tests** with different ad creatives, messaging, and offers. This data-driven approach allows you to refine your strategy based on real user behavior.

Elements to Test:

- **Ad Copy**: Experiment with different headlines, calls-to-action, and messaging to see which version drives the most clicks and conversions.
  - Example: Test "Get 15% Off Now!" vs. "Claim Your Exclusive Discount Today" to find the more effective phrasing.
- **Visuals**: Try various images, videos, or carousel formats to identify the visuals that generate the most engagement.
  - Example: Use product photos in one ad and lifestyle images in another to see which resonates more with your audience.
- **Offers**: Test different incentives, such as percentage discounts, free shipping, or bonus products, to find the most persuasive offer for your audience.
  - Example: Compare the performance of ads offering "Free Shipping" against those offering "10% Off."

By systematically testing different elements, you can optimize your retargeting campaigns for higher performance.

2. Adjusting Ad Frequency and Budget

Retargeting works best when ads are shown frequently enough to keep your offer top-of-mind, but not so often that they become annoying. Monitor your **ad frequency** to ensure a balanced approach.

Ad Frequency Guidelines:

- **Frequency Cap**: Set a frequency cap to limit how often the same user sees your ads within a given time frame (e.g., no more than 3 times per week). This prevents ad fatigue and keeps your ads fresh.
    - Example: "Cap ad frequency at 3 impressions per week to avoid overexposure."
- **Adjust Budget Based on Performance**: Allocate more budget to the best-performing segments and ads, while scaling back or pausing underperforming ones.
    - Example: "Increase the budget for ads targeting cart abandoners with a 5x ROAS, and reduce spend on ads for website visitors with low engagement."

By managing ad frequency and budget effectively, you maintain a positive user experience while maximizing the effectiveness of your retargeting campaigns.

3. Scaling Successful Retargeting Campaigns

Once you've identified high-performing retargeting campaigns, the next step is to **scale** them to reach more of your target audience and recover additional sales.

Scaling Strategies:

- **Expand Retargeting Windows**: Adjust the time frame for your retargeting audiences to capture users who visited your site within the last 30, 60, or even 90 days, depending on your product's sales cycle.

- ◦ Example: "Expand the retargeting window to 60 days for high-ticket offers, allowing for longer decision-making periods."
- **Lookalike Audiences**: Use data from your retargeting campaigns to create lookalike audiences, targeting users who have similar characteristics to those who converted through retargeting ads.
  - ◦ Example: "Create a 1% lookalike audience based on users who completed purchases after seeing retargeting ads."
- **Introduce New Creative**: Refresh your ads with new visuals, copy, or incentives to keep your retargeting campaigns engaging and effective over time.
  - ◦ Example: "Update ad creatives every 4 weeks to prevent ad fatigue and maintain high engagement rates."

By scaling and continuously optimizing your retargeting strategy, you can recover more lost sales and significantly boost your overall revenue.

Conclusion

Mastering retargeting is a critical skill for recovering lost sales and maximizing your revenue potential. By understanding how to set up effective retargeting campaigns, segment your audience, craft compelling ads, and optimize for performance, you can turn prospects who initially hesitated into paying customers.

Retargeting keeps your brand and offer in front of potential buyers, reinforcing your value proposition and addressing objections. With a well-executed retargeting strategy, you can increase your conversion rates, improve your return on ad spend (ROAS), and scale your business effectively. By implementing the tactics covered in this chapter, you'll be well-equipped to harness the power of retargeting and drive consistent, profitable results for your business.

Chapter 33: The Power of Joint Ventures

Joint ventures (JVs) are a powerful way to expand your reach, tap into new audiences, and increase sales by leveraging the networks, resources, and expertise of other entrepreneurs. When done right, joint ventures can create win-win situations for both parties, providing mutual value and significantly boosting revenue.

This chapter will guide you through understanding the dynamics of joint ventures, how to identify ideal partners, the best practices for setting up collaborations, and strategies to ensure a smooth, profitable partnership. By the end, you'll have the tools and knowledge to establish joint ventures that amplify your business growth.

Step 1: Understanding Joint Ventures and Their Benefits

A joint venture involves **collaborating with another business or entrepreneur** to achieve a common goal, typically involving a shared promotional campaign, product launch, or marketing effort. Unlike partnerships, which are long-term and often involve shared equity, JVs are typically **short-term collaborations** designed for specific campaigns or projects.

1. The Benefits of Joint Ventures

Joint ventures offer a range of benefits for entrepreneurs looking to grow their businesses, particularly in reaching new audiences and boosting sales:

Key Advantages:

- **Expanded Reach**: By collaborating with another business, you gain access to their established audience, allowing you to introduce your product to new potential customers who might not have found you otherwise.
  - Example: If you sell a fitness product, partnering with a popular nutrition coach exposes your product to their audience, which is likely already interested in health and wellness.

- **Credibility and Trust**: Associating with a reputable partner can enhance your credibility. When a trusted entrepreneur endorses your product to their audience, it increases trust and reduces buying hesitation.
  - Example: "When [Influencer Name] promotes our product to their followers, it instantly boosts our credibility because their audience trusts their recommendations."
- **Cost-Effective Marketing**: JVs often involve **revenue-sharing** or **cross-promotion**, which means you can leverage your partner's marketing channels without incurring high upfront costs. This can be much more cost-effective than traditional advertising methods.
  - Example: "Instead of spending thousands on Facebook ads, we collaborate with a JV partner to promote our product through their email list in exchange for a commission on sales."
- **Diverse Expertise**: Your JV partner may bring different skills, insights, and marketing strategies to the table, helping you create a more effective and comprehensive promotional campaign.
  - Example: "While we focus on product creation, our JV partner handles the social media promotion, leveraging their expertise to increase campaign visibility."

2. Types of Joint Ventures

Joint ventures can take many forms, depending on the objectives and strengths of the partners involved. Some common types of JVs include:

JV Types:

- **Product Launch Collaborations**: Partnering with another entrepreneur to co-launch a product or service. This could involve bundling products together or jointly developing a new offering.
  - Example: A fitness coach and a nutritionist team up to launch a "30-Day Health and Fitness Challenge" that in-

cludes meal plans, workout guides, and exclusive online support.

- **Cross-Promotion**: Each partner promotes the other's products or services to their respective audiences. This is often done through email marketing, social media, webinars, or podcasts.
  - Example: "We send an email promoting our partner's online course to our subscribers, and in return, they promote our product during their next webinar."
- **Affiliate Partnerships**: In an affiliate JV, one partner (the affiliate) promotes the other's product and earns a commission for each sale made through their unique affiliate link.
  - Example: A business coach promotes a financial management software to their clients and earns a 30% commission on every sale made through their referral link.
- **Content Collaboration**: Co-creating content, such as a webinar, ebook, podcast, or video series, where both partners contribute their expertise. This content is then promoted to both audiences.
  - Example: "We co-host a live webinar with a social media marketing expert to provide valuable insights to both of our audiences, and at the end, we each promote our respective services."

Understanding these different types of JVs will help you identify the best approach for your business and tailor your strategy accordingly.

Step 2: Finding and Vetting the Right Joint Venture Partners

The success of a joint venture heavily depends on finding the **right partner**. You want to collaborate with someone whose audience aligns with your target market, who has a solid reputation, and whose products or services complement—not compete with—your own.

1. Identifying Ideal JV Partners

When looking for potential JV partners, consider the following criteria to ensure a mutually beneficial collaboration:

Qualities of an Ideal JV Partner:

- **Audience Alignment**: Your partner's audience should overlap with your target market. Their followers, customers, or subscribers should have a genuine interest in what you offer.
    - Example: If you sell productivity tools, a business coach whose audience consists of entrepreneurs and professionals would be an ideal partner.
- **Complementary Products or Services**: Choose partners whose products or services complement, rather than compete with, your own. This allows you to provide more value to the customer without causing conflicts.
    - Example: "A nutrition coach would be a perfect JV partner for our fitness product, as their meal plans complement our workout guides."
- **Reputation and Trust**: Collaborate with partners who have a positive reputation in their industry and a loyal following. Their endorsement should carry weight and credibility with their audience.
    - Example: "We chose to partner with an established influencer in the wellness industry because their audience trusts their product recommendations."

2. Approaching Potential JV Partners

Once you've identified potential JV partners, the next step is to approach them with a well-crafted proposal that clearly outlines the benefits of collaboration.

Tips for Approaching JV Partners:

- **Personalized Outreach**: Customize your approach to show that you understand their business and audience. Mention specific aspects of their work that you admire and how your products or services align with their brand.

- ◦ Example: "I've been following your work for a while and love how you empower entrepreneurs. I think our productivity tools would provide great value to your audience."
- **Clear Value Proposition**: Highlight the benefits of the joint venture for them. Emphasize how the collaboration will help them achieve their goals, whether it's revenue generation, audience growth, or brand enhancement.
  - ◦ Example: "By promoting our upcoming course, your audience will gain access to exclusive content, and you'll earn a 30% commission on each sale."
- **Keep It Simple**: Start with a straightforward collaboration idea that requires minimal commitment. This lowers the risk for your potential partner and makes them more likely to agree to a trial collaboration.
  - ◦ Example: "Would you be open to cross-promoting our products during our next webinar? We can offer a special discount code for your audience."

By making your proposal clear, beneficial, and easy to implement, you increase the chances of forming a successful joint venture partnership.

3. Vetting Potential Partners

Before entering into a JV, thoroughly vet potential partners to ensure their business values, practices, and audience engagement align with yours.

Vetting Process:

- **Review Their Content**: Examine the quality of their content, products, and services to ensure they meet your standards and align with your brand.
  - ◦ Example: "Check their social media profiles, website, and customer reviews to gauge the quality of their work and audience engagement."

- **Assess Audience Engagement**: Look at how actively their audience engages with their content. High engagement indicates a loyal and responsive following, which is crucial for successful cross-promotion.
  - Example: "If their social media posts have high engagement rates and their email newsletters receive strong open rates, it's a good sign of an active audience."
- **Discuss Goals and Expectations**: Have a candid conversation about the goals, expectations, and logistics of the collaboration. Ensure both parties are on the same page regarding timelines, responsibilities, and revenue-sharing models.

A thorough vetting process helps prevent potential issues and ensures a smooth collaboration.

Step 3: Structuring and Setting Up a Successful Joint Venture

Once you've secured a joint venture partnership, the next step is to **structure the collaboration** in a way that benefits both parties and sets clear expectations. This involves planning the logistics, defining roles, and setting up marketing materials for the joint campaign.

1. Defining Roles and Responsibilities

Clarity is key to a successful JV. Both parties need to understand their roles, responsibilities, and contributions to the campaign to avoid misunderstandings and ensure a seamless collaboration.

Assigning Roles:

- **Content Creation**: Determine who will be responsible for creating marketing content, such as emails, social media posts, landing pages, and promotional materials.
  - Example: "We'll create the promotional email copy, while our partner will handle social media posts to promote the webinar."

- **Promotion Channels**: Agree on which platforms and channels each partner will use for promotion. This could include email marketing, social media, webinars, or podcasts.
  - Example: "Our partner will send a dedicated email to their list, and we'll promote the collaboration through Facebook Ads and Instagram Stories."
- **Customer Support**: Decide who will handle customer inquiries related to the campaign. If you're offering a bundled product, ensure both parties can address questions about their respective offerings.
  - Example: "We'll manage customer support for our product, and our partner will handle inquiries related to their coaching services."

2. Creating a Revenue-Sharing Model

One of the most critical aspects of a JV is establishing a **revenue-sharing model** that fairly compensates both parties. The structure of this model will depend on the nature of the collaboration and the products or services involved.

Common Revenue-Sharing Models:

- **Affiliate Commission**: One partner promotes the other's product and earns a commission on each sale made through their referral. This model is straightforward and aligns incentives for both parties.
  - Example: "Our partner will receive a 30% commission on every sale generated through their unique affiliate link."
- **Profit Split**: For co-created products or bundled offers, consider a profit-splitting arrangement where both parties share the net profits after expenses.
  - Example: "We'll split the net profits 50/50 for our co-created online course, after deducting marketing expenses."

- **Fixed Fee Plus Commission**: In some cases, you may offer a fixed fee for promotion plus a commission on sales. This can provide the partner with an upfront incentive to participate.
  - Example: "We'll pay a $500 upfront fee for the webinar promotion, plus a 20% commission on every sale made during the event."

Ensure that the revenue-sharing model is mutually beneficial and agreed upon before launching the campaign.

3. Creating Marketing Materials

To streamline the promotional process, prepare **marketing materials** in advance and provide them to your JV partner. This includes email copy, social media graphics, product images, and any other content needed for the campaign.

Marketing Materials Checklist:

- **Email Templates**: Create pre-written email templates that your partner can send to their list, including subject lines, body copy, and call-to-action links.
- **Social Media Graphics**: Provide a set of high-quality social media graphics and suggested captions that your partner can use to promote the collaboration.
- **Landing Pages**: If applicable, design a dedicated landing page for the joint venture promotion. This page should include both partners' branding and a compelling call to action.
- **Affiliate Links**: Set up unique affiliate links for tracking sales and commissions, ensuring your partner receives credit for the customers they refer.

By providing ready-made marketing materials, you make it easy for your partner to promote the collaboration effectively.

Step 4: Executing the Joint Venture Campaign

With all the planning and materials in place, it's time to **execute the campaign**. This involves launching the promotional activities, monitoring performance, and maintaining open communication with your JV partner.

1. Coordinated Launch and Promotion

The success of a joint venture relies on **coordinated efforts** to maximize reach and impact. Set a clear timeline for each promotional activity, and ensure both partners are aligned.

Launch Checklist:

- **Email Marketing**: Schedule email campaigns to go out on both partners' lists simultaneously to create buzz and anticipation.
  - Example: "We'll send the initial launch email on Monday at 9 AM, and our partner will follow up with a reminder email on Wednesday."
- **Social Media Posts**: Plan a series of social media posts to promote the collaboration across both partners' platforms. Use consistent branding and messaging to reinforce the partnership.
  - Example: "Post countdown graphics on Instagram Stories in the days leading up to the webinar launch."
- **Webinars and Live Events**: If hosting a joint webinar or live event, coordinate the event's promotion and execution, ensuring both parties actively engage with the audience during the event.

2. Monitoring Performance

During the campaign, closely **monitor performance** to assess what's working and where adjustments may be needed. Use analytics tools to track key metrics such as clicks, conversions, and sales.

Key Metrics to Monitor:

- **Email Open and Click Rates**: Measure the performance of email promotions to determine how effectively the campaign is reaching and engaging the audience.
- **Sales and Conversion Rates**: Track sales and conversions through unique affiliate links or tracking pixels to measure the success of the collaboration.
- **Return on Investment (ROI)**: Calculate the ROI for each promotional channel to assess the profitability of the joint venture.

Regularly share performance updates with your partner to keep them informed and maintain transparency throughout the campaign.

Step 5: Post-Campaign Evaluation and Follow-Up

After the joint venture campaign concludes, it's important to conduct a **post-campaign evaluation** to assess its success and identify opportunities for improvement. This process helps refine future collaborations and strengthens your relationship with the JV partner.

1. Analyzing Campaign Results

Review the results of the JV campaign in detail, focusing on key performance indicators (KPIs) such as sales volume, conversion rates, and customer acquisition costs.

Post-Campaign Analysis:

- **What Worked**: Identify the most effective elements of the campaign, such as high-converting email copy, successful social media posts, or compelling offers.
  - Example: "Our limited-time discount offer generated the highest conversions, indicating that urgency was a key motivator for our audience."
- **Areas for Improvement**: Note any challenges or areas where performance fell short of expectations. Discuss potential solutions with your partner to improve future collaborations.

 ◦ Example: "Email open rates were lower than expected; we may need to test different subject lines in our next campaign."

2. Debrief with Your JV Partner

Hold a **debrief meeting** with your JV partner to review the campaign's performance, share insights, and discuss potential next steps. This open communication helps strengthen the partnership and sets the stage for future collaborations.

Debrief Questions:

- "What aspects of the campaign were most successful?"
- "Were there any unexpected challenges or obstacles?"
- "How can we improve our collaboration for future campaigns?"

3. Nurturing the Partnership for Future Ventures

A successful joint venture often opens the door to **long-term partnerships**. Keep the lines of communication open with your partner, and consider exploring additional opportunities for collaboration.

Future Collaboration Ideas:

- **Recurring Promotions**: Discuss the possibility of making the JV campaign a recurring event, such as an annual or seasonal promotion.
- **New Joint Offers**: Brainstorm new products, services, or bundles that you can co-create and promote together.
- **Cross-Branding Opportunities**: Explore opportunities to cross-brand each other's products in future marketing materials, enhancing both brands' visibility and credibility.

By nurturing the relationship, you can establish a network of JV partners that supports ongoing growth and mutual success.

Conclusion

Joint ventures are a powerful strategy for expanding your reach, increasing sales, and growing your business by leveraging the networks and resources of other entrepreneurs. By finding the right partners, structuring collaborations effectively, and executing coordinated campaigns, you can tap into new markets and amplify your impact.

A successful JV isn't just a one-time event; it can lead to long-term partnerships and a network of collaborators who help propel your business to new heights. With the strategies and best practices outlined in this chapter, you're equipped to master the art of joint ventures and unlock a new level of growth for your business.

Chapter 34: Hosting a Flash Masterclass

Flash masterclasses are powerful, high-impact events that provide immense value to attendees in a short time while positioning you as an expert in your niche. These live, value-packed sessions are an ideal way to engage with your audience, showcase your expertise, and build trust—all while setting up a compelling **high-ticket upsell** for those who are ready to take the next step. When executed effectively, a flash masterclass can generate a surge in sales and expand your customer base rapidly.

In this chapter, we'll explore the step-by-step process of hosting a flash masterclass, including planning, promotion, content delivery, and seamlessly transitioning into a high-ticket offer. By the end, you'll know how to create a compelling masterclass experience that not only educates your audience but also drives significant revenue.

Step 1: Planning Your Flash Masterclass

The success of your flash masterclass depends heavily on strategic planning. The goal is to provide **valuable content** that addresses a key pain point for your target audience while leading seamlessly into your high-ticket offer.

1. Choosing a High-Impact Topic

Selecting the right topic is the cornerstone of a successful masterclass. The topic should address a specific, pressing problem that your audience faces and promise a clear, actionable solution. It should be relevant to your high-ticket offer, creating a natural progression from the free masterclass to the paid program or product.

Criteria for Selecting Your Topic:

- **Specific and Niche**: Choose a topic that is specific enough to attract your ideal customers. A narrow focus ensures that attendees have a keen interest in the subject matter.

- Example: Instead of a general topic like "Boost Your Business," opt for a more targeted topic like "How to Generate 10 High-Paying Clients in 30 Days."
- **Actionable Outcomes**: Ensure the masterclass offers a tangible, actionable outcome that attendees can achieve by the end of the session.
  - Example: "By the end of this masterclass, you will have a 5-step strategy to identify and close high-paying clients using LinkedIn."
- **Aligned with Your Upsell**: The content of the masterclass should naturally set the stage for your high-ticket offer, solving a piece of the problem while the upsell provides the full solution.
  - Example: If your high-ticket offer is a comprehensive 12-week coaching program, the masterclass could cover a specific technique that's part of the larger program, giving attendees a taste of the transformation they can achieve.

2. Structuring the Masterclass

A well-structured masterclass keeps attendees engaged, builds credibility, and smoothly transitions into the upsell. Plan a session that is **60-90 minutes** long, balancing valuable insights with storytelling, engagement, and your offer.

Suggested Structure:

- **Introduction (5-10 minutes)**: Start with a brief introduction to yourself, your credentials, and why you're qualified to teach this masterclass. Share your personal story to build rapport and establish credibility.
  - Example: "Hi, I'm Jane Doe, a business growth strategist who has helped over 200 entrepreneurs double their revenue in 12 months. Today, I'm here to teach you my proven strategy for attracting high-paying clients."

- **Problem Identification (10 minutes)**: Outline the problem or challenge that your audience faces. Use real-life examples, statistics, or stories to illustrate the problem and create an emotional connection with your attendees.
  - Example: "Many entrepreneurs struggle to find high-paying clients because they're focusing on the wrong strategies. Sound familiar?"
- **Teaching (30-40 minutes)**: Deliver high-value content by teaching key strategies, frameworks, or techniques that provide a **quick win** for your audience. This should be actionable, insightful, and relevant to the high-ticket offer.
  - Example: "Here's my 5-step method for building a LinkedIn profile that attracts premium clients. I'll walk you through each step in detail, so you can implement this immediately."
- **Case Studies and Success Stories (5-10 minutes)**: Share success stories of clients or students who have applied your methods and achieved results. This social proof reinforces the effectiveness of your strategies and builds credibility for the upsell.
  - Example: "One of my clients, Sarah, used this exact strategy to close five high-ticket clients within her first month."
- **Transition to the Upsell (10-15 minutes)**: Segue into your high-ticket offer by explaining that while the masterclass provides a foundational strategy, the upsell (e.g., a coaching program, course, or membership) offers the full solution. Emphasize the benefits and transformation attendees can achieve by investing in the next step.
  - Example: "Now that you have a taste of what's possible, imagine having a complete roadmap and personal support to attract high-paying clients consistently. That's exactly what my 12-week coaching program provides."

3. Setting Up the Logistics

To host a professional, smooth-running masterclass, you'll need to set up the necessary tools and technology.

Logistics Checklist:

- **Platform**: Choose a reliable webinar or live streaming platform such as Zoom, WebinarJam, or Demio. Ensure the platform allows for screen sharing, Q&A sessions, and attendee interaction.
    - Example: "Use Zoom for its ease of use and interactive features like polls, chat, and breakout rooms."
- **Registration Page**: Create a registration page where attendees can sign up for the masterclass. Include key information about the topic, date, time, and what attendees will learn.
    - Example: "Join my free masterclass, 'How to Generate 10 High-Paying Clients in 30 Days,' on March 15th at 2 PM EST. Reserve your spot now!"
- **Email Reminders**: Set up an email sequence to send reminders to registrants, including a confirmation email, a day-before reminder, and an hour-before reminder to maximize attendance.
- **Slides and Visuals**: Prepare slides or visuals to support your presentation. Include key points, data, case studies, and images to make the masterclass engaging and easy to follow.

By planning these elements in advance, you ensure a seamless and professional masterclass experience for your attendees.

Step 2: Promoting Your Flash Masterclass

A successful masterclass requires effective promotion to attract the right audience. The more targeted your promotion efforts, the more likely you are to attract attendees who are interested in both the masterclass and your high-ticket upsell.

1. Crafting a Compelling Registration Page

Your masterclass registration page is a critical element in attracting attendees. It should clearly outline the **benefits** of attending and create excitement around the topic.

Key Elements of a Registration Page:

- **Headline**: Use a powerful headline that highlights the main benefit or outcome attendees will achieve by joining the masterclass.
  - Example: "Learn the 5 Proven Steps to Attract High-Paying Clients and Double Your Revenue!"
- **Bullet Points**: Include a list of bullet points describing what attendees will learn, emphasizing actionable strategies and outcomes.
  - Example: "In this 60-minute masterclass, you'll discover how to: optimize your LinkedIn profile for client attraction, craft compelling outreach messages, and close deals with confidence."
- **Urgency and Scarcity**: Create urgency by mentioning that spots are limited or the masterclass is happening soon. This encourages people to register right away.
  - Example: "Only 100 spots available—secure your seat now before it's too late!"
- **Call to Action (CTA)**: Use a clear CTA button for registration, such as "Reserve My Spot Now" or "Join the Masterclass."

2. Leveraging Multiple Promotion Channels

To reach a broad yet targeted audience, promote your masterclass across various marketing channels. Use a mix of organic and paid methods to maximize your reach.

Promotion Channels:

- **Email Marketing**: Send promotional emails to your existing list, highlighting the value and outcomes of the masterclass. Follow up with reminder emails to increase attendance.
    - Example: "Are you ready to attract high-paying clients? Join my free masterclass and learn the exact strategies I use to help entrepreneurs grow their revenue."
- **Social Media**: Promote the masterclass on social media platforms, using eye-catching graphics and compelling copy. Create countdown posts as the date approaches to build excitement.
    - Example: "Join me live this Thursday for a free masterclass on attracting premium clients. Learn the strategies that have helped my clients generate consistent five-figure months!"
- **Paid Ads**: Use Facebook, Instagram, or LinkedIn ads to target a specific audience likely to benefit from the masterclass. Create ad copy that speaks to their pain points and the solutions they'll gain by attending.
    - Example: "Struggling to find high-paying clients? Join my free masterclass and discover a proven 5-step strategy. Spots are filling up fast—reserve yours now!"
- **Partnerships and Affiliates**: Collaborate with industry peers, influencers, or affiliates to promote your masterclass to their audiences in exchange for a commission on any upsell sales.

By leveraging these promotion channels, you'll attract a high-quality audience that's more likely to engage with the masterclass and be interested in your upsell.

Step 3: Delivering a High-Value Masterclass

The **delivery** of your masterclass is crucial for engaging your audience, building trust, and setting up the upsell. Focus on providing actionable insights while establishing your authority and demonstrating the value of your high-ticket offer.

1. Engaging Your Audience Throughout the Session

Keep your audience engaged from start to finish using interactive elements, storytelling, and clear, actionable steps.

Engagement Techniques:

- **Start with a Story**: Begin your masterclass with a personal story that resonates with your audience and establishes credibility.
    - Example: "I remember when I was struggling to find high-paying clients. I tried countless strategies, but nothing worked until I discovered the 5-step method I'm about to teach you."
- **Ask Questions**: Throughout the session, ask questions that encourage attendees to reflect on their own experiences. Use polls or the chat feature to make the session interactive.
    - Example: "How many of you have felt overwhelmed trying to find clients? Type 'yes' in the chat if you can relate."
- **Provide Actionable Tips**: Share practical, step-by-step advice that attendees can implement immediately. This positions you as a knowledgeable expert and gives them a taste of the value they'll receive in your upsell.
    - Example: "Step 1: Optimize your LinkedIn headline to include your niche and the problem you solve. Here's how to do it..."

2. Transitioning to the Upsell

The transition from teaching to selling should feel natural and seamless. Focus on the gap between what they've learned in the masterclass and the comprehensive solution your high-ticket offer provides.

Effective Transition Techniques:

- **Highlight the Next Steps**: Emphasize that the masterclass covered foundational strategies, but to achieve the full transformation, attendees need a complete roadmap.
    - Example: "Today, I've given you the basic steps to attract high-paying clients. But to create a consistent, scalable system, you need a comprehensive strategy—and that's exactly what my 12-week coaching program offers."
- **Introduce Your Offer**: Present your high-ticket offer as the logical next step for those who want to dive deeper and achieve even greater results. Clearly outline the features, benefits, and outcomes of the offer.
    - Example: "Introducing my 'Client Attraction Accelerator' program—a 12-week coaching experience that will take you from struggling to thriving, with personalized support every step of the way."
- **Offer an Incentive**: Provide a limited-time incentive, such as a discount, bonus, or exclusive access, for attendees who sign up during or immediately after the masterclass.
    - Example: "Enroll in the next 48 hours, and you'll receive a free 1-on-1 strategy session worth $500."

Step 4: Following Up and Maximizing Conversions

The follow-up process is just as important as the masterclass itself. Many attendees may need a little more time or information before committing to your high-ticket offer. A well-crafted follow-up sequence can significantly increase conversions.

1. Post-Masterclass Email Sequence

Set up an automated email sequence to nurture attendees after the masterclass. Use these emails to provide additional value, address objections, and remind them of the offer.

Email Sequence Outline:

- **Email 1: Replay and Recap (Sent Immediately After)**: Share the masterclass replay and summarize key takeaways. Include a reminder about your high-ticket offer and the limited-time incentive.
    - Example: "In case you missed it, here's the replay of today's masterclass. Remember, my 'Client Attraction Accelerator' program is now open, with an exclusive bonus for the next 48 hours."
- **Email 2: Address Objections (Day 1 Post-Masterclass)**: Tackle common objections or concerns, using testimonials and case studies to reinforce the value of your offer.
    - Example: "Worried about the time commitment? Here's how one of my clients fit the program into their busy schedule and achieved incredible results."
- **Email 3: Highlight the Benefits (Day 2 Post-Masterclass)**: Focus on the outcomes and transformation they'll experience by joining your high-ticket program.
    - Example: "Imagine consistently attracting high-paying clients who value your expertise. That's the reality our program makes possible."
- **Email 4: Last Chance Reminder (Day 3 Post-Masterclass)**: Send a final reminder about the limited-time incentive and the closing of the offer.
    - Example: "This is your last chance to enroll and receive the exclusive bonus. Doors close tonight at midnight!"

2. Personal Outreach

For a more personal touch, reach out to engaged attendees who showed strong interest during the masterclass or asked insightful questions. Offer to answer any further questions or schedule a discovery call to discuss their goals.

Personal Outreach Message:

- "Hi [Attendee Name], I noticed you were actively engaged during the masterclass. I'd love to answer any questions you have about the 'Client Attraction Accelerator' program. Would you like to hop on a quick call to discuss how it can help you achieve your goals?"

Conclusion

Hosting a flash masterclass is an effective way to deliver immediate value to your audience while setting up a high-ticket upsell. By providing actionable insights, establishing trust, and offering a compelling next step, you can convert engaged attendees into high-paying clients.

With strategic planning, targeted promotion, engaging delivery, and timely follow-up, a flash masterclass can become a powerful component of your business growth strategy. The techniques outlined in this chapter equip you to run masterclasses that not only educate and inspire but also drive significant revenue and client acquisition for your high-ticket offerings.

Conclusion: Your Path to Wealth and Freedom

Congratulations! You've reached the final chapter of this transformative journey, equipped with the knowledge, strategies, and tools to generate $100,000 in 24 hours and beyond. As you reflect on the chapters you've explored, it's clear that this method isn't just about making money quickly—it's about building a **sustainable, high-impact business model** that can revolutionize your life and set you on a path to wealth and freedom.

When you adopt this high-income mindset and implement these proven strategies, you take control of your financial future, break free from traditional limitations, and open up new possibilities for personal and professional growth. This conclusion will remind you of the life-changing potential of this method, inspire you to take action, and outline how these strategies can empower you to generate consistent, scalable income.

1. The Life-Changing Potential of This Method

The strategies you've learned are designed to help you break the common myths around money-making and business growth. Many people believe that accumulating wealth is a slow and arduous process, but you now know that with the right approach, **large sums of money can be generated in a short amount of time**. By implementing these methods, you have the power to change not only your financial situation but also your lifestyle and future prospects.

1.1 Breaking Free from Financial Constraints

One of the most liberating aspects of this method is the ability to break free from the traditional 9-to-5 grind. No longer do you have to rely solely on a paycheck or be limited by trading hours for dollars. By mastering high-ticket sales, creating valuable digital products, leveraging joint ventures, and hosting flash masterclasses, you open up multiple streams of income that can work for you **around the clock**.

The Benefits of Financial Freedom:

- **Flexibility**: Work on your terms, choosing when, where, and how you operate your business. Whether you prefer working from a beach in Bali or a cozy home office, you have the flexibility to design a lifestyle that suits you.
- **Security**: A diversified business model with multiple income streams provides a safety net, reducing financial stress and uncertainty. You're no longer dependent on a single source of income, making you more resilient in the face of economic changes.
- **Opportunity**: With financial freedom comes the ability to invest in personal and professional development, travel, pursue passions, and make decisions based on what truly matters to you, rather than being constrained by monetary limitations.

1.2 Building a Business That Scales

The beauty of the strategies in this book is that they are designed for **scalability**. You've learned how to create digital products, host high-value webinars, leverage joint ventures, and utilize retargeting to grow your revenue exponentially. By leveraging technology, automation, and strategic marketing, your business can grow beyond the confines of time and effort.

The Potential for Consistent, Scalable Income:

- **Digital Products**: Once you create a high-value digital product—whether it's an online course, eBook, or software—it can be sold an unlimited number of times without the need for additional resources. This is the essence of passive income.
- **High-Ticket Offers**: By mastering the art of high-ticket sales through webinars, masterclasses, and targeted marketing, you can significantly increase your revenue with fewer customers, focusing on delivering deep value to a select group of clients.

- **Automated Sales Funnels**: Automated funnels allow you to capture leads, nurture prospects, and make sales 24/7. Even while you sleep, your business continues to work for you, bringing in revenue and building a loyal customer base.

With these scalable income models, you're not just making money quickly—you're laying the foundation for a **sustainable business** that continues to grow and thrive.

2. Taking Action: Your Journey Starts Here

Knowledge is powerful, but it's **action** that creates change. The path to wealth and freedom doesn't happen overnight, nor does it come from simply reading about success strategies. It's the **consistent implementation** of these methods, learning from each experience, and refining your approach that will lead to lasting results. Your journey to wealth and freedom starts with the decision to take action.

2.1 Implementing What You've Learned

You now have a roadmap for creating $100,000 in 24 hours, from identifying market opportunities and crafting irresistible offers to mastering high-converting sales funnels and leveraging joint ventures. As you prepare to implement these strategies, keep the following steps in mind to ensure a successful launch:

Your Action Plan:

1. **Define Your Goal**: Start by setting clear, measurable income goals. Whether your target is a six-figure launch or building a consistent monthly income, clarity is key to staying focused and motivated.

2. **Choose Your Niche and Offer**: Select a niche that aligns with your passions and expertise, then develop a high-value offer that addresses a specific problem within that niche.

3. **Build Your Sales Funnel**: Create a streamlined sales funnel that captures leads, nurtures prospects, and drives conversions. Lever-

age tools like email marketing, retargeting ads, and landing pages to optimize the customer journey.

4. **Leverage Partnerships**: Seek out joint venture partners, affiliates, and influencers who can help you reach new audiences and amplify your marketing efforts.

5. **Host a Flash Masterclass or Webinar**: Use live sessions to engage with your audience, deliver actionable value, and transition into your high-ticket upsell with confidence.

6. **Analyze and Refine**: After each campaign or launch, analyze the data to identify what worked and where improvements can be made. This cycle of continuous refinement is the key to scaling your business.

As you implement these steps, remember that consistency, adaptability, and persistence are the keys to success. Every launch and every campaign will provide valuable insights that will help you refine your strategies and achieve even greater results in the future.

2.2 Overcoming Challenges

The journey to financial freedom will have its challenges, and there will be moments of uncertainty or setbacks. However, it's essential to embrace these challenges as **learning opportunities** rather than obstacles. Each setback is a chance to gain insights, grow your skills, and strengthen your business.

Mindset Shifts for Success:

- **Resilience**: Accept that not every campaign will be a home run. Use each experience as a stepping stone to greater success. The key is to stay committed, adapt your strategies, and keep moving forward.

- **Focus on Value**: The most successful businesses focus on delivering genuine value to their customers. When you prioritize solving real problems and enriching the lives of your clients, the revenue will naturally follow.

- **Celebrate Progress**: Every milestone, no matter how small, is a testament to your efforts. Celebrate your wins, learn from your challenges, and keep your eyes on the ultimate goal—financial freedom and a life designed by you.

3. Your Path to Wealth and Freedom Awaits

The strategies you've learned have the power to change your life. By generating consistent income through high-ticket offers, automated sales funnels, and strategic collaborations, you're not just building a business—you're creating a pathway to **wealth and freedom**. Imagine waking up each day with the financial security to pursue your passions, support your loved ones, and explore the world on your terms.

3.1 Envisioning Your Future

Picture your future self: a successful entrepreneur who confidently launches new products, hosts value-packed events, and collaborates with industry leaders. You have built a business that runs efficiently, providing you with the freedom to focus on what truly matters. Whether that's traveling the world, spending more time with family, or giving back to your community, the choice is yours.

This vision is within your reach, and the strategies you've learned are the key to making it a reality. Your path to wealth and freedom is not just a dream; it's a **step-by-step process** that you can start implementing today.

3.2 The Next Step: Take Action Today

The only thing standing between you and your ideal life is **action**. Don't wait for the "perfect moment" or for everything to feel ready. Start with what you have, implement the strategies in this guide, and refine as you go. Success is built on a foundation of small, consistent actions taken with determination and confidence.

- **Make a Commitment**: Right now, commit to taking the first step. Whether it's outlining your first high-ticket offer, setting up your webinar, or reaching out to potential JV partners, make a decision to act today.

- **Stay Focused on Your Vision**: Keep your vision of wealth and freedom at the forefront of your mind. When challenges arise, remind yourself why you started and the life you're building.

Your path to wealth and freedom begins with the steps you take now. With the strategies in this guide and a commitment to action, you have the power to transform your business, your finances, and your life.

Now is your moment. Embrace it, take action, and start creating the wealth and freedom you deserve. Your future self will thank you for the choices you make today. Here's to your **unstoppable success**!

Bonus Chapter: The 24-Hour Launch Checklist

This bonus chapter presents a **comprehensive checklist** to guide you through every crucial step of your 24-hour launch, ensuring a smooth, flawless execution. A meticulously planned launch increases your chances of hitting the $100,000 mark, minimizing potential pitfalls and maximizing your revenue. Use this checklist as a step-by-step blueprint to prepare, execute, and optimize your launch for success.

The checklist is divided into **four main phases**: Preparation (pre-launch planning), Promotion (building anticipation and buzz), Launch Day Execution, and Post-Launch Follow-Up. Each phase includes detailed steps to guide you through the process, from crafting your offer to executing your sales funnel and following up with potential customers.

Phase 1: Preparation (4-6 Weeks Before Launch)

Preparation is the most critical phase of your launch. In this stage, you will define your goals, create your offer, and set up all necessary systems to ensure a seamless experience for your audience.

1. Define Your Launch Goal and Strategy

- **Set a Revenue Goal**: Decide on your launch goal, such as hitting $100,000 in 24 hours, and break down how many units you need to sell to achieve that target.
    - Example: "To hit $100,000, we need to sell 100 units of our $1,000 offer or 200 units of our $500 offer."
- **Choose Your Product or Offer**: Select the high-value product, service, or bundle you'll be launching. Ensure it aligns with your target audience's needs and provides a clear transformation.
- **Determine Your Sales Funnel**: Plan the funnel you'll use to capture leads and convert sales. Choose whether to use a webinar, flash masterclass, sales page, or live event as your primary conversion tool.
- **Create a Launch Timeline**: Outline a detailed timeline for your launch, including key milestones like content creation, promotional activities, and follow-up sequences.

2. Craft Your Irresistible Offer

- **Design the Core Offer**: Outline the key features, benefits, and unique selling points of your product or service.
- **Add Bonuses**: Create additional bonuses (e.g., eBooks, 1-on-1 sessions, exclusive webinars) that increase the perceived value of your offer.
- **Develop Scarcity and Urgency**: Define any limited-time bonuses, discounts, or limited spots to create a sense of urgency during your launch.
- **Set Your Price**: Choose a price that reflects the value of your offer. Consider including payment plans to make your offer accessible to a broader audience.

3. Build Your Sales Funnel

- **Create Landing Pages**: Design a high-converting landing page that captures leads and showcases the benefits of your offer. Include testimonials, case studies, and compelling CTAs.
- **Design Your Sales Page**: Develop a detailed sales page that provides an in-depth overview of your product, features, benefits, pricing, and bonuses.
- **Set Up the Checkout Process**: Integrate a seamless checkout system with secure payment options. Test the process to ensure there are no technical issues.
- **Develop Upsell and Downsell Offers**: Plan any upsell or downsell offers that will be presented after the initial purchase to increase your average order value (AOV).
- **Create Email Sequences**: Write and schedule your pre-launch, launch day, and follow-up email sequences, including reminders, countdowns, and last-chance offers.

4. Prepare Promotional Content

- **Create Ads**: Design eye-catching ads for platforms like Facebook, Instagram, Google, and LinkedIn. Develop multiple variations to test during the promotion phase.
- **Write Social Media Posts**: Craft engaging posts for all your social media channels, highlighting key aspects of your offer and building excitement.
- **Record Video Content**: Produce video content (e.g., teasers, behind-the-scenes, testimonials) to promote your launch on social media and in emails.
- **Design Webinars or Masterclasses**: If hosting a live event, prepare the presentation, including slides, key points, engagement elements, and the transition to your offer.

5. Set Up Tracking and Analytics

- **Install Tracking Pixels**: Add Facebook Pixel, Google Ads Pixel, or other tracking codes to your website to monitor traffic, conversions, and retargeting.
- **Set Up Google Analytics**: Configure Google Analytics to track user behavior, page views, and sales funnel performance.
- **Create Custom Reports**: Set up dashboards in analytics tools to track key metrics, such as traffic sources, conversion rates, cart abandonment, and sales.

Phase 2: Promotion (1-2 Weeks Before Launch)

Promotion is about building anticipation and excitement around your upcoming launch. This phase is crucial for warming up your audience and priming them for the big day.

6. Announce Your Launch to Your Audience

- **Email Your List**: Send an announcement email to your subscribers, revealing the date of your launch and teasing what's coming.
  - Example: "Something big is coming! Mark your calendar for March 15th and get ready for an exclusive offer that will transform your business."
- **Create a Landing Page**: Direct your audience to a pre-launch landing page with a signup form to capture leads interested in your upcoming offer.
- **Use Social Media**: Post teasers, countdowns, and behind-the-scenes content on all social media channels to generate buzz and anticipation.

7. Warm Up Your Audience

- **Host a Pre-Launch Webinar or Live Session**: Offer a free webinar or live Q&A session to provide value, engage with your audience, and introduce the problem your upcoming offer solves.
- **Share Testimonials and Success Stories**: Post customer success stories and testimonials that highlight the benefits of your product or service.
- **Release Free Content**: Share valuable content (e.g., blog posts, podcasts, video tutorials) related to your launch topic to showcase your expertise and build interest.

8. Run Paid Advertising Campaigns

- **Set Up Pre-Launch Ads**: Run ads targeting your existing audience, email subscribers, and website visitors to drive traffic to your pre-launch landing page.

- **Create Retargeting Campaigns**: Set up retargeting ads for website visitors and social media engagers to keep your offer top-of-mind.

Phase 3: Launch Day Execution (24 Hours)

Launch day is the culmination of your hard work. This phase focuses on executing your sales strategy, engaging your audience, and driving conversions.

9. Kick Off the Launch

- **Send Launch Emails**: Send the launch announcement email to your list, including details about the offer, bonuses, scarcity elements, and a clear call to action.
  - Example: "The doors are officially open! For the next 24 hours, get access to [Product Name] plus exclusive bonuses valued at $1,500."
- **Update Social Media**: Post the launch announcement on all social media platforms, using stories, reels, and live videos to engage with your audience.
- **Activate Your Ads**: Launch your paid ad campaigns targeting your warmed-up audience segments. Use retargeting ads to reach those who have shown previous interest.

10. Engage and Create Urgency

- **Host a Live Event**: If using a webinar or masterclass as part of your launch strategy, go live to deliver value, engage with attendees, and introduce your offer.
- **Post Regular Updates**: Throughout the day, post updates on social media, share customer testimonials, and answer questions in the comments to maintain engagement.
- **Leverage Urgency**: Send reminder emails and social media posts highlighting the limited-time nature of the offer and bonuses.

- ◦ Example: "Only 8 hours left to grab [Product Name] with all the exclusive bonuses. Don't miss out!"

11. Monitor Performance and Optimize

- **Track Sales**: Monitor real-time sales performance, including conversion rates, cart abandonment, and revenue generated.
- **Adjust Ad Spend**: Allocate more budget to top-performing ads and pause underperforming ones to maximize ROI.
- **Respond to Inquiries**: Be active on social media and in email to answer questions, address concerns, and encourage hesitant prospects to take action.

Phase 4: Post-Launch Follow-Up (1-3 Days After Launch)

The post-launch phase is crucial for maximizing revenue, nurturing customer relationships, and gathering feedback for future launches.

12. Send Follow-Up Emails

- **Thank You Email**: Send a thank-you email to customers who purchased during the launch, expressing appreciation and providing information on what to expect next.
- **Cart Abandonment Emails**: Send a reminder email to those who visited the sales page but didn't complete the purchase, addressing common objections and offering an incentive to buy.
  - ◦ Example: "We noticed you left [Product Name] in your cart. Complete your purchase in the next 24 hours and receive a free bonus!"
- **Last Chance Email**: If your offer includes a limited-time bonus or discount, send a final "last chance" email to your list.
  - ◦ Example: "This is your final reminder—the bonuses expire at midnight tonight. Don't miss your chance!"

13. Analyze Launch Performance

- **Review Sales Data**: Analyze your sales data to assess overall performance, including total revenue, conversion rates, and customer demographics.
- **Evaluate Marketing Channels**: Identify which marketing channels (email, ads, social media) contributed most to sales and engagement.
- **Gather Customer Feedback**: Reach out to new customers for feedback on their purchase experience, identifying areas for improvement in future launches.

14. Nurture New Customers

- **Onboard New Customers**: Send a welcome email sequence to onboard customers, guiding them through how to access and make the most of your product or service.
- **Upsell and Cross-Sell**: Present additional products, services, or memberships to new customers as part of a post-purchase upsell strategy.
  - Example: "Thank you for joining our program! Enhance your experience with our VIP 1-on-1 coaching sessions—available exclusively to new members."

Conclusion: Your Blueprint for a Flawless Launch

This comprehensive 24-hour launch checklist provides you with a **step-by-step guide** to execute a flawless, high-impact launch. By following this blueprint, you set the stage for a successful, revenue-generating event that not only reaches your $100,000 goal but also lays the foundation for future profitable launches.

Remember, the key to a successful launch lies in **thorough preparation, strategic promotion, engaging delivery**, and **effective follow-**

up. As you use this checklist to guide your launch efforts, you'll gain valuable insights into what works best for your audience, empowering you to refine your strategy and achieve even greater success in the future.

Your path to a six-figure launch is now within reach—follow these steps, take action, and watch your business grow!

<u>Message from the Author:</u>

I hope you enjoyed this book, I love astrology and knew there was not a book such as this out on the shelf. I love metaphysical items as well. Please check out my other books:

-Life of Government Benefits

-My life of Hell

-My life with Hydrocephalus

-Red Sky

-World Domination:Woman's rule

-World Domination:Woman's Rule 2: The War

-Life and Banishment of Apophis: book 1

-The Kidney Friendly Diet

-The Ultimate Hemp Cookbook

-Creating a Dispensary(legally)

-Cleanliness throughout life: the importance of showering from childhood to adulthood.

-Strong Roots: The Risks of Overcoddling children

-Hemp Horoscopes: Cosmic Insights and Earthly Healing

- Celestial Hemp Navigating the Zodiac: Through the Green Cosmos

-Astrological Hemp: Aligning The Stars with Earth's Ancient Herb

-The Astrological Guide to Hemp: Stars, Signs, and Sacred Leaves

-Green Growth: Innovative Marketing Strategies for your Hemp Products and Dispensary

-Cosmic Cannabis

-Astrological Munchies

-Henry The Hemp

-Zodiacal Roots: The Astrological Soul Of Hemp

- **Green Constellations: Intersection of Hemp and Zodiac**

-Hemp in The Houses: An astrological Adventure Through The Cannabis Galaxy

-Galactic Ganja Guide

Heavenly Hemp

Zodiac Leaves

Doctor Who Astrology

Cannastrology

Stellar Satvias and Cosmic Indicas

Celestial Cannabis: A Zodiac Journey

AstroHerbology: The Sky and The Soil: Volume 1

AstroHerbology:Celestial Cannabis:Volume 2

Cosmic Cannabis Cultivation

The Starry Guide to Herbal Harmony: Volume 1

The Starry Guide to Herbal Harmony: Cannabis Universe: Volume 2

Yugioh Astrology: Astrological Guide to Deck, Duels and more

Nightmare Mansion: Echoes of The Abyss

Nightmare Mansion 2: Legacy of Shadows

Nightmare Mansion 3: Shadows of the Forgotten

Nightmare Mansion 4: Echoes of the Damned

The Life and Banishment of Apophis: Book 2

Nightmare Mansion: Halls of Despair

Healing with Herb: Cannabis and Hydrocephalus

Planetary Pot: Aligning with Astrological Herbs: Volume 1

Fast Track to Freedom: 30 Days to Financial Independence Using AI, Assets, and Agile Hustles

Cosmic Hemp Pathways

How to Become Financially Free in 30 Days: 10,000 Paths to Prosperity

Zodiacal Herbage: Astrological Insights: Volume 1

Nightmare Mansion: Whispers in the Walls

The Daleks Invade Atlantis

Henry the hemp and Hydrocephalus

10X The Kidney Friendly Diet

Cannabis Universe: Adult coloring book

Hemp Astrology: The Healing Power of the Stars

Zodiacal Herbage: Astrological Insights: Cannabis Universe: Volume 2

Planetary Pot: Aligning with Astrological Herbs: Cannabis Universes: Volume 2

Doctor Who Meets the Replicators and SG-1: The Ultimate Battle for Survival

Nightmare Mansion: Curse of the Blood Moon

The Celestial Stoner: A Guide to the Zodiac

Cosmic Pleasures: Sex Toy Astrology for Every Sign

Hydrocephalus Astrology: Navigating the Stars and Healing Waters

Lapis and the Mischievous Chocolate Bar

Celestial Positions: Sexual Astrology for Every Sign

Apophis's Shadow Work Journal: : A Journey of Self-Discovery and Healing

Kinky Cosmos: Sexual Kink Astrology for Every Sign

Digital Cosmos: The Astrological Digimon Compendium

Stellar Seeds: The Cosmic Guide to Growing with Astrology

Apophis's Daily Gratitude Journal

Cat Astrology: Feline Mysteries of the Cosmos

The Cosmic Kama Sutra: An Astrological Guide to Sexual Positions

Unleash Your Potential: A Guided Journal Powered by AI Insights

Whispers of the Enchanted Grove

Cosmic Pleasures: An Astrological Guide to Sexual Kinks

369, 12 Manifestation Journal

Whisper of the nocturne journal(blank journal for writing or drawing)

The Boogey Book

Locked In Reflection: A Chastity Journey Through Locktober

If you want solar for your home go here: https://www.harborso-lar.live/apophisenterprises/

Get Some Tarot cards: https://www.makeplayingcards.com/sell/
apophis-occult-shop

<u>Get   some   shirts: https://www.bonfire.com/store/apophis-shirt-emporium/</u>

<u>Instagrams:</u>
@apophis_enterprises,
@apophisbookemporium,
@apophisscardshop
Twitter: @apophisenterpr1
Tiktok:@apophisenterprise
Youtube: @sg1fan23477, @FiresideRetreatKingdom

Podcast: Apophis Chat Zone: https://open.spotify.com/show/5zXbrCLEV2xzCp8ybrfHsk?si=fb4d4fdbdce44dec

Newsletter: https://apophiss-newsletter-27c897.beehiiv.com/

* 9 7 9 8 3 3 0 4 4 8 8 9 0 *